LORETTE WILMOT LIBRARY
Nazareth College of Rochester

Rochester City Ballet

American Indian Ballerinas

American Indian Ballerinas

By Lili Cockerille Livingston

UNIVERSITY OF OKLAHOMA PRESS : NORMAN AND LONDON

Library of Congress Cataloging-in Publication Data

Livingston, Lili Cockerille, 1945–
    American Indian ballerinas / Lili Cockerille Livingston.
        p.   cm.
    Includes bibliographical references and index.
    ISBN 0–8061–2896–8 (alk. paper)
    1. Tallchief, Maria. 2. Chouteau, Yvonne. 3. Tallchief,
Marjorie. 4. Hightower, Rosella. 5. Indian ballerinas—United
States—Biography. I. Title.
    GV1785.A1L526   1997
    792.8'028'0922—dc20
[B]   96–32307
                                                            CIP

Text design by Debora Hackworth.

The paper in this book meets the guidelines for permanence and
durability of the Committee on Production Guidelines for Book
Longevity of the Council on Library Resources, Inc. ∞

1 2 3 4 5 6 7 8 9 10

In humble gratitude to Alexandra Danilova and
Frederic Franklin for teaching me to be a
dancer and a lady

Contents

Contents

Illustrations

PLATES

Illustrations

Marjorie Tallchief and George Skibine in *Idylle,* 1954
Marjorie Tallchief in *Giselle,* 1957
Maria Tallchief and Erik Bruhn in a studio portrait of
   Giselle, 1958

FIGURES

Preface

This is a book about four women who set out from the Oklahoma prairies of their American Indian ancestors to achieve greatness in an art form born in France, raised in Russia, and redefined in America. *American Indian Ballerinas* is an authorized biography of the legendary ballerinas Maria Tallchief, Rosella Hightower, Marjorie Tallchief, and Yvonne Chouteau. It is not, however, a dance book in the traditional sense.

Rather than render detailed accounts of each woman's career and a comprehensive list of the roles that catapulted each to fame, I have presented each individual's view of her accomplishments, emphasizing those that she regarded with the greatest pride. *American Indian Ballerinas* thus offers a kaleidoscope of memories, anecdotes, and reflections as we follow Maria Tallchief, Rosella Hightower, Marjorie Tallchief, and Yvonne Chouteau on their personal trails to fame.

My initial and most extensive interviews with the women were conducted between December 1988 and November 1989. When in 1995 I asked each of them to help me update the material, they responded enthusiastically and once again spoke with joy and laughter about their lives, families, work, and views.

My personal exposure to the women began in 1955, when I had the opportunity to perform the role of Clara in the Ballet Russe de Monte Carlo's one-act production of *The Nutcracker* during a summer engagement at the Carter Barron Amphitheater in Washington, D.C. Because I was a student of the Fokine-Slavenska studios, my selection for the honor had more to do with Leon Fokine and the fact that I fit into the costume than the potential I showed as a young dance student. My most cherished memory of that experience is being introduced to Yvonne Chouteau. I had never met a ballerina before, and I have never forgotten the impression left by the kind, reed-thin young woman with blond hair who leaned down to whisper "Good luck" before I took my first steps on the stage of a professional ballet company. I would not see Yvonne Chouteau again until 1973, when I had retired from my career in dance and moved to Oklahoma.

Three years later, I again performed the role of Clara, this time in George Balanchine's full-length production of the work presented by New York City Ballet (NYCB) in the nation's capital. By that point, I was enrolled at the Washington School of Ballet studying under Mary Day, Lisa Gardiner, and a star-studded roster of guest teachers that included Alexandra Danilova, Frederic Franklin, and Edward Caton. My selection for the leading child role in the NYCB production had little to do with the size of the costume. NYCB ballet mistress Vida Brown held citywide auditions and subsequently prepared those selected to perform with Balanchine's company during a two-week engagement at the Capitol Theatre.

Among the ballerinas I watched perform the Sugar Plum Fairy from my second-act perch on the stage was Maria Tallchief, who had created the role the previous year. I distinctly remember that there was a special electricity on the stage and in the wings that was missing when others performed the role. I had the opportunity to study with Maria Tallchief after being awarded a Ford Foundation Regional Scholarship by Balanchine in 1961 to study at the School of American Ballet (SAB).

Preface

After serving my apprenticeship with NYCB during the 1962 winter season at the City Center Theatre, I joined the newly formed Harkness Ballet in 1963. During my first four years with the company, Marjorie Tallchief was its leading ballerina. Her husband, George Skibine, was its artistic director. Jeannot Cerrone served as company manager, and for a brief period my former teacher Leon Fokine held the post of ballet master. The first stop on the company's inaugural European tour was an extended residency in Cannes, France.

It was in France that I met Rosella Hightower. In addition to providing our company rehearsal space and a home away from home at her studios, Rosella had taken on the responsibility of serving as guest teacher.

At some point, after making Oklahoma home and turning my efforts to writing, I realized that of all the contemporary ballerinas I was exposed to during my career, the four women from Oklahoma had left the strongest impression on me. I also became aware that although their individuality was clearly defined, they were similar in some special way. When in 1978 Yvonne Chouteau suggested that I write a book about their lives with respect to their Oklahoma roots, I knew that I would come to accept that challenge.

During the ten years between that moment and the time this book became a viable project, I took advantage of an opportunity to pursue a career as an arts writer and dance critic with the *Tulsa Tribune*. In addition to gaining a decade's worth of experience writing for a daily newspaper, my assignments allowed me to travel throughout Oklahoma and become acquainted with the diverse cultures of the state, including its indigenous peoples.

The fortitude, resilience, and pride exhibited by the American Indian people who were forced time and again to tame vast expanses of wilderness for generations of white men's children are apparent in the personalities of the women who are the subjects of this book. But this is not the source of their similarity. Nor can one postulate that their simultaneous emergence as leading forces in the world of ballet was a cosmically ordained phenomenon.

I saw them together only once, when they attended the November 1991 dedication of a mural installed in the Great Rotunda in the Oklahoma State Capitol. After the ceremony, they stubbornly refused to stop signing autographs until everyone in line had been accommodated. As a result, the Tallchiefs, the Paschens, and Rosella Hightower had to be driven to the airport with a police escort to make their flights. Perhaps their similarity lies in their strong wills.

Much like the history of dance, the history of Oklahoma and her people is a study in divergent perceptions fueled by the power of human potential. These ethereal creatures took their place on stage through the strength of their own talent, will, and dedication to the pursuit of excellence. My sincere hope is that my efforts will encourage others to seek further knowledge of the contributions made by Maria Tallchief, Rosella Hightower, Marjorie Tallchief, and Yvonne Chouteau to the world of dance as well as to the legacy of the sovereign Osage, Choctaw, and Cherokee-Shawnee nations in Indian Territory.

Acknowledgments

At long last, I have the opportunity to thank my family, Maria Tallchief, Marjorie Tallchief, Rosella Hightower and Yvonne Choteau and their families, and all of the friends who have helped bring this book to fruition. Among the latter I would like first to express my gratitude to Anatoly Armais Arutunoff—Toly, as he is known familiarly—a discerning patron of dance, a globe-trotting vintage sports car collector and racer, and the first person to open a Honda dealership in Oklahoma.

Next I wish to thank Barbara Palfy, whom I met in 1988 through Jack Anderson, an authority on the Ballet Russe era, a poet, and a dance critic for the *New York Times*. I met Barbara before I started the research and interview phase of the project. She liked the concept enough to volunteer her assistance. She has been invaluable in guiding me through the proper research channels, reading countless drafts of the manuscript, and keeping me convinced that the book would be a significant contribution to the written history of dance.

I am also very grateful to my friend Barbara Horgan, the president of the George Balanchine Foundation, for directing me to Nancy Lassalle, who in turn allowed me to work with Jane Emerson in accessing the archival collection of New York City Ballet known as Ballet Society. Likewise I extend my appreciation to my friend, the choreographer Margo Sappington, for introducing me to Kate Wimpfheimer, a member of the family that cofounded Random House. Kate gave me her guest room, her energy, and the opportunity to meet her friends from the literary world during the time I spent gathering research at the Dance Collection of the New York Public Library for the Performing Arts at Lincoln Center.

My good friend and former roommate, Judith Jamison, artistic director of the Alvin Ailey American Dance Theater, also played an important role by introducing me to the poet and biographer Howard Kaplan. Thanks to Kaplan, my manuscript was read by the late Jacqueline Onassis. Less than a month before her death, she sent me a letter of recommendation to help me acquire a publisher for what she considered "a wonderful achievement."

Paul Patton, director of the Tulsa County Medical Society, political consultant, and beekeeper, picked up the thread there. He turned to his mentor and avid supporter of the University of Oklahoma Press, Julian Rothbaum. Through Rothbaum, the manuscript ended up on the desk of George Bauer, director of the press.

Dance Magazine's late Bill Como and Joe Mazo as well as Richard Philp, current editor-in-chief, Marilyn Hunt, Gary Parks, Gloria Fokine, Leon Fokine's widow, and Robert Johnson, former news editor, also helped me tremendously. Likewise, I have Windsor Ridenour and Mary Hargrove of the now-defunct *Tulsa Tribune* to thank for giving me an on-the-job degree in journalism and David Lloyd Jones for hiring me.

I also am grateful to "Saginaw" Morgan Grant, a Sac and Fox wise man, poet, and powwow straight dancer, for introducing me to the cultural perspective of the American Indian in a white man's world. And to Jim Smith, vice president of Clear Channel Communications, for being a reader.

Acknowledgments

My thanks also are extended to everyone who granted me interviews and recalled memories with such enthusiasm. And a special thank-you to my husband, Stanley, my daughter, Alton, and my son, Zachary, for putting up with me during the eight years it took for *American Indian Ballerinas* to be published.

Regrets

I have honored the request of Moscelyne Larkin Jasinski to be excluded from this book.

A native of Miami, Oklahoma, of Peoria-Shawnee heritage, Larkin began her professional career in 1941 as a member of Colonel W. de Basil's Original Ballet Russe. She married premier danseur Roman Jasinski and attained the rank of ballerina after the couple joined Sergei Denham's Ballet Russe de Monte Carlo in 1948. Shortly after the birth of their son, Roman Larkin Jasinski, in 1952, Larkin resumed her position with the Ballet Russe touring ensemble sent out by Columbia Artists during the troupe's hiatus from performing. Larkin also was engaged as guest ballerina by Radio City Music Hall and toured the Orient in 1954 with Alexandra Danilova's "Great Moments in Dance."

At the conclusion of that tour, Larkin and Jasinski retired from performing and focused their energies on developing a home for classical ballet in the style of the Ballets Russes in Tulsa, Oklahoma. Through their tireless efforts, Tulsa boasts a nationally acclaimed regionally based professional dance company known today as Tulsa Ballet Theatre. In 1995, under the direction of Marcello Angelini, the company employs twenty-nine dancers, boasts an annual budget of $2.2 million, and owns a 38,000-square-foot, state-of-the-art dance facility, which was dedicated in memory of the late Roman Jasinski in 1992.

Larkin's efforts to gain recognition for the state's American Indian ballerinas resulted in three highly successful Oklahoma Indian Ballerina Festivals.

Part I

Childhood

Chapter One

Durwood, Oklahoma, 1920

People in Durwood will tell you not much has changed since January 20, 1920, when smoke curling uninterrupted from the chimney at Doc Fanning's place meant something special was happening. Whatever fees the good doctor collected then for tending the needs of the citizenry and livestock in Carter County were hardly enough to keep a fire burning hot all day without good reason. Although Doc had brought more than his share of babies into the world, the arrival of the first Fanning-Hightower was cause for celebration. Doc Fanning is not around anymore, but there has been a historical marker erected to honor the baby he delivered that day.

Making ends meet in the heart of southern Oklahoma farm and

ranch country is not much easier than it was seventy-five years ago. That is why both families approved when in 1918 Charles Edgar Hightower, known as C.E., began guiding his horse south across twenty miles of limestone-streaked red clay gullies dotted with wild heather to call on Miss Eula May Fanning. In time, the soft-spoken ways of the tall, lanky Choctaw won the heart of the diminutive, high-spirited Irish girl. Their marriage united the two families in their efforts to survive. With Hightowers and Fannings tending each other's fields and livestock, the labors of the spring and summer months brought greater harvest yields. Whether working the Fanning livestock, cultivating the Hightower soft-shell pecan farm, or raising and putting up food crops for the family, everyone earned a seat at the supper table.

Winter in southern Oklahoma can be fierce, but it begins late and usually spends its might during the first quarter of the new year. With fields lying dormant and livestock needing little attention other than protection from unexpected storms, there were few chores that could not be put aside when news arrived that Eula May had gone into labor. Between the clatter of relatives coming and going and the organized chaos of preparing for the birth, the normally complacent C.E. grew visibly excited. Following Doc Fanning's announcement that a healthy baby girl had been born, C.E. exploded untypically into a lengthy, impassioned explanation of the name that had been chosen. The baby would be named, he proclaimed, in honor of a great lady in the history of the Choctaw Nation, Rosella Hightower.

Tribal heritage was paramount in Hightower family life. Rosella's great-grandmother, thought to be in her nineties by 1920, was the last of the clan born east of the Mississippi. She had been among the 19,559 Choctaws ordered by the United States government to begin the exodus of all southeastern tribes to the west in the 1830s. Being driven as an infant from the family's well-cultivated Southern plantation by covered wagon to carve a new existence from the undeveloped, arid lands set aside as Indian Territory had not embittered her toward the white man. The hardships endured by the tribe, resulting from a treaty signed with the United States government exactly one hundred years prior to her great-granddaughter's birth, had simply taught her that the white man's treaties could not be trusted.

Of her great-grandmother Rosella says,

I still remember when she called the last of the big family reunions. High-towers from all branches of the family came from all over to hear what she had to say. There were at least four hundred gathered when she announced that she would not register on the Mississippi Choctaw rolls with the Of-fice of Indian Affairs. As the elder, her refusal to file meant that no High-tower could ever qualify for payments or pensions owed the tribe under land purchase agreements made with the federal government. There was no discussion. Her word was final and the issue was settled, forever.

Shaking her head, Rosella adds, "It's always the dramatic moments that you remember as a child. What I really saw in my great-grand-mother was not an iron hand. I saw a woman of tremendous inner strength, patience, and wisdom. Although I was too young to un-derstand a lot of what I saw and heard, being in her presence taught me that life goes good, life goes bad, and you must live through both phases."

The history of the Choctaw is a fascinating study in survival dat-ing back to the mid-1500s. The tribe suffered such great losses fighting to protect its legendary Chief Tuskalusa against Hernando de Soto's forces in 1540 that it disappeared from the historical record for close to two hundred years. By the early eighteenth century, English, French, and Spanish traders noted 115 villages established by the Choctaw, in the region known today as Winston County, Mississippi. Subdivisions within the early tribe, thought to have numbered close to twenty thousand, included the Okla falaya, or Tall People; Okla tannap, or People of the Other Side, also known as the Haiyip tuklo, or Two Lakes; the Ahe pat okla, or Potato-eating People; the Okla hannai, or Six Town People; and the powerful southeastern Kun/sha group.

Tribal origins of the Choctaw, a deeply ritualistic people, are de-picted in elaborate legends of great spirits carrying them forth from the moment of creation. According to tribal legend, existence began after the creation of Nanih Waya, or Productive Mountain, by a great red man who descended from the heavens above to a muddy area of the plains. Upon completion of his task, he is said to have called forth a race of red people known as the Chahta, a derivative of the Creek word *cate,* meaning red. The eventual transliteration to Choctaw is thought to have been influenced by the Spanish word *chato,* mean-ing flat, to reflect the ancient tribal practice of flattening the foreheads of male infants. Of medium height and slender build, the typical Choctaw has a narrow bone structure, long limbs, and a narrow face overshadowed by hard-edged cheekbones.

The Choctaw were the most successful agriculturalists of the southeastern tribes and were known for their patience, keen diplomacy, and tremendous strength as defensive warriors. They were mild people who became outstanding leaders in the field of education and established a school system later adopted by the Creek, Chickasaw, and Seminole nations.

Following the arrival of French and English trading operations in the Louisiana area, the tribe became embroiled in the fight for supremacy waged by the foreign traders, often pitting Choctaw against Choctaw on the battlefield. In 1750, the tribe was reunited under the French flag and removed itself from the conflict. Although all southeastern tribes came under British rule in 1765, the French influence had become an integral part of Choctaw life. Intermarriage and a blending of cultures had formed bonds that could not be severed by a transference of rule.

The tribe remained preeminent in the agricultural industry and entered into a treaty with Spain in 1784 to establish trade limitations that required that all traders be licensed by the Spanish government. Two years later, the tribe signed its first treaty with the United States government in Hopewell, South Carolina. The agreement defined the boundaries of Choctaw hunting grounds, opened trade relations with the United States government, and allowed trading posts to be established within Choctaw lands. By 1800 dwindling herds forced hunting parties west and eventually up the Red River into Oklahoma, but the tribe continued to focus its agricultural enterprises in the Mississippi Valley. Nanih Waya mound, located ten miles southeast of Noxapater, Mississippi, also remained the focal point of tribal sacred rituals until forced removal to Indian Territory began in 1831.

Following completion of the Louisiana Purchase, in 1804 the United States Congress authorized President Thomas Jefferson to begin negotiations to acquire all southeastern lands held by Indian tribes in exchange for a permanent, designated country for each tribe in the vast frontier west of the Mississippi. Sixteen years later, as an appointee of the U.S. secretary of war, General Andrew Jackson signed a treaty with the Choctaw Nation at Doaks Stand, Mississippi.

Ten years later, that treaty allowed Jackson, then president of the United States, to approve a congressional act calling for the removal of the southeastern tribes to lands designated by the federal government as Indian Territory in 1830.

The tremendous cultural, educational, and industrial advances the Choctaw Nation had made in the twenty years since the treaty at Doaks Stand had been signed were of no consequence to the government. In 1831 removal to the west began, and the Choctaw led the march along the route known today as the Trail of Tears. Except for a small band of renegades who took refuge in remote areas of Neshoba County, the removal of the Choctaw Nation was completed by 1836. The tribe, which had left the Mississippi Valley 19,559 strong, numbered 12,500 at the end of the forced march.

Even as removal was under way, the Choctaw set about establishing an organized government and educational system within the boundaries of their new lands. By 1834 the tribe had written and adopted the first constitution in Indian Territory and by 1838 had twelve schools in operation within the Choctaw Nation. Among Choctaws prominent in early Oklahoma history, Allen Wright, who served as principal chief from 1866 to 1870, is credited with giving Indian Territory the name Oklahoma. At the 1866 Choctaw-Chickasaw Treaty negotiations, Wright referred to Indian Territory in his native language using the words *okla,* meaning people, and *homma,* meaning red. That same year, the Office of Indian Affairs deemed the educational and social structure of the Choctaw, Chickasaw, Cherokee, Creek, and Seminole nations sufficient to create a division within Indian Territory known as the Five Civilized Tribes. Although the term is still in use today, it no longer reflects the distinction of cultural, social, and behavioral sophistication it once did.

Removal to the west struck the death knell for the ancient Choctaw tribal clan system in more ways than one. Under conditions of the Doaks Stand Treaty, the Chickasaw had purchased the right to settle among the Choctaw following removal to Indian Territory. Once again, bloodlines and familial ties became obliterated through intermarriage and cohabitation. After valuable coal and asphalt reserves were discovered within the Choctaw Nation in the early 1870s, the federal government made several attempts to sort out the mixed bloodlines and property holdings between the two tribes. Agreements to set new rights of registry for the equitable distribution of funds owed members of both tribes from the sale of jointly held properties were ratified by all three parties in 1897 and 1902. Between the lack of cooperation extended by the Mississippi Choctaw, who like Rosella's great-grandmother would not register on the new rolls, and mishandling of the process by the federal government, the first payment was not issued until 1950.

The Choctaw and Chickasaw continue to live in peace and harmony today on lands originally designated the Choctaw Nation. Although the Choctaw have been prominent in education, politics, medicine, military service, literature, and the arts, their primary industry remains agriculture. For most Oklahoma Choctaw, survival continues to revolve around farming and ranching, as it did for the Fannings and Hightowers.

Growing up on a farm suited Rosella. A wisp of a child, she delighted in doing chores considered too difficult and strenuous for her size. Rosella recalls, "As soon as I could walk and was strong enough to drag a sack behind me, I started picking cotton. Everyone picked cotton and, to me, it was fun. Getting paid at weigh-in was fantastic, and then the adults made such a big fuss over me because I was working and carrying my own sack. It became how I made myself interesting."

Being recognized as a productive member of the family was important. By the time she could count, Rosella remembers, twenty-five sat at the family supper table. The work at hand dictated who worked where and, in some cases, who lived where. An eager child, Rosella quickly learned to be where she was needed.

At the Hightower farm I spent my time in the kitchen with my father's mother. Like my father, Grandmother Cumy was quiet. She also had more patience than anyone I have ever met in my life. You never knew what she was doing or thinking, but somehow she always managed to take care of everyone and get everything done. She taught me how to churn butter and to can food and put up preserves. There were always quilting parties and 4-H Club meetings, and I took part in all of that.

At the Fanning ranch Rosella worked outside with her mother's father, Sammie. "He taught me to work with the horses and livestock. I learned to ride, check the fences, distribute feed and water, and help when the animals gave birth. We also gathered eggs, killed the snakes we found in the henhouse, and patched holes to keep the chickens in and everything else out." Except for church on Sunday, which she remembers as more of a social affair than a religious experience, Rosella recalls there were as many outside diversions as there were idle moments.

Durwood, five miles east of the Fanning place, was and remains today little more than a cluster of churches, a cemetery, and a schoolhouse. Nine miles to the west lies Ardmore, where the railroad once served as the only link for area farmers and ranchers to markets across the nation. With diminished rail service, once-thriving processing plants for local pecan and dairy products became rusted and deserted beside the tracks. During the 1920s, stores along Main Street offered what could not be bought by mail order and the town's single movie theater did a booming business.

As hard as the family worked, life in Carter County was a constant struggle. Sitting up straight in her chair, Rosella comments,

I was lucky because I learned the value of a dollar early. There was no such thing as an allowance in those days. For a long time my dad gave me ten cents a week for the work I did. Finally, it got up to twenty-five cents, which was enough for one movie a week. Of course, I forgot most of what I learned to do on the farm, but being able to darn pointe shoes, mend practice clothes, and exist on small amounts of money proved essential during the early years of my career. What comes to mind when I think about Oklahoma is the image of what you dream about when you imagine running away from everything. Learning to work the land and handle the animals was fun, and there was always something new to do. Most of my cousins were boys, and when we finished our chores we would go off into the woods to find good places to fish and explore the countryside. It was a special time in my life. It was an adventure.

Chapter Two

Kansas City, Kansas, 1925

In late 1924 Rosella's father decided to take a job in Kansas City with the Missouri-Kansas-Texas Railroad. The salary and benefits offered by the railroad promised a better future and held more potential than working the family land. Leaving Eula May and Rosella behind, C.E. headed for Kansas City to assume his duties. As soon as he had saved enough money to secure a lease on a modest apartment, he returned for his wife and daughter. When the day arrived to leave Durwood, Rosella remembers being too excited by the prospect of going to live in Kansas City to feel anything else: "I was only five, and moving to the city was the beginning of a new adventure." With their belongings packed into Doc Fanning's four-cylinder 1923 Buick and Eula

May's brother John along to return the car, they began the three-hundred-mile trip leading straight up central Oklahoma to the Kansas border. Before passing the Carter County line, heavy rain began to fall. Rural dirt roads and crudely built wooden bridges along the way became impassable, and the trip stretched into a four-day journey.

Once settled in Kansas City, it became apparent that the family could not live on C.E.'s salary. Eula May would have to take a full-time job. Figuring out who would take care of Rosella presented no serious dilemma. C.E. sent for his youngest sister, Maxine. Rosella says, "That was what started everything. Aunt Maxine was only sixteen or seventeen when she joined us in Kansas City. Having lived her entire life in the country, she was determined to see everything the city offered. Because she was there to take care of me, she took me with her."

The state's second-largest metropolis, Kansas City was as much of a "dream town" as Rodgers and Hammerstein would depict it in their 1943 Broadway hit *Oklahoma!* Everything was "up-to-date in Kansas City" in 1925 and recreation opportunities ran the gamut from bawdy houses to fine arts museums. "Somehow Aunt Maxine always managed to get tickets and we went to wrestling matches and vaudeville shows and anything that came through town. Whatever we saw, we'd try to copy when we came home. We'd sing and dance and make music until we exhausted ourselves and everyone else's patience."

Rosella still remembers the ukelele her aunt brought with her from Oklahoma and the family eventually acquiring a Victrola and piano. When there were no shows to see, the two listened to records and emulated singers from the world of opera to the Moulin Rouge. At her aunt's urging, Rosella also mastered the Charleston. The latter became something of an issue with Aunt Maxine, who encouraged her young charge to enter Charleston competitions and cheered loudly each time she walked away with first prize. "Aunt Maxine was a wonderful girl, and she introduced me to the entire world of entertainment."

In 1933, René Blum and Colonel W. de Basil's Ballets Russes brought the wonders of Russian ballet to America for the first time since Serge Diaghilev toured his legendary troupe from coast to coast in 1915. One of several companies organized after Diaghilev's death, de Basil's company boasted Leonide Massine and George Balanchine as resident choreographers, Serge Grigoriev as *régisseur,* and a roster of ballerinas that included Alexandra Danilova, Irina Baronova, Tatiana Riabouchinska, and Tamara Toumanova. Although the Blum–de Basil alliance erupted into one of the ballet world's most vehemently fought battles a few months later, it succeeded in giving classical ballet a foothold in America. News of the troupe's successful debut at New York's St. James Theatre, under Sol Hurok's management, preceded its arrival in each city. Not one to miss anything new on the cultural horizon, Aunt Maxine promptly secured tickets and prepared her thirteen-year-old niece for a new experience. Rosella recalls, "I had never seen anything like it in my life. I decided then that that was what I was going to do with my life. My mind was made up. I even followed the company to Chicago to see another performance."

Because her father worked for the railroad, Rosella and her aunt could ride the train free. Once she found out the company was going on to Chicago, she had no difficulty convincing her aunt the trip was a necessity. Her instant infatuation with ballet was not taken lightly. In the seven years she had been going to the theater, Rosella had never shown any real commitment to anything. Outside of the performances she attended with her aunt and going to school, she dedicated most of her free time to playing baseball: "Participating in sports was encouraged very strongly by the school system and baseball was big. I was a star player on the school team and also played as a regular member on the team my father organized for the men in our neighborhood. I remember being small for a long time, but I was fast and could always get there to catch the ball."

Responding to her niece's apparent conviction to pursue ballet wherever it might lead her, Aunt Maxine launched a campaign to convince Eula May that Rosella should be given a chance to study ballet under Dorothy Perkins. "My mother could see how much it meant to me, so she went along with it. My father did not know about it and would not for a long time." Although thirteen is generally considered late for a girl to begin studying ballet, it posed no problems for Rosella. In addition to having set her mind on becoming a dancer, she had developed speed and agility as an athlete and had not yet reached her full height. Making a terrible face, she remarks, "I remember being put into corrective shoes. My mother had enlarged bunions that caused severe problems. It was hereditary. But I have to admit, as much as I hated those big, awful black shoes, they did their job. I never developed problems with my feet."

Rosella credits her first teacher, whom she refers to as Perky, with having the greatest impact on her career.

She is still the major influence on my work. What I learned from her is very much a part of my school today. She gave her students a cultural education along with the basic positions and steps. As a young dancer, Perky had studied under Michel Fokine and Enrico Cecchetti, been a stand-in for Mary Pickford, and traveled extensively to see all the great dancers of the Diaghilev era. She loved to talk and painted a vivid picture of the Ballet Russe and the entire culture of dance.

Perky taught from a chair. A tiny woman, who Rosella contends weighed no more than sixty pounds, Miss Perkins had been paralyzed from the waist down in a fluke accident in New York City. "A gust of wind hit her and she fell on the ice. In those days, they didn't know a lot about the human body. There was no rehabilitation therapy or working through serious injuries. Of course, she did walk again but only because of what she did on her own." Determined to keep up with developments in dance as well as advances being made in the area of dance therapy, Perky spent her summers working with others teaching the Cecchetti method in New York and England and spent a good deal of time studying eurythmics with Émile Jaques-Dalcroze in Switzerland and teachers involved in kinesthetic studies.

Rosella contends that learning ballet from a teacher who could not demonstrate gave her a tremendous advantage. "She always picked one student to translate what she was getting at into movement for the rest of the class. I was that person for five or six years, and picking up combinations of steps by movements of the hand and a few words became a habit." One of Rosella's strongest assets at the onset of her career was an uncanny ability to work with choreographers. The kinesthetic awareness she had learned demonstrating for her wheelchair-bound teacher instilled an innate sense of associating words with physical movement. "All a choreographer had to show me was the start of a gesture and talk it through for me to know what he or she meant. That was invaluable."

Kansas City, Kansas, 1925

During the summer months when Perky was off expanding her own horizons, Rosella remembers studying with guest teachers.

That helped balance our training and changed the pace. It also exposed us to some of her former students who had gone on to establish successful careers. I remember Eula Sharon, who became quite successful dancing in shows and revues in England. As a working professional, she was more concerned with our technical and virtuoso skills than the broad, comprehensive approach Perky took. She knew what we needed to be able to do to get a job and drilled it into us. We needed some of both and we got it.

Performing in Kansas City and surrounding communities also was part of the training offered under Perky's guidance. Rosella's face flushes with laughter when reminded of an impromptu encore she took upon herself to present during one of her first public appearances. "Evidently, after we had finished our routine and everyone had left the stage, I came back out and continued dancing as long as the music played. I loved being in front of an audience. And I felt in my place onstage."

Chapter Three

Monte Carlo, Monaco, 1938

Sitting in her office buried in the basement of the white stucco high-rise apartment building housing her Centre de Danse International in Cannes, France, Rosella gestures to her surroundings with a sweep of her arms. "This all started when I was fourteen. That's when I taught my first class. A very private, very exclusive preschool in Kansas City asked Perky for someone to teach a basic movement class. She sent me. Working with children four and five years old was good for me because I had to figure out how to keep them amused and try to make little dances for them." The school also employed a woman who taught the children introductory French. "I was fascinated by the sound of the words. As soon as possible, I enrolled in

French and Spanish courses at school. Of course, I didn't remember any of it later on, but at least I had had some exposure to foreign languages."

The same year, Rosella remembers going to study in New York for the first time. "Perky said, 'Michel Fokine is there and you must go.'" Getting approval from home to make the trip to New York took more than saying that Perky thought she was ready. By this time her father knew as much about his daughter's plans to become a dancer as everyone else in the family. "He was very much against the whole idea at first. So sending me to New York to study seemed to be carrying the whole thing too far. But his way of dealing with things he didn't like was to make his opinion known and then sit back and watch everything work out for the best. After he made it clear how he felt, he said it was okay." Train passes were secured, and arrangements to stay with a distant relative in New York were made.

Remembering her first class in a New York studio, Rosella takes a short breath. "That was an eye-opener. I had never seen as many dancers my age as good or better than I was. It was extremely important because it gave me an idea of what I had to learn before I could consider myself ready [to audition]. Of course, I thought I was ready when I arrived, but after seeing what the dancers around me could do, I realized I needed about two more years of hard work."

From age fourteen to seventeen Rosella spent as many weeks of her summer vacation taking ballet classes in New York City as her family could afford. Although Fokine's classes remained the nucleus of her daily schedule, she took classes with as many different teachers as possible. She was, admittedly, beginning to assemble a small cadre of teachers to expand her technical abilities. Throughout her career she would return to many of the teachers she had established relationships with during her teen years. At Fokine's studio she began working with the great choreographer's sister-in-law, Madame Alexandra Fedorova. Years later Fedorova would coach her in one of her most famous virtuoso roles, the "Black Swan" pas de deux. Rosella remembers, "She had a very rough approach to teaching. She was phenomenal. Her attitude was simple. If she could do it, you could do it. And that was that."

Taking class with dancers who rivaled her abilities gave Rosella something to remember all year long. Her experience in New York also taught her the importance of taking advantage of any learning opportunities that were available. "I ran from one class to the next, the entire time I was there. I must have taken at least one class in every studio in Manhattan."

Soon after her first New York trip, Rosella began trying to work out a schedule at school to give her more time for classes with Perky. As an excellent student, she qualified for special dispensations and was granted morning class time to work at the studio.

Perky dedicated those one-on-one sessions to floor exercises, stretches, and working every part of the body. What I learned during that time came back to me throughout my career. It was invaluable training as far as learning how and what makes the body work, how to prepare the body for working, and how to train muscles to do what they needed to do. I am convinced it was the main reason why I was never seriously injured during my career.

Having made the decision to become a dancer on her own, Rosella was comfortable pursuing her goal without a constant mentor. She knew, or believed, that as long as she kept sight of her original goal during difficult times, everything would ultimately work out as planned. She credits herself with having always been able to see the direction her career was heading and knowing when she needed to change course. "I always had a plan. I remember someone asking me what I thought my future held when I was fourteen or fifteen. They probably regretted asking because I launched into a detailed explanation of what I was going to do for the next thirty years. It carried me all the way to what I'm doing now. And it has all come true."

In 1937, Sol Hurok launched the de Basil Ballets Russes on another cross-country tour of America. The tour would bypass Kansas City but was scheduled to stop in St. Louis. Word was out that Massine, who was finishing out his contract as director under de Basil before heading back to Monte Carlo to begin his own ballet company, was looking for dancers and would be holding auditions. Permission to skip school, train passes, and Perky's support were secured. "I didn't really think he would give me an audition," Rosella says. "I was so thrilled that he did, I was too excited to concentrate on everything he said to me afterward. All I know is that he told me to come to Monte Carlo and join his company. He told me I could get there fairly inexpensively on a third-class ship named the *Berengaria* and when I needed to be there."

Rosella did not need to hear anything else. At eighteen, she had passed her first audition with flying colors and had a job waiting for her in Monte Carlo. She was going to dance in essentially the same company that had sent her to ballet class in the first place. Time could not move fast enough. The news was received with great trepidation at home, however. "Even my mother thought the idea of going to Europe by myself to become a dancer was crazy. Then it became obvious I had no intention of letting the opportunity go by. There was the question of money, which I knew had to be dealt with because I had to pay my own way over and have money to live on for a while after I got there."

As usual, the family eventually went along with the plan and Perky led the way to the next phase of Rosella's career. The Kansas City *Times* published a picture and an announcement of Rosella's big break into show business and the scramble to raise funds for the journey began. The family cashed in an insurance policy and sold the piano. Perky donated her own funds and secured contributions from several local arts patrons.

Rosella was ready to begin her professional career. Having to travel halfway around the world to do so, she admits, had its good and bad points. Getting to Monte Carlo from Kansas City involved taking a train to New York, spending ten days crossing the Atlantic Ocean, taking a train from the port of arrival to Paris, and taking another train to the south of France and the principality of Monaco. Rosella was not intimidated. "I did not speak a word of French, but I had my train schedules written out on a card in French so I could make the right connections after we docked at Le Havre and once I got to Paris. I packed one black dress for going out, a few everyday things, what pointe shoes I had, and hundreds of practice clothes. I even wore those awful big black corrective shoes because they were sturdy."

Going to Europe on an overcrowded third-class ship in 1938 was not a pleasant experience. More concerned with where she was going than how she was getting there, Rosella spent the voyage sharing her unbridled enthusiasm with an American couple she met onboard. The train ride from Le Havre to Paris remains a treasured memory. "Coming in to Paris and seeing the city from the train was absolutely fantastic. The city looked magical with its huge buildings and tall spires and everything seemed to be a different color from anything I had ever seen before." She remembers her relief at making the connection to the train headed for Monte Carlo without any problem. Then the nightmare began.

After the train made its first stop, I realized there was no one calling out the names of the stations. I had no idea how many stops there were between Paris and Monte Carlo, so I immediately became terrified of missing my stop. I sat up all night in anguish, staring out the window trying to read the names of the stations as the train slowed to a stop. I kept my bag within reach, ready to get off at every stop. I think the trip took ten or twelve hours because I remember the sun was up when I finally saw the sea. Then, for the first time all night, I knew we hadn't passed Monte Carlo. I was exhausted, but I arrived in one piece.

Chapter Four

Fairfax, Oklahoma, 1925

The road to Fairfax winds through gently rolling hills dappled with the faint hue of bluestem grass splashed with occasional clusters of shade trees and isolated patches of wheat. One of five townsites established on Osage reservation land in 1905, the small agricultural community in northeastern Oklahoma sits tucked beneath towering oak, pecan, and hackberry trees. Highwater creeks teeming with lush flowering vines and thick wild cane lend a tropical ambience while trapping moisture needed to combat the ravages of the searing Oklahoma sun. Large stately homes surrounded by impeccably manicured lawns, well-tended flower beds, and masses of brilliant green ground cover flank wide, red brick streets extending eight square blocks uphill from Main Street to the entrance of a sprawling, sixty-acre private estate. Perched atop the highest ridge in sight, the Tall Chief family home commands a panoramic view of the countryside. Today, the speckled beige brick house with a terra-cotta tile roof remains the familial link of the Tall Chief clan and home of George and Vaden Tall Chief, an Osage Nation historian and former principal chief and current president of the Osage Nation, respectively.

Unlike the French corruption of the tribe's Indian name *wazha'zhe* to Osage, the Tall Chief family name reflects the consistency of their tribal leadership. Along with their Bigheart relatives through marriage, the Tall Chiefs have wielded influence in tribal affairs since the first recorded mention of the tribe by Father Jacques Marquette in 1673.

The Osage were hunters of outstanding repute among the Great Plains tribes, and their early life revolved around the buffalo. A nomadic people, they followed the herds from the Virginias to the Mississippi Valley and west to the area known today as Oklahoma long before the United States government became involved in Indian affairs. Osage warriors were known for their combative nature, superior skills in battle, and unrelenting courage. As confident as they were fearless, the early warriors often set out for battle on foot to return victorious astride horses seized from their enemies. Acts of aggression against the Osage were rare. By 1810 summer hunting excursions into Oklahoma and Kansas drew entire Osage villages west to vacation and share in the spoils of the hunt.

The Osage are above average in height, possess an imposing profile, and are aristocratic in bearing. The typical Osage has a well-defined jaw, high cheekbones, prominent forehead, and dark, piercing eyes separated by a delicately bridged nose. The superior attitude evidenced in their gait and direct stare has been noted by observers since Osage settlements were first discovered along the Osage River in present-day Missouri.

Using legendary tribal division names to denote geographic separation rather than physical distinctions between two bands, the Pahatsi, or Great Osage, settled near the mouth of the Marmaton River and the Utseha, or Little Osage, settled six miles to the west along the banks of the Osage River. The innate business skills of the tribe, which continue to bring the Osage unparalleled success in the white man's world, were evident in their dealings with the early French and Spanish traders. Long before the "oil-rich Osage" became a part of American history, the tribe had carved a position of respect and prominence in the economic development of the nation.

As recently as late August 1995, the Osage signed a $5 million agreement with Chevron USA and the Tulsa-based Davis Brothers Oil Producers, Inc., that was hailed by some in the industry as the largest mid-continent deal since 1965. Under terms of the agreement, Chevron will pay in excess of $1 million as an advance payment for a seismic option on up to 414,720 acres owned by the tribe through mid-December 1995. At that time, normal leasing operations will resume on all Osage land not chosen by Chevron. An additional $4 million will be spent by Chevron to conduct 3-D seismic explorations on selected Osage lands. The latter marks the first techologically sophisticated exploration program to be conducted on Osage lands and to allow reaching oil-bearing formations that have remained untouched. As a gesture of friendship and respect, Chevron also will replace an elm tree known as the "million dollar elm" at the site where the Osage conducted early lease auctions during the height of the oil boom. Ironically, the famous elm died during the late 1980s when oil production hit an all-time low and the industry nearly collapsed.

It was in 1808, however, that the first treaty ratified by the Osage and the United States government was signed far from Oklahoma, at Fort Clark, located in present-day Jackson County, Missouri. The treaty allowed federal acquisition of various tribal holdings along the Osage River and vast expanses of land in Missouri and northern Arkansas in exchange for a fifty-mile reservation tract along the Neosha River in Kansas. By 1825 the federal government had gained possession of all Osage land exclusive of the Kansas tract. The tribe remained in Kansas until 1872, making exceptional advances in education and embracing the Roman Catholic religion. The Civil War drove a wedge between the two major divisions of the tribe and incurred great loss of property and life. At war's end the Osage were forced to cede additional lands in Kansas and were put under pressure to relinquish further holdings to allow the opening of all Indian lands in the state to white settlers.

In 1870 Congress authorized the sale of Osage land in Kansas to underwrite the purchase of a new Osage reservation in Indian Territory. The move south took two years and reduced the population of the tribe by one-half. Recovery was slow and survival required new skills. Although Osage farming and stock-raising efforts faced an uphill battle against poor soil and weather conditions, the bluestem grasslands covering the majority of the tribe's northern Oklahoma reservation proved to be ideal for grazing. By the time cattle raising became a major industry in the late 1880s, Osage lands were prime grazing areas for leading commercial range operators.

Under the authorization of the tribal council, hundreds of thousands of acres of Osage pasturelands were leased and the profits divided equally among tribe members. In addition to income derived from pasture leases, the interest due the tribe on funds held in trust by the U.S. Treasury increased significantly. Between 1880 and 1891, proceeds from the sale of Osage lands in Kansas raised the total trust amount from $2 million to $8 million and increased annual tribal interest earnings from $90,648 to $409,490.

When the Osage National Council convened in Pawhuska in 1881 to adopt a written constitution, select a legislative council, and elect its first principal chief, citizenship requirements for the Osage Nation were of primary concern. Not bound by the terms of the Congressional Allotment Act of 1887, the Osage were approached by the United States Cherokee Commission in 1893 to negotiate an agreement providing for the allocation of tribal lands and funds based on the existing tribal roll. Representing the fullblood members of the tribe and speaking in perfect English, Osage Principal Chief James Bigheart demanded action be delayed until the Office of Indian Affairs had succeeded in ascertaining a correct tribal roll. No action resulted and no agreement was reached.

Bigheart, the first principal chief elected by the tribe, was a half-Osage who held formidable strength at the negotiating table. In 1886, using his command of the English language and superior business acumen, Bigheart secured a ten-year comprehensive lease covering all Osage lands thought to be rich in oil and natural gas, guaranteeing a one-tenth royalty on all oil produced on leased lands and an annual fee of $50 per gas well. The initial lease, negotiated with Osage council member Edwin B. Foster and subsequently known as the Foster Lease, established a foundation for the unprecedented financial security the Osage Nation continues to enjoy today. Income from oil and gas recovery, and pasture leases and other real estate holdings proved lucrative for the Osage through the opening of Indian Territory to white settlers in 1889. Two years before Oklahoma was granted statehood, the Foster Lease was renewed by an act of Congress with the annual payment for operating gas wells increased to $100 and the royalty amount earned on all oil and gas produced raised to one-eighth.

In 1907 the Osage tribal roll was closed with a total of 2,229 Osage registered, and guidelines were set for distributing fullblood headrights in perpetuity among heirs of the original allottees. By year end the Osage had devised a system of allocating tribal property interests that was taken to Washington in early 1908 by a delegation headed by Bigheart. Ratified by Congress as the Osage Allotment Act, the agreement contained a provision stipulating that both the mineral and the surface rights to tribal lands would remain common property of the Osage Nation. Although mineral rights to 1.5 million acres of land in northeastern Oklahoma remain common property of the Osage Nation today, surface rights of 640 acres, or one square mile per headright, were allocated to enrolled Osage in 1909.

The percentage of individual headrights assigned to heirs of the original allotees is still based on actual blood ties and the number of immediate family members. As a result, headrights passed from generation to generation represent only fractional rights to profits derived from the original allotment. Oil production on Osage land was without precedent. By 1906 more than five million barrels of oil had been recovered. It was not until the discovery of the billion-dollar Burbank Field in 1920, however, that the tribe's extensive oil wealth attracted national attention. A tumultuous period of rampant spending and unscrupulous attempts to wrest control of Osage headrights ensued.

Taking the sudden influx of wealth in stride, the Tall Chief family refrained from excessive displays of extravagance and remained essentially unscathed. The family embraced its share of luxuries but led a lifestyle more aptly described as comfortable. Alexander Joseph Tall Chief, groomed to continue the legacy of the family name, was in his early teens when his uncle, James Bigheart, headed the negotiations that resulted in the ratification of the Osage Allotment Act. Although offered a full academic scholarship to attend a

The Alex J. Tall Chief home in Fairfax, Oklahoma. The photo was taken in the mid-1950s. (Personal collection.)

prestigious Ivy League university, Alex opted for continuing his pursuits in Fairfax over life on the East Coast. He enjoyed the ways of the Osage and the leisurely affluence of life in Fairfax. A widower with three young children when he married Ruth Porter, Alex had long since developed a complacent approach to life. Ruth did not share her husband's outlook. An ambitious woman with a yen for getting the most out of every opportunity, she became active in developing a social circle in Fairfax. Her inexhaustible ability to get things done made her an integral part of the community and reflected well on the family.

The family lived well. In addition to maintaining the original Tall Chief home after construction was completed on the brick mansion on the hill above Fairfax, the Tall Chiefs rented a summer home in Manitou Springs, a small community on the outskirts of Colorado Springs, Colorado. While Ruth deplored the lack of drive among the Osage, which she attributed to financial independence, she recognized its merits. Being able to concentrate her energies on raising a family within a structure that could provide whatever was needed to develop and nurture individual potential made up for a lot of faults. And it offered the chance to alter the course of the future.

After the arrival of her first child, Gerald, Ruth introduced a new ingredient—music—to the traditional pattern of raising offspring in the Tall Chief family. Although her husband was an accomplished saxophone player, he had not discovered music until his teens. Among Ruth's peers music lessons for children were something of a status symbol, and finding a teacher with a good reputation in the community was no problem. As soon as Gerald could handle a child-sized trumpet, he began private lessons at home.

Considering the family's prominent position in Fairfax, the circumstances surrounding the birth of Alex and Ruth Tall Chief's second child on January 24, 1925, should have been avoided. Exactly what transpired when the couple arrived at Fairfax Memorial Hospital is unclear, but the story, remembered by family members, is that the doctor showed up in a somewhat inebriated state. A farm girl from Kansas of Scotch, Irish, and Dutch descent, Ruth Porter Tall Chief had little regard for doctors. The incident lent credence to her contention that the medical profession was unworthy of being taken seriously in Fairfax or anywhere else. Despite the circumstances, Elizabeth Marie Tall Chief entered the world without complications.

The world that Betty Marie entered, however, was not without its complications. "I think Mother's whole life was a reaction to what she had seen happen to the Osage after they discovered oil," Maria says. Sinking gracefully into a deep-cushioned armchair surrounded by an impressive display of contemporary art in her spacious Chicago apartment overlooking Lake Michigan, Maria mentions having shortened Betty Marie to Maria in 1943.

Mother could never accept that because of the oil money my father had not continued his education past high school. My mother was determined to see that we did more with our lives. She knew about the families who were killed for their headrights and all of that too. I remember hearing about a family related to us that was murdered, except for one child who was spending the night at a friend's house. Insurance scams were generally the way it happened, and the man who was behind those murders had come around trying to sell insurance to my grandmother, Eliza Tall Chief. She had sent him away because she didn't get involved with people like that. My mother was determined to see that we did more with our lives.

Chapter Five

Hollywood, California, 1930

Before Betty Marie's first birthday, it became apparent that another Tall Chief was on the way. Once again, Ruth came up short in her dealings with the medical profession. Five weeks short, to be exact. Trusting her doctor's calculations, Ruth decided to accompany the family on its annual trek to Colorado. Since their return to Fairfax was scheduled several weeks ahead of her projected due date, spending the latter months of her pregnancy six hundred miles from the stifling Oklahoma summer weather made sense. To Ruth's dismay, her third child had a different agenda. Determined though Ruth was that all of her children be born in Oklahoma, she wasted no time getting to a hospital in Denver after feeling the first twinges of labor. Driving seventy miles to give birth in a strange hospital under the supervision of an unfamiliar doctor was not what Ruth had had in mind. But she took the situation in stride. Concern that the infant might be premature was dispelled within minutes of the arrival of an obviously full-term, healthy baby girl on October 19, 1927. The infant was promptly named Marjorie, and Alex and Ruth gathered what was needed to care for the newborn before returning to the family retreat. News of Marjorie's unexpected arrival was sent back to Fairfax immediately, and plans were launched for a swift return home.

Almost from the beginning the physical similarities between Betty Marie and Marjorie created confusion among friends and relatives. After Ruth began dressing them alike, it became almost impossible to tell the girls apart with a casual glance. The resemblance between the two has never been more than superficial, however. Ruth encouraged them to develop strong individual personalities. They did. Today both laugh about the fact that they were always too busy competing *with* each other, as opposed to *against* each other, to get involved in sibling rivalries. The only subject they sincerely disagree about is the dates of their births. Marjorie insists that she was born in 1926, and her sister is equally adament that she was born in 1925. To my chagrin, efforts to locate hospital records or other legal documentation proved futile.

The intensely rigid childhood they shared nurtured a mutual trust and friendship that remains integral to their lives today. Prior to Marjorie's decision to move to Boca Raton, Florida, in 1989 to direct the ballet faculty of the fledgling Harid Conservatory, it was not uncommon for the two women to meet regularly at a fashionable Chicago department store restaurant for lunch, order the same entrée, and spend the afternoon trying on the same clothes. They also share a sense of humor when they are mistaken for each other by people unaccustomed to looking past the similar hairstyles and commanding presence.

As children, it was Betty Marie who first gave evidence of possessing significant potential.

I was very young when I started studying the piano. I think I was still in diapers! Well, the teachers explained to my mother that I had perfect pitch and that was very rare. Mother was a very demanding woman, and once she

Marjorie *(left),* Maria *(right),* and Ruth Tall Chief celebrate Maria's induction into the Oklahoma Hall of Fame, 1972. (Personal collection.)

became aware that you were capable of something, you did it. If she knew you could make straight A's in school, you made straight A's. The music teachers had told her I had extraordinary potential at the piano so I played the piano.

Soon after beginning piano, Betty Marie took her first dance lessons. At such an early age, she recalls having been too shy to look anyone in the eye, much less question an adult's order. "So, when the teacher told me to point my toes out in opposite directions, I couldn't believe it. But I did it."

Whatever innate talent Betty Marie displayed in her first dance classes did not measure up to the potential she showed at the piano.

Mother didn't know anything about dance. But she had become somewhat of a social leader of Fairfax. So when a teacher came through town offering private dance lessons, Mother arranged for me to have private lessons from Mrs. Sabin. And that was how it started. In the beginning, she came to the house twice a week and taught class in the basement. As soon as Marjorie was old enough, she started too, and we had great fun jumping

Circa 1927. *Left,* Marjorie and her father, Alex Tall Chief, Fairfax, Oklahoma; *right,* Betty Marie and Marjorie with their mother, Ruth Tall Chief, at the stone gate of their Fairfax home. (Personal collection.)

around and dancing on our toes. Of course, we were put into pointe shoes way too early, but somehow we managed to get up there and spin around like tops.

Marjorie admits that her enthusiasm for dance classes far exceeded her interest in the piano.

I didn't have any special musical talents and I didn't like to sit still at the piano. I took my lessons and practiced the way I was supposed to, but I never took it seriously. Dancing class was different. I was very limber and loved acrobatics. I was a contortionist at a very young age and did a lot of tumbling, which I am convinced was very helpful later. Acrobatics taught

34

Circa 1930. *Left,* Betty Marie Tallchief in her Highland Fling costume; *right,* Marjorie Tallchief on pointe at the Tall Chief home in Fairfax, Oklahoma. (Personal collection.)

me balance and control and showed me how to use my full strength. Mother didn't quite know what to make of it, but she was happy that I showed so much interest.

Under Mrs. Sabin's guidance several routines were arranged, and Betty Marie and Marjorie began performing at benefits for the Boy Scouts, community events, county fairs, and just about anywhere else Ruth could wrangle an appearance. Today Maria remembers, "Mother thought it was good for us to perform, so we did. Sometimes I would play the piano and then Marjorie and I would dance. Most of the time, though, we just did a dance number. I think mother thought that a sister act was a good introduction to show business even if we were the intermission act at the rodeo."

35

Marjorie takes equal delight in describing her earliest memories of performing. "I remember one of our most popular routines, *Stars and Stripes Forever*. The grand finale always got a big round of applause. Maria wore a cape that had an American flag sewn into the lining. At the end she would do fouettés holding the cape open while I did walk-overs around her in a circle. As silly as it all was, people always wanted us to come back. So I guess we were successful."

Reflecting on their mother's dislike of doctors, both women remember an incident that happened on one of their out-of-town engagements. "I got sick," Maria says. "And, rather than call a doctor, Mother put me in a hot shower. I fainted and Marjorie had to go out and dance my part and hers. As it turned out, I had strep throat, and as soon as I got better, Marjorie came down with it and I had to do double duty. Mother never did take us to a doctor. I'm sure we must have had all the children's diseases such as chicken pox and measles, but none of us ever went to a doctor while we lived at home."

An interesting element missing from their childhood performing careers was the inclusion of any authentic Indian dances. According to Maria, "about as close as we came to doing anything that reflected our heritage was a routine we did in Indian costumes. We had bells on our ankles and hopped around in headpieces decorated with feathers. Obviously, it had nothing to do with traditional Indian dances. As I remember them, the authentic Osage dances were kind of lethargic, and I don't think Mother thought they were suitable for showcasing our best attributes."

The Tall Chief sisters became somewhat of a fixture at social and charity events in Fairfax and the surrounding area. Both clearly remember performing in the Tall Chief Theatre in Fairfax and being considered the budding young stars of the community. By the time Betty Marie was ready to start second grade, Ruth had reached the conclusion that Betty Marie's continuing progress at the piano and the potential both she and Marjorie had shown in their dance classes demanded better training. As far as Ruth was concerned, better teachers and the possibility of being discovered by a big-time producer were lurking in the hills of Hollywood. Alex had no qualms about moving to California. "He loved to play golf," Maria says. "And he knew he could play golf more in California than Oklahoma or Colorado, so he was all for it." The family home and farm was left in the capable hands of Alex's older children under the supervision of his mother. Arrangements were made to locate a home in the hills above Los Angeles, and the five Tall Chiefs headed west.

Ruth Tall Chief was not the kind of person to let what she did not know slow her down. Although she had been apprised of several reputable music schools, including the music department at the University of California at Los Angeles, by Betty Marie's piano teacher in Fairfax, Mrs. Sabin had been unable to come up with a list of dance studios. "Looking back I can't believe it," Maria says. "Mother asked a clerk in the drugstore a few blocks from our house to recommend a good dance studio! Fortunately, he recommended Ernest Belcher's studio."

Belcher, a distinguished teacher with unlimited integrity, promptly informed Ruth that the girls would have to go back to beginners class and throw out their pointe shoes or he would not accept them in his school. Impressed by photographs of known performers and movie stars lining the hallway of Belcher's Hollywood studio and the steady stream of students going from class to class, Ruth enrolled Betty Marie and Marjorie. Going back to the basics and learning how to point their toes in opposite directions all over again was not a thrilling experience for either of them. "We had to unlearn everything we had been taught," Marjorie says.

He was very strict too, and we weren't used to that. I was so young, and there were so many differences between going to his school and studying at home that I did not pay much attention to how different the actual classes were. What I do remember, though, was the day he told me I had to stop doing contortions. He could see I was getting so overstretched that it was working against building strength so he finally said "Enough." Since there was no question in anyone's mind that I was going to be a ballet dancer at that point, I stopped.

Although Marjorie's participation in acrobatics was severely curtailed, both girls took tap, acrobatics, and Spanish dancing in addition to their ballet classes at Belcher's studio. "It was very difficult at first," Maria says. "But Mother said that if he hadn't thought we were very talented, he wouldn't have bothered to send us back. So we worked as hard as we could and caught up fairly quickly. It was a difficult experience but very valuable."

37

At the same time the girls were wrestling to overcome bad habits in the dance studio, they ran into similar problems on the academic front. Although Betty Marie was two years ahead of Marjorie in school, they were both put into the same class. "It was called an 'Opportunity Class,'" Maria explains. "But the whole idea was to let us do whatever we wanted to do. I didn't like that, but Marjorie did. We were very different. She never liked school and I loved it."

Chapter Six

New York, New York, 1942

As the move to California had been made to offer Betty Marie and Marjorie an opportunity to pursue their potential in the professional world of music and dance, family life revolved around their studies. "I practiced the piano for an hour before school in the morning and an hour after school in the afternoon and then we dashed into the car to get to our dancing lessons," Maria says. "There wasn't much time for anything else, but Mother made sure we learned to sew and cook and those kinds of things. I remember everyone helped in the kitchen, and there was never any attitude about who was supposed to do what." Marjorie recalls having been only mildly aware of the difference between living in Fairfax and living in Los Angeles. "I was too young to be able to make a comparison. I don't think I even saw the difference between Mr. Belcher and Mrs. Sabin. Except, of course, that he took away our pointe shoes. All I remember was that we were near the ocean, we ate a lot more fruit and vegetables, and there were all kinds of plants and flowers. I liked the climate because it was warmer but never seemed to get as hot as Fairfax."

It was not until later that Maria remembers becoming aware that being Indian was viewed differently in California than it was in Oklahoma. "I do not think it became an issue until high school, but I remember the kids at school making a big deal about the way we spelled our name. Wanting to be as much like everyone else as I could, I changed it to one word. I can't remember what my parents thought about that, but they must have gone along with it because Marjorie started spelling it that way too."

Maria also vividly recalls seeing her first ballet performance in Los Angeles.

We started attending performances presented by the Los Angeles Philharmonic and the Ballets Russes de Monte Carlo came and I still remember *Gaîté Parisienne*. Oh, it was so romantic. George Zoritch and Leonide Massine and Alexandra Danilova were all dancing, and I thought to myself, that's the kind of world I want to be in. Alicia Markova must have been with the company too, because I remember seeing her perform *Giselle*. I think seeing the Ballets Russes was what started me thinking about becoming a dancer instead of a pianist. Danilova and Markova made an incredible impression on me and really opened my eyes to what ballet was.

Although performing opportunities were not as easy to come by as they had been in Fairfax, the girls made their California debut at the Sacramento State Fair and appeared in the MGM feature film *Presenting Lily Mars*, starring Judy Garland. Betty Marie's progress at the piano led to solo recitals and appearances with the chamber music quartet at the University of California at Los Angeles. Before Betty Marie's twelfth birthday, Ruth decided it was time to move the girls to the Hollywood studio of the legendary Russian expatriate Bronislava Nijinska. The studio boasted an impressive roster of guest teachers including the ballerinas Mia Slavenska and Tatiana Riabouchinska and the latter's husband, dancer-choreographer David

Lichine. The parting with Belcher was amicable and not an uncommon occurrence in the daily existence of Hollywood studios.

"Mme Nijinska was completely different from anyone we had ever been exposed to," Marjorie says, sitting bolt upright in her chair. "The entire time you were in class you had to totally focus on what was going on. When you were waiting for your turn to do a center combination, you stood with your arms in first position or you left the class. There was no leaning on the barre or looking away from whoever was dancing." The sister of the legendary Vaslav Nijinsky and a highly acclaimed choreographer in her own right, Nijinska had graduated from the Imperial School of Ballet in St. Petersburg in 1908. She was a featured dancer with the famed Maryinsky ballet company but succeeded in obtaining extended leaves of absence to appear as a guest with Diaghilev's Ballets Russes before leaving Russia for good in 1918. Revered as the grande dame of Russian ballet in America, Nijinska held a position of great influence in the world of ballet. Her dedication to continuing the legacy of classical Russian ballet drove her to teach. Deriving the lion's share of her income from her work as a choreographer and ballet mistress, Nijinska had the luxury of being able to pick and choose her students.

Arching her neck majestically, Maria says, "When you walked into her class it was like going to church. You didn't go into class prepared to do anything less than your maximum effort. There was no 'I don't feel like doing anything today.' You did everything full out, or you were out. And you stayed out." Relaxing her position, Maria describes Nijinska with fondness. "Here she was, a roly-poly little woman who could jump and move like lightning. She had tiny feet and they were so fast. Her batterie and footwork were incredible, but she was more concerned with training the arms and upper body and teaching you to breathe, which was so very important. In some ways, I think she was really more of a choreographer in class than a teacher."

A combination of Betty Marie's and Marjorie's technical strengths and eagerness to improve put them in the good graces of Nijinska and her impressive faculty. "My sister had a much more natural talent than I," Maria remarks. "She was so limber, she could wrap her leg around her head and all that. For me, it was a big struggle. I didn't start out with a supple body. I had to really stretch it out and work for everything. It was hard. I had small hips and no natural turnout. It was difficult. But maybe that's all the more reason why I worked so hard."

Working hard paid off. While Betty Marie continued to gain recognition as a pianist, Marjorie gained popularity working in films and the two joined the small group of students Nijinska allowed to appear in Los Angeles Light Opera productions and local concerts. In 1940 both appeared in a gala evening of dance presented at the Hollywood Bowl. For Betty Marie, the performance held tremendous significance and marked her debut in a major role. Performing the second lead in Nijinska's *Chopin Concerto* opposite Cyd Charisse in front of an audience of twenty thousand touched a nerve that no piano performance had ever reached. Despite the fact that everything that could have gone wrong did, Maria still considers the performance a landmark in her career. "We got stuck in traffic on the way to the theater, so Marjorie and I had to run up the hill to the dressing room to get into our costumes in time for the curtain. Then I made my entrance and promptly slipped. After the performance, I remember Mme Nijinska said that she was pleased and that I had recovered very well, so it didn't bother me."

Audience reaction was excellent, and Betty Marie's performance was praised by the reigning arts observers. A few weeks after the performance, Maria remembers writing an essay at school about making a decision between two careers. "I loved the piano, but I didn't like having to practice for hours in a room by myself. I liked people and being around people and that's what ballet offered. I don't think I ever came out and said it that directly at home, but from that moment on I was determined to prove to my mother that I should be a dancer and not a pianist."

As far as Marjorie was concerned, not having to divide her energies between ballet and music was just fine. "By the time I entered Beverly Hills High School, I knew my future was in ballet and I was devoted to dance. I did quite a bit of work in films and enjoyed it, but I always knew it was part of my training for a career in ballet." Having exhibited the single-minded determination needed to succeed as professional dancers in addition to their abundant talents, Betty Marie and Marjorie quickly gained star-pupil status at Nijinska's studio.

During Betty Marie's senior year in high school, the intensity of

Betty Marie and Marjorie Tallchief, 1933. (Personal collection.)

her training increased. Regardless of how talented she was, there was no getting around the fact that if she was to pursue a career in ballet, she would need to get into a company as soon after graduating as possible. Whether or not Ruth Tall Chief was aware of the significance of what was happening, she allowed Betty Marie to audition for Sergei Denham's Ballet Russe de Monte Carlo in 1942.

As company premier danseur and ballet master at the time,

Frederic Franklin was on the audition committee during the troupe's California auditions. His recollection is vivid.

The company desperately needed girls. Because of the war, we had terrible problems because we had so many dancers who didn't have American passports. The company was booked on a Canadian tour and we were going to have to leave a dozen or so dancers behind. Maria, or Betty Marie as she was known then, looked just like all the other girls we had seen in every city we stopped in when she came into the room. She put her pointe shoes on and without any fuss went into a prepared routine. By the time she had finished, it was very quiet in the room.

She was absolutely amazing. Even though everything was rough around the edges, she could do anything. Her technical strength didn't please everyone on the audition committee, but I pushed very hard back in New York to make sure she was hired.

Maria remembers little more than being excited and a little nervous until she started dancing. No contract or specific offer was made, but she was told that Mr. Denham would be interested in seeing her after she graduated from high school. As far as Betty Marie was concerned, no further encouragement was needed. She would celebrate her eighteenth birthday as a member of the Ballet Russe de Monte Carlo!

To what degree Nijinska and her illustrious colleagues manipulated the circumstances will never be known. But the legendary ballerina Tatiana Riabouchinska paid a visit to the Tall Chief home a few days before she was to leave for New York to join Denham's company as a guest artist. On the spur of the moment, she suggested that since Betty Marie had just graduated from high school, perhaps she should accompany her to New York and see if Denham was really serious. Ruth quickly agreed.

Mother had it all arranged before I graduated that I would start college in the fall to pursue a career in music. As far as she was concerned, going to New York would be a nice change of scenery and give me a chance to buy a new wardrobe for college. Well, when I got to New York, it turned out that Denham needed dancers for the Canadian tour because of the "nansens," as we used to call the Russians without passports. So he hired twelve of us as apprentices and told us we had the tour to prove worthy of being hired as regular company members.

Betty Marie's request for permission to sign with Denham was not greeted with great elation at home. After lengthy discussions, Ruth agreed to let her seventeen-year-old daughter join the company but insisted that her potential career as a concert pianist would not be put to rest simply because she had gotten a job as a dancer first. With the Canadian tour to earn a first-year contract from Denham and a year's grace to convince her mother that ballet would offer greater rewards than a career in music, Betty Marie Tallchief entered the professional world of ballet.

Chapter Seven

Hollywood, California, 1944

As thrilled as Marjorie was for her sister, she remembers it had little effect on her own life. "We were very close and I missed her, but we had both gone off on our own paths by that point. Even though we had been in the same classes at Nijinska's studio and had performed together in some concerts, everything else was pretty much separate. Of course, I didn't mind being able to have my own room for the first time in my life."

With a year of high school left to complete and a full schedule of ballet classes, film engagements, and concert appearances beckoning, Marjorie recalls seizing an opportunity to shorten her academic career by six months. "I enrolled in a special horticulture class that involved growing specific kinds of plants at home for extra credit. Mr. Gooch, who taught the course, would come by to monitor the status of the plants and determine your grade from what he saw. I remember Maria coming home for a visit and saying something about the house looking like a tropical forest, but Mr. Gooch gave me an 'A' and I finished my senior year six months ahead of my class." In retrospect, she admits having been quite amazed by the entire experience. "Considering how much time I didn't spend in school, I still find it incredible I actually graduated early!"

Without having to divide her time pursuing two potential careers, Marjorie had made a name for herself in the movies and seemed well on her way to a full-blown film career.

I had become very popular with several of the studios and established myself to the point that I was offered a long-term contract to stay on. After the Judy Garland spectacular, I was accepted as one of the regular studio dancers and appeared in at least half a dozen films. I remember one starring Eleanor Powell that involved a horse. Mother never let us near horses in Fairfax because Gerald had had a serious accident as a very young child and she was afraid we would get hurt. Of course, that made us afraid of horses and when this huge animal appeared on the set next to me, it terrified me. I still remember him struggling to get his feet under him a few inches from me on the slippery stage, which had been coated with wax to reflect the lights. It was terrible because I was convinced he was going to fall on me the entire time.

Sitting in her sun-drenched living room in Chicago filled with Russian icons and framed sketches of original sets and costumes, Marjorie admits that she would like to forget some of the publicity stunts arranged by the studios as much as her experience with the horse. Her first taste of Hollywood-style glamor was being named the Pin-up Girl for the 414th Air Squadron in 1944. "It was part of a studio promotion and I guess I had to do it."

Regardless of her success in the movies, Marjorie had no illusions of pursuing a career on the silver screen. "Underneath it all, I think Mother had always wanted to be a dancer. And that was part of it." Although Marjorie continued working in films, no long-term contract was signed. Instead, the focus of her energies was turned to preparing for her debut in the professional world of ballet. Unlike

Studio portrait of Marjorie Tallchief, Hollywood, California, 1945. (Personal collection.)

her sister's off-handed departure for New York and inauspicious debut with the Ballet Russe de Monte Carlo eighteen months earlier, Marjorie's transition to the professional world was carefully orchestrated. The question of which company Marjorie should join became the focus of attention at home and at the studio.

Once high school was out of the way, Marjorie spent her free time working predominantly with Nijinska and Lichine.

That's when I started learning the Competition Dance from Lichine's *Graduation Ball*. It was a wonderful variation for me and really showed off my best points. There were lots of fouettés and fast, high kicks that I had always done well, so I enjoyed it too. Of course, Lichine wanted me to learn it because he knew he was going to be setting it for Ballet Theatre's fall season in New York and that it would be a suitable audition piece for me.

As it turned out, I never did audition. Mr. Denham invited me to join Maria in the Ballet Russe de Monte Carlo and impresario Sol Hurok offered me a soloist contract with Ballet Theatre.

Before Ruth Tall Chief had time to reach a conclusion, Nijinska intervened.

Madame Nijinska rarely had much to say, but she made an issue out of the fact that I should not go to the same company where Maria was. She took Mother aside to explain that going to Denham's company was not a good idea. She was adamant that because Maria and I were so much alike technically, I would never be given the chance to do a significant role first. And, of course, Madame Nijinska was right. Maria had rank and seniority, and because there were so few roles, I wouldn't have had a chance.

Lichine and Riabouchinska agreed. Having signed with Hurok themselves to appear as featured guest artists during Ballet Theatre's 1944 fall New York season, the couple encouraged Ruth to take Nijinska's advice. In addition to performing, Lichine also pointed to the fact that he and Nijinska had been engaged to join the troupe's illustrious roster of guest choreographers for the season. There was little room for argument. Nijinska's opinion was uncontested. Denham's offer was politely declined and Marjorie signed with Hurok and Ballet Theatre. Although the company was under the direction of Lucia Chase and Richard Pleasant, Hurok was an integral part of management and wielded a good measure of artistic control. According to the terms of her contract Marjorie would join the company as a soloist but would also perform roles in the corps de ballet. She was guaranteed the role she had learned in *Graduation Ball* and a stipend from Hurok to augment her salary from Ballet Theatre.

Ruth Tall Chief was pleased with the terms of Marjorie's starting contract and signed the parental permission documents without resistance. This time, however, she did not wave good-bye at the train station. She went along. "My mother went with me on tour, and it was a good thing because the dancers Hurok brought into the company did not exactly win any popularity contests. I might not have had a roommate if she hadn't been there. And she wasn't the only mother traveling with the company. I remember Tommy Rall's mother was there and a few others. So we left my father and brother in California and headed off to join the company in Canada."

Maria remembers being thrilled by the news that Marjorie had signed as a soloist with Ballet Theatre. That Ballet Theatre and the Ballet Russe de Monte Carlo would both be presenting fall seasons in New York also meant that there would be time to celebrate the direction their careers had taken. "We took every opportunity we could to see each other perform," Maria says. "And we both watched Lichine and Riabouchinska from the wings at the Met."

Marjorie concurs.

It was very special, and seeing them on stage was an incredible experience. The Ballet Russe was performing at City Center and a group of us from Ballet Theatre used to sneak into the theater to see performances. I thought I had mastered getting by the ushers without being noticed because I never got caught. But on my way out of the theater the last performance of the season the manager stopped me in the lobby and said, "Good-bye Miss Tallchief, I'm glad you could join us." He was so sweet and apparently took great delight in watching all of us scurrying up the back steps to the balcony the entire season! Years later, I remember laughing when I heard the tradition of sneaking into City Center was still going on and that no one ever got caught.

Following the conclusion of the Ballet Theatre and Ballet Russe seasons, Ruth Tall Chief returned to California and the family's home in Beverly Hills. Within a year and a half of Marjorie's Canadian debut with Ballet Theatre, Ruth, Alex, and Gerald headed back to Fairfax and the house on the hill. The decade they had spent in California had fulfilled Ruth's goal and catapulted both girls into the international world of ballet where their future remained to unfold.

51

Chapter Eight

Vinita, Oklahoma, 1929

Barely fifty miles from the Arkansas, Missouri, and Kansas state lines, the northeastern Oklahoma agricultural community of Vinita bears little resemblance to the far western and southwestern areas of the state. Untamed thickets of scrub oak, cottonwood, and hackberry give way to jagged sandstone cliffs flanking the sandy shoreline of an intricate network of lakes stretching as far as the eye can see. Driving by huge expanses of grazing lands and fields of corn, soybeans, and wheat the countryside appears to be endowed with unlimited potential.

Northeastern Oklahoma also is Chouteau country. Highway signs, town names, dams, bridges, roadside scenic overlooks, and historical markers attest that it was here in 1796 that Major Jean Pierre Chouteau built the first white settlement in what would become the forty-sixth state of the Union. Heading an expedition for the Chouteau Brothers Trading Company into the uncharted wilderness southwest of St. Louis, Chouteau carved a path by foot and horseback some four hundred miles through dense forest and towering cliffs before coming upon a river known to his Osage guides as Neo'zha. It was, the Osage assured Chouteau, the first of three great rivers that converged farther south that could yield a new route between St. Louis and New Orleans. Fashioning a crude dugout canoe from a cottonwood tree, the party proceeded downstream by land and water. Two days later, Chouteau discovered a coldwater stream leading to an inland spring within a stone's throw of the riverbank.

Gathering his men together, he began building a permanent settlement named La Saline. Although little remains of the original rough-hewn outpost, a plaque honoring Major Chouteau as the Father of Oklahoma marks the site now incorporated in the city limits of Salina in Mayes County, Oklahoma. Considering that Major Chouteau's elder brother, Auguste, is credited with cofounding the city of St. Louis, one wonders what shape the American frontier might have taken had the Chouteau brothers decided to make a go of their father's unsuccessful bakery in New Orleans.

The history of the Chouteau family in northeastern Oklahoma is a superior example of the blending of cultures through intermarriage that fostered a frontier life untainted by social or racial bias and free of conflict between the white man and the Indian. Loyalties built on trust and respect served the Chouteaus, the Osage, the Shawnee, and the Cherokee well, fueling familial and philosophical ties that remain intact today. As a result, the Chouteau family tree is extremely complex but clearly reveals the bloodlines and adoption practices linking the Oklahoma Chouteau, the Shawnee, and the Cherokee.

In 1856, William Meyer Chouteau, great-grandson of Jean Pierre Chouteau, married a Shawnee maiden, Mary Silverheels. Thirteen years later the roughly seven hundred Shawnees remaining in Oklahoma were adopted by the Cherokee Nation in a formal ritual. Since 1869, the Shawnee have registered on the Cherokee roll as adopted tribal members. Among the seven children born to William and Mary Silverheels Chouteau was a son named Edmond, born blind. Edmond Choteau was a musician of local acclaim. He married Myra Fields Ware and the couple had two sons, Byron Ware and Corbett Edward. The latter, known familiarly as C.E., married Lucy Arnett, a schoolteacher. The couple had one child, Myra Yvonne. The Chouteau legacy bequeathed little in terms of financial wealth but bred a pride of birthright and ancestry no earthly riches could buy.

In 1928 C.E. found himself facing an uphill battle by attempting to continue the long-standing family tradition of farming. When the first wave of the Great Depression swept through Vinita in the latter days of Calvin Coolidge's reign of prosperity, C.E. had the opportunity to take a job with an oil company based in Fort Worth, Texas. Deeply concerned by the rapidly deteriorating world economy and the fact that he and his young wife were expecting their first child, C.E. decided that leaving his native Vinita was a small price to pay for financial security. The loss of revenue from area farms and ranches already had idled more able-bodied men and boys than the community could support and the odds of landing a job as close to home as Texas were few and far between. Lucy agreed, as did his mother.

As matriarch of the family, Myra Ware Chouteau had no intention of allowing the newest member of the Chouteau clan to enter the world anywhere except the family home in Vinita. A widow by that time, Mme Chouteau had a reputation for telling everyone, including her children, exactly what she expected of them whether they liked it or not. Not one to discuss matters, she often turned on her heels and left after stating her position. Such was the case in 1928. C.E. would go to Fort Worth and Lucy would stay in Vinita until the baby was born.

Initially, the arrangement worked out well. A Mississippi-born schoolteacher with tremendous interest in American Indians and their cultures, Lucy had met her husband while teaching at a Navaho reservation school in Fort Defiance, Arizona. She respected the traditions of the Chouteau family without question and raised no objections to the decision. Lucy accepted her assigned tasks and prepared the nursery as decreed by her mother-in-law without complaint, but she availed herself of every opportunity to visit her husband in Fort Worth. Either both women miscalculated the due date of the child or Mother Nature intervened, for an early spring visit to Fort Worth brought an unexpected dividend.

On March 7, 1929, Myra Yvonne Chouteau arrived healthy and happy in a Fort Worth hospital. "My grandmother never forgave my mother for that. Daddy was very upset and so was my mother, but that's what happened." Making room for her yellow Labrador retriever, Nigel, on a long couch nestled beneath a sunny window, Yvonne remembers hearing stories about her grandmother's reaction to the news. "Grandmother was furious. She insisted that my great-great-great-grandfather, Major Jean Pierre Chouteau, would have been upset, along with every other Chouteau down the list. My grandmother wasn't exactly an easy person to live with and Mother went to Fort Worth as much to get away from her as she did to see my father. But the last thing she wanted to do was give birth there." Patting Nigel's broad head she adds, "My father always used to say I was born in Vinita and everyone in the family went along with him. But I wasn't. Of course, as soon as the doctor said it was safe to travel, we returned to Vinita and Grandmother."

Just as Mme Chouteau had voiced her rancor at the unexpected turn of events, she fussed and fluttered over the newborn. Neither Lucy nor C.E. stood a chance of monopolizing time in the nursery. Yvonne's wispy blond hair and delicate features became the highlight of her grandmother's life at a time when economic destruction threatened to destroy the world she had known to be safe, secure, and solvent. Breaking into a haunting, rhythmic chant of syllabic phrases resembling "nyah, nyah, oya nyah," Yvonne says, "I still remember Grandmother putting me on her lap and singing Indian songs to me while she churned buttermilk. Underneath the harsh exterior, she was an incredible woman. We called her Grand Mamère because she had such a way of saying things and telling you what to do. And because she was a grand lady."

Mme Chouteau may have ruled with an iron hand, but there were few alternatives when it came to keeping both the family's gracious Vinita residence and the mile-square Chouteau farm twenty miles away unscathed by the grim realities of a world economy gone bust. The events of Monday, October 28, 1929, had no impact on the solvency of the Chouteaus and sent little more than a minor shiver through the streets of Vinita. Dwindling food markets and the threat of foreclosure already had prompted men and boys, who had never been more than a hundred miles from where they were born, to seek jobs as far afield as California. And while the American economy tumbled into disarray much like a barn hit broadside by a tornado, little Yvonne played in the fields and grasped at the musical instrument that had been her grandfather's life.

"Even before I could walk, I was allowed to touch things that made sound. Grandpa Edmond died before I was born, but Grandmother told me people came from all over Oklahoma and faraway places to take piano, violin, and singing lessons from him. I always wanted to play the harp, but I never had the chance," Yvonne adds, gracefully extricating herself from Nigel's body now stretched out prone on the couch.

Looking back, it's amazing to me that I never saw the fear or concern that must have been going through my parents' minds. Now I realize that life in Vinita was a different world from what was happening everywhere else. And I'm sure that's why I spent so much time there.

My father went from job to job for some time and there was a lot of going back and forth, so there were long periods that I stayed with Grandmother. Because of that, my earliest memories are of a happy time filled with so many things to discover and enjoy. The house, which is no longer there, had a magnificent porch that wrapped around the front and sides. We would sit out there and watch the birds and the fireflies and listen to the wind rustling through the trees. And there always was music playing. My grandfather had collected recordings of the great operas and the great orchestras that I heard over and over again. Later, Daddy always told people that he had made up his mind I would be an opera singer or a ballerina before I was born. I have a feeling that Grand Mamère had the same idea!

Endowed with the high brow, slightly elongated oval face, and medium frame of the Shawnee, C.E. bore his lineage to Mary Silverheels as proudly as he bore the name Chouteau. The family embraced its American Indian heritage with sincere fervor.

Grandmother loved the tribal legends and Mother taught me many of the Indian ways and customs. There were a lot of Indian artifacts in the house and we were always visiting Indian artists in the area. Willard Stone, the sculptor, was a good friend of the family, and even as a child, I remember being deeply impressed by his work and its tremendous closeness with nature. My father

Yvonne Chouteau: at age eight. (Personal collection.)

knew everyone and because he had worked for the Bureau of Indian Affairs on and off for years, he was very involved with the tribal governments. In many ways, he followed in the footsteps of the pioneer Chouteaus who had served as agents for the Osage and mediated for them in Washington. It is possible that the ability of the early Chouteaus to live in peace and harmony with the Indian tribes they encountered along the pioneer front might well have been a gift of humanity passed on from generation to generation.

Vinita, Oklahoma, 1929

Long before classical ballet would make its way to Oklahoma, C.E. introduced his daughter to the traditional ceremonial dances of her Indian ancestry.

I couldn't have been more than few months old when Daddy took me to my first powwow. He had been raised in Vinita, which is barely forty miles from the headquarters of the Cherokee Nation in Tahlequah, and spent his childhood attending powwows and taking part in tribal celebrations. I still find it difficult to describe the experience of watching the pageantry of men, women, and children in full tribal regalia executing traditional ceremonial dances to the accompaniment of Indian drums and wind instruments. It is a powerful experience that brings feelings and emotions to the surface that words cannot explain. And it is not just the dances or the music or the mass of people gathered together. There is an aura of mysticism that comes with celebrating ancient customs of worship as they have been passed down through the centuries. Being part of that touched something very deep inside.

Explaining that the traditional dances of her ancestors provided the foundation for her interest in dance, Yvonne points to a framed color photograph of a young blond child clad in an ornately beaded and feathered costume.

My parents spent hundreds of dollars having costumes made for me in California and we went to small towns all over Oklahoma so that I could learn the traditional dances of the different tribes from the authentic sources. It was an exhausting and expensive venture, but that is what performing on the powwow circuit is. Each dance has its own meaning, costume, and tradition. The powwow dancers of today are the same, and because of them the legacy will continue.

Chapter Nine

Oklahoma City, Oklahoma, 1932–1940

Before his daughter would make her first appearance as a powwow dancer, C.E. left the oil business and rejoined the Bureau of Indian Affairs. His first assignment was in Oklahoma City, where Lucy and Yvonne joined him. Yvonne says, "We moved into a huge house owned by a German Roman Catholic family. The Aarons had twelve children and we lived in separate quarters upstairs in the back of the house. I became very close with several of the children and Judy Aaron remains one of my closest friends today." It was the Aarons, Yvonne admits, who inspired her interest in the Roman Catholic faith.

Although the early Chouteaus had been Roman Catholic, the majority of the Oklahoma Chouteaus adopted the Methodist faith.

Of course, being from Mississippi, my mother was a Baptist. My parents shared a strong belief in God, but there was little emphasis placed on attending services. They never objected to my going to Mass with the Aarons and later enrolled me in Villa Teresa, which is a school in Oklahoma City run by the Carmelite nuns. So they had no qualms about my attraction to Catholicism.

My parents were not demonstrative people and rarely expressed their feelings about anything. As much love as I felt in the home, I don't remember ever getting a bear hug or more than a kiss on the cheek. That was just the way they were, and it had no effect on the warmth or closeness we had as a family.

As much as Yvonne enjoyed adjusting to living in Oklahoma City and making new friends, she still treasured her visits to her grandmother. She says, "I don't think it was more than a year or two after we moved to the city that Grandmother became ill. As little as I was, I knew that she was going to die. I still clearly remember the day she motioned for me to climb up the bedstool to reach her. She held me in her arms, told me how much she loved me, and said good-bye." After her grandmother's death, trips to Vinita became rare.

My father was very close to his brother Byron, but the distance became an intrusion. Plus, I don't think Momma was very excited about Daddy and Byron spending a lot of time together. So, except at powwow time, we rarely visited Vinita.

I don't exactly remember when, but the house was destroyed by fire. I still own one hundred twenty acres of the original parcel and really don't know what I'm going to do with it. The couple who leased it all these years to run cattle and horses are thinking about retiring. It is pretty land. And my husband and I always have talked about building a house on the property for our daughters and their children to enjoy. But we'll have to see. As soon as the rainy season is over, I'm going up for a visit. It's interesting because I didn't spend all that much time there, but it is home to me. I guess I'll always feel that way about it.

Rising to let Nigel out in the yard behind the two-story colonial in Northwest Oklahoma City where she and her husband raised their

Yvonne Chouteau: at age twelve. (Personal collection.)

daughters, Christina and Lisa, Yvonne stops to retrieve a snapshot from a neat stack of papers resting by the phone.

These are the latest pictures of Christie with the grandchildren, Sean and Ryan. Their momma didn't go on with her dancing. And as much as it hurt when both girls stopped, I was determined to let them make up their own mind about what they wanted to do. They were both quite talented and always seemed to enjoy the Indian dances I taught them as well as their ballet classes. But they had more traditional childhoods and when faced with the decision between ballet or cheerleading, ballet lost out.

Calling Nigel back in as a light drizzle begins to fall, Yvonne deftly spreads a throw over the end of the couch before he can resume his perch. "I was very fortunate to have the opportunities I did. My father was very careful that what I performed was authentic, and he made sure that I was noticed." On November 16, 1932, Yvonne got her first taste of major public attention. Although smitten by the pageantry of the day, she does recall being vaguely aware of the honor attached to leading the Silver Anniversary Statehood Day parade through the streets of the state capital from her own float. She remembers that performing at both the annual Statehood Day dinner and the Hall of Fame ceremonies later that evening was different from any performances she had ever given. "I had been performing at powwows all over the state by then, but it was the first time I danced in front of a nonparticipating audience. It was completely quiet during my solo dances, and when I finished everyone applauded!"

After her Statehood Day debut, Yvonne suddenly found herself on the path to stardom. In addition to being deluged by requests to appear in parades across the state, the pint-sized trouper was selected to represent the state of Oklahoma during the American Indian Day celebrations at the 1933 Century of Progress World's Fair in Chicago. Two years later, she was named by then Oklahoma governor E. W. Marland to represent his office at the San Diego Exposition. In addition to all the parades and continuing appearances on the powwow circuit and at festivals across the nation, Yvonne was enrolled in Fronnie Asher's Oklahoma City School of Dance. There she discovered a new way of moving and a new world of dance.

I remember my parents taking me to see the René Blum and Colonel W. de Basil Ballets Russes de Monte Carlo when it came through town in 1934. I had just turned five and I sat there absolutely mesmerized. I started reading books on dance and came upon an autobiography written by Anna Pavlova, which I still have. She wrote that her goal was "to make people happy with her dancing and to give them a taste of something beautiful." After reading that, I decided that I, too, wanted to make people happy!

Oklahoma City, Oklahoma, 1932–1940

Yvonne's decision to become a ballet dancer was welcomed by her father. He would, it appeared, someday see his dream come true.

Of course, my parents were not about to let ballet take me away from my Indian dancing, but they made it possible for me to do both. Looking back, that was very wise, because the recognition I had gained as an Indian dancer offered me tremendous opportunities to perform. I think the San Diego Exposition was the first place that I did both ballet and Indian solos. From then on, I rarely did my exhibition Indian dances without at least one ballet piece. As far as I was concerned, the two were very similar. At that age, I hadn't been exposed to the complex technique of classical ballet and all I saw was that the steps were different. I had been taught the sanctity of dance as it is seen in the eyes of the Indian and approached ballet the same way. So later I didn't have to learn that classical ballet, in its purest form, demands spiritual focus as well as technical ability. There is much more to ballet than steps, and what makes it art comes from deep inside.

Starting school added another element to Yvonne's life. Having learned to read long before she entered the first grade, Yvonne enjoyed the challenge of school. "I was very curious as a child, and since my mother had been a schoolteacher, I was aware of the value of an education. I never had difficulty and always got good grades."

Yvonne's progress in ballet class also pleased her teacher and her parents. Having developed an exceptional memory for movement, she learned the rudiments of classical ballet with tremendous speed. Her natural agility and ethereal quality of expression were viewed as potential talent of immeasurable depth. Yvonne had gained a sense of confidence and decorum from the years of performing and being in the public eye that caught the attention of visiting teachers and dance world luminaries. A brief audience with Leonide Massine, deftly arranged by C.E. during a late 1936 engagement of the Blum–de Basil Ballets Russes in St. Louis, resulted in a recommendation that Yvonne be taken to New York City so that her training could be completed under the best of teachers. A slightly different version of Massine's recommendation was made in 1938 by a visiting teacher and former partner of Anna Pavlova, Veronine Vestoff. Vestoff offered to go into business with C.E. and establish a ballet studio in Oklahoma City where Yvonne and other aspiring classical dancers could be trained.

Knowing full well that the center of the professional ballet world would remain in New York regardless of how many great teachers were willing to come to Oklahoma, C.E. decided against capitalizing a venture of such limited appeal. Keeping vigil on his daughter's training, he ventured first to Dorothy Perkins's studio in Kansas City. Yvonne explains, "Rosella [Hightower] already had left and was in a company by then, but Miss Perkins talked about her constantly. For me, hearing about Rosella was inspiring and it was very encouraging for my parents. Rosella's mother and my mother became good friends. Later, after I went off on tour, Mrs. Hightower made it much easier for Momma because she had been through the same thing. They wrote back and forth constantly and developed a great friendship."

The pace of balancing school, daily classes at Asher's studio, and regular jaunts to Kansas City to work with Perkins didn't faze Yvonne. "I loved to dance, which is why I loved summer break. Then I could take more classes, powwow season was at its height, and my parents started taking me to studios outside Oklahoma to study for two weeks." Among her favorite summer memories, Yvonne talks of going to study with Ernest Belcher in Los Angeles. "Maria and Marjorie were there, and I remember how much it meant to meet the 'Tallchief sisters' from Oklahoma. Of course, they were much more advanced than I was at that point, but we got along quite well."

Although her ballet training was fast becoming the central focus of her life, Yvonne continued to be a major attraction as an exhibition Indian dancer. "I appeared at every world's fair held on this continent from 1933 to 1941. In every publicity piece Daddy ever wrote, he always put that at the top. And it was an honor because my designation as a representative of Oklahoma always came from the governor's office!"

Yvonne's career was not the only mission in C.E.'s life. Since his mother's death, he had taken over as the family historian and was deeply committed to bringing statewide attention to the achievements of his great-great-grandfather, Major Jean Pierre Chouteau. His efforts were rewarded through a series of statewide events during the term of Governor E. W. Marland, beginning with the 1936 installation of a historical marker in Salina, Oklahoma, honoring Chouteau as the Father of Oklahoma. Prior to leaving office in 1939, Marland established a precedent in the state legislature by designating the day of Chouteau's birth, October 10 (1758), Oklahoma Historical Day in perpetuity. Although statewide observances of the first legislated commemorative day would not be held until 1940, a daylong celebration was held in Salina beginning with a parade down Main Street. "My father, Momma, and I wore pioneer garb and rode in the lead float. It was a very exciting day for the entire family. At long last, my father succeeded in gaining the recognition the Chouteau name deserved. It was great fun and I was elated to see my father benefit from the fruits of his labor." During the evening festivities, Governor Marland named C.E. an honorary colonel and Yvonne a major on his staff. To her delight, the governor presented Yvonne with a custom-made replica of the state's honor guard uniform. With her father's help, Yvonne composed the following poem at age ten to express her gratitude to the governor:

THE LITTLE MAJOR

I'm an Honorary Major
On Governor Marland's staff;
But that's not all the story
It isn't even half!

He said he had a little suit,
Which wouldn't fit the rest,
That he would like to see me in,
If I'd expand my chest.

"Now girls don't make good soldiers,"
Said my mother with a smile,
But the Governor knew they did—
At least once in a while!

And father said, "Of course they did!
Soldiers that take commands!
Have you forgot Joan de Arc,
And how she saved her land?"

So now I have a uniform,
Brass buttons, cap, and all!

American Indian Ballerinas

I think I wear it very well,
For one not very tall!

I know what "Forward, march!" means now!
But the order I like best,
At least when I am tired—so tired,
Is "Company, halt! At rest!"

I like to hear the bugle's call!
I like the sharp commands!
Yet even a Major tires at last—
But my Governor understands!

He tells me I'm "his right-hand man"
Must help protect our State!
That the flower of the nation blooms out here,
Untouched by the hand of hate!

But I'm afraid—if danger came,
I might forget and flee—
And wake to find, to my chagrin,
The State protecting me!

Yet a great big State, and great big man,
And a little girl like me,
Could rout the foe any day I know
In the cause of democracy!

It's fun to be a Major
For a great big man like him!
To hear him give his orders
And watch the staff "Fall in!"

Yes, it's great to be a Major
On the staff of a State like this!
I give it my love—with a snappy salute
From an Oklahoma Miss!

Oklahoma City, Oklahoma, 1932–1940

Despite her celebrity status, Yvonne does not remember it being a problem among her peers.

I got along well at school. There was never much time to socialize, but I had some good friends and they thought it was great that I rode in parades and danced all over the country. As hectic a childhood as it was, I enjoyed all of it. I loved what I was doing, and except for the time I shared with my grandmother, performing was really the only existence I knew. How difficult it was at times for my parents I'll never know. But they were the ones who made sacrifices so that I could dance.

Chapter Ten

New York, New York, 1941

Before her tenth birthday Yvonne was performing ballet solos at concerts on a regular basis. Her delicate classical line, elegant grace, and superior musicality added a new dimension to the recognition she had received on the powwow circuit. Her talent was fast exceeding the realm of ceremonial dances and her parents wisely began revising the plans for her future. In early 1941 C.E. decided it was time to take Yvonne to New York. There were many studios accepting students for limited study, and he arranged for her to spend two weeks in late summer studying at the Vilzak-Shollar studio.

Prior to the family's departure Yvonne was honored by the Oklahoma legislature as the state's most celebrated twelve-year-old and officially designated a "Daughter of Oklahoma, Goodwill Ambassadress of Oklahoma to the World at Large." Although Yvonne considered going to New York an exciting prospect, she resented having to pursue her training outside of Oklahoma. "I accepted the fact that you had to go to New York before you could get into a company. Everybody had to do that. I just didn't like having to go away to study. Of course, my white Eskimo spitz, Fluffy, went with me!"

From the moment she could see the New York skyline from the back seat of her father's gold tone DeSoto, Yvonne remembers being overwhelmed by excitement. "When we got there, Daddy drove straight to the studio, which was in Steinway Hall," she says, squeezing her eyes shut. "He parked the car in front of the Automat across the street, but I was too excited to eat. I got my dance bag out and made sure everything I needed was there and we went upstairs to the studio." Two hours later, Yvonne slid back into the back seat of the DeSoto with a bruised ego, blood blisters on her toes, and a burning desire to be a dancer. Her first class with Mme Shollar had been a total disaster.

I had never had a full class on pointe before in my life. It was August, the studio was very hot, and my feet started to hurt terribly. Mme Shollar wouldn't let me take my pointe shoes off. She insisted I go on, even after you could see blood showing through the satin. I guess she thought I was a spoiled little brat from Oklahoma who had been allowed to go on pointe too early and needed to find out that ballet was serious business. It was humiliating, but I finished the class and came back the next day for more.

Having studied with Vestoff, Yvonne was not surprised by Shollar's harsh approach.

A lot of the Russian teachers were very severe. That's just the way they were, so you either got used to it or you went back home. What really shocked me was being in a class with people my own age who, for the most part, sized each other up with such coldness and acted as if getting into the front line was a life or death matter.

Not one to measure her progress against that of others, Yvonne was neither threatened nor intimidated by the attitude of her peers. The savvy she had acquired from performing since the age of two and a half had instilled the ability to channel the adrenaline or proverbial jitters triggered by competitive situations into a positive source of energy. Putting her first day's experiences behind her, Yvonne thrust herself into a full schedule of classes. Midway through her second week at the studio, she overheard conversations about an audition. "The School of American Ballet [SAB] was holding scholarship auditions, and my parents agreed to let me go for the experience."

Undaunted by the sight of more than one hundred other qualified entrants on hand for the annual SAB audition, Yvonne gingerly demonstrated her skills under the intense gaze of George Balanchine, Alexandra Danilova, and Leonide Massine. To her utter amazement, she was called to return before the judges. She had, they explained, been selected as the sole recipient of a lifetime scholarship to Balanchine's school. Dumbfounded, Yvonne mustered a bright smile for pictures with the legendary Danilova and held her award tightly during group photographs with the other scholarship winners and all three judges. "It was a dream come true. Alexandra Danilova presented me my award! I had seen her dance in Oklahoma City and I couldn't believe how beautiful she was in person. She encouraged me to work hard and said I was very talented."

As thrilled as her parents were, Yvonne remembers the situation put them into a difficult predicament.

We were supposed to be getting ready to start the trip home, but all of a sudden everything changed. Of course, Daddy came up with a way to make it work. He decided Momma would stay with me, he would go back to his job in Oklahoma and send us money to live on. The school arranged for me to enroll in the Professional Children's School [PCS] and we found affordable rooms in a huge apartment on West 58th Street. It was a boardinghouse run by a wonderful little Irish lady named Miss Anne O'Sullivan.

Fluffy was allowed to stay, but C.E. headed home after moving Lucy and Yvonne into the apartment. "That's when I became a devoted letter writer, Yvonne adds. "Momma taught me what was important to hear from someone faraway and let me start a diary. Daddy would come to visit and brought what we needed from home, but we were such a close family it was a difficult adjustment."

As a scholarship student at SAB, Yvonne's training fell under the

Alexandra Danilova presents Yvonne Chouteau a lifetime scholarship to the School of American Ballet, New York City, 1941. (Personal collection.)

scrutiny of Balanchine. "Occasionally, he would teach class. He was very different from the other teachers. With him, we worked very slowly and did simple combinations. I was too young to grasp a lot of what he said, but he talked a lot and very softly." Among the regular faculty, Yvonne credits Pierre Vladimirov and Anatole Oboukhoff as having the greatest influence on her development.

They taught the students who were "interested" variations as they had learned them in Russia. Most of my favorite memories of the time I spent at SAB revolves around my two best girl friends. We all lived to dance and we were always "invited" to variations class.

My closest friend was Enrica Soma. Her father owned a famous night-club called Tony's. She went on to dance with Ballet Theatre, but retired very early. She married John Huston, of Hollywood fame, and gave birth to a daughter who they named Angelica. My other best friend was Tanaquil LeClercq, who became one of New York City Ballet's greatest ballerinas and married Balanchine. Tanaquil's career ended abruptly in 1956 when she was infected by a polio virus. But we had great fun together at SAB and each of us had our own idols. Enrica wanted to be [Irina] Baronova, Tanaquil wanted to be [Tamara] Toumanova, and, of course, I wanted to be Alexandra Danilova.

Pressing her temples, Yvonne says, "There were so many things that made SAB special. I remember Vera Nemchinova coming to class in a white tutu and trying not to stare at her. And there were times when Mme Danilova and Vera Zorina took class or Massine was in the studio. Most of the dancers who were working with Balanchine took our class and I even ended up working with Nicholas Magallanes in pas de deux class!" SAB's resemblance to the Russian Imperial School was not limited to the classroom. "We were taught to curtsy and 'extend the hand.' And you paid proper respect to your elders and superiors or you were sent home. I loved it and wish there was just a little of that still around today!"

Although Yvonne admits that she did well in her academic studies, she never adjusted to going to the Professional Children's School. "It was completely different from what I was accustomed to in Oklahoma. There were a bunch of us from SAB who went, and none of us really wanted to be there. But it was required, so we went and kept our grades up." As fate would have it, a lunchtime conversation at

PCS thrust her career into a new phase. "I still remember the way it happened," she says with a mischievous glint in her eyes. "It was near the end of my second year in New York and somebody asked if anyone had the nerve to cut class at PCS to go to an audition for Sergei Denham's Ballet Russe de Monte Carlo. It sounded like a good idea, so I called Momma and she gave me permission to go." Cutting an academic class to go to an audition was fine, but when Yvonne realized that waiting for the results would make her late for variations class at SAB, she left. "I had filled out the information sheet when I arrived, and since Mme Danilova was one of the judges, I figured if they wanted to get hold of me they could. So I did a variation from *Coppélia* and left."

When she arrived home after class, Yvonne was stunned to hear that the Ballet Russe company manager, Jeannot Cerrone, had called. "He asked Momma why I had run away and she said I had left to go to class. Then he told her that Mme Danilova had been interested in me and that Mr. Denham wanted to hire me!" Cautioning her fourteen-year-old daughter not to get too excited, Lucy explained that mothers were not allowed to travel with the company and she was not about to let "her little girl go on the road with a bunch of gypsies." "But," Yvonne explained, "the decision was up to Daddy. When Momma told him the news, he insisted it was exactly the opportunity he always dreamed I would have. He agreed with Momma's concerns but said he was sure the details could be worked out to ensure that I was taken care of properly."

Before her mother had a chance to call Cerrone back, she received a call from Mr. Denham. "Well, Mme Danilova had stepped in and agreed to act as my guardian! Since I was only fourteen, her British secretary, Elizabeth Twysden, would serve as my chaperone. Mr. Denham agreed to all of Momma's other requests and made sure she fully understood why it was an opportunity of a lifetime and what it would mean for my career." By the way her mother hung up the phone, Yvonne knew instantly she would be allowed to join the Ballet Russe de Monte Carlo. With a faraway look in her eyes, Yvonne adds softly, "It was one of those moments when you aren't sure if you're awake or dreaming. I was ecstatic, and when I saw Momma smile, I knew she was too!"

Part II

The Performing Years

Chapter Eleven

Maria Tallchief
Professional Debut

When Betty Marie Tallchief made her debut in the corps de ballet of Sergei Denham's Ballet Russe de Monte Carlo in 1942, American dancers were not considered ballerina material. The company's success at the box office depended on the roster of Russian and European stars Denham had assembled to validate the artistic integrity of his product— Russian ballet. American audiences would buy tickets to see Russian ballet, danced by Russian stars. A rigid star system determined individual status and power within the company and created sharp definitions between ranks. The majority of the company had been trained in Russia or Europe, and to them the image and potential of the American dancer was that of a thigh-slapping, gum-chewing tap dancer.

Having been trained by Nijinska in the traditions of Russia's Imperial School of Ballet, Betty Marie did not fit the stereotype. Being treated with disdain and denied recognition of her individual potential because of her birthright left a lasting impression. Today, she attributes an overdeveloped sensitivity to the image of American dancers around the world to her initial experience in the Ballet Russe. During all the foreign tours she made under the auspices of the U.S. State Department, including her 1960 guest appearances with American Ballet Theatre in Russia, Maria admits having made a concerted effort to present the antithesis of the negative image of the American dancer.

It was very difficult. I remember Mme Slavenska talking to me before I left California. She said "You know, you must not pay attention to anybody. You must not make enemies. You must do your work and not let anything bother you." She was absolutely right. But because I had always been well liked and made friends easily, I didn't realize how right she was until I was there. Because of the hostile atmosphere, I made very good friends with the American dancers, and those friendships have lasted a lifetime. Vida Brown and I were roommates, and together with Helen Kramer, Gertrude Tyven, and a few others, we had our own little group. We were always being thrown on stage in new roles, so we would practice ballets in our hotel rooms. You didn't wait to be told to learn new parts. You did it on your own. The night I made my debut in the company in Massine's *Gaîté Parisienne,* I found out I was dancing in three new ballets the next night.

Learning roles on short notice was a part of life in Denham's company that Betty Marie relished and accomplished with ease. Although her ability to do well under pressure and her voracious appetite for hard work did nothing for her popularity, it was well appreciated by management. Frederic Franklin recalls watching her adjust to her life in the company. "From the day she joined the company you could see that she knew what she wanted and was determined to get it. She didn't have to be told what to work on and learned very quickly. When she wasn't onstage, she was in the wings watching, taking it all in like a sponge."

Following the Canadian tour, Nijinska joined the company to set several of her ballets. Maria says, "Well, Mme Nijinska didn't let anybody tell her what to do. About anything! So she cast me as the Tar-

tar Girl in *Ancient Russia.* Then she announced I would be Nathalie Krassovska's understudy in the second ballerina role in *Chopin Concerto* and Lubov Rostova's understudy as Spring in *Snow Maiden.* Needless to say, that did not go over well with the Russians. For them, Nijinska was the goddess of Russian ballet and for her to consider a first-year American corps de ballet girl her protégée was unbelievable. It created quite a scandal."

As if she did not have enough strikes against her in the eyes of the Russians, Sasha Goudovitch fell in love with Betty Marie. "He was my first beau, and it made the Russians furious because he was the darling of the company." Armed with the conviction that hard work could overcome any obstacle, Betty Marie became skilled at avoiding direct confrontations with her detractors and plunged headlong into the opportunities she was given. "But no matter how horrible some of them were to me, I never lost my respect for their artistry."

Other than the cold weather, Betty Marie enjoyed the rigors of life on tour.

We traveled by passenger train, but not one with sleeping cars, so we sat up all night. At that age, sleep didn't matter much, so it was okay. We were all poor. I think we made something like $32.50 a week and had to pay our own hotel bills. So none of us ate properly. It was so bad, there was a wonderful doctor in Philadelphia who used to have roast chickens delivered to the stage door for me instead of flowers! My parents would send me a five- or ten-dollar bill in a letter occasionally, but I never used it. Some people said the only reason I was doing well in the company was because my father was a rich Indian and paying Denham to give me parts. So I put away the money from home.

Maria remembers gradually being given a chance to perform more roles and making the most of each new opportunity. "That first year in the company, you had to be ready to do anything. You never showed that anything was wrong, and if you were tired or hurt, you learned from it." Eight months after making her debut in the Ballet Russe, Betty Marie stepped in as a last-minute replacement for Krassovska in *Chopin Concerto.* Although she had been told to prepare to perform the role several times during the tour, each time she had been denied the opportunity at the last minute with no explanation. Fully expecting the usual disappointment, Betty Marie prepared herself but did not believe she would actually take her place onstage opposite the company's leading ballerina, Alexandra Danilova.

In his dual role as leading male dancer and ballet master, Franklin was involved in the ultimate decision. He recalls,

By the time we realized Krassovska was not going to be able to perform, it was too late to prepare anyone else. Of course, as soon as it became obvious that Betty Marie was going on, the furor began. In those days you didn't put a first-year corps dancer on equal footing with a ballerina without hearing about it. Krassovska was livid and there was quite a scene. Outwardly, Betty Marie appeared calm. But I do think she reached that terrifying moment in the wings when you wonder why you're there. Then you remind yourself, you wouldn't be there if someone didn't think you could do it. And, therefore, you do. And she did.

After pushing Betty Marie out of the wings himself, Franklin watched her give "the performance of a lifetime. She held her own magnificently, the critics were there, and that's when it all started." Knowing full well that this was her first big break and that her future in Denham's company depended on how well she did, Betty Marie kept her focus firmly on the role she was performing. "I didn't really remember anything afterward. The entire time I was onstage, I was concentrating so hard I was unaware of anything except the ballet. I knew from the the reaction of the audience it must have gone well. And then Freddie and my friends kept telling me how well I did. It was quite an experience."

Although little was made of her triumph within the company, management had carefully taken note of the exceptional composure and technical command Betty Marie Tallchief had exhibited. Several weeks later, Krassovska became embroiled in a contract dispute with Denham that prompted her unexpected departure from the company. Word came from Denham that Betty Marie would perform the *Chopin Concerto* role during the troupe's upcoming New York season and rehearsals would be scheduled. Denham's decision clarified his opinion of Betty Marie's abilities and potential as one of the troupe's up-and-coming young stars. No one knew better than Denham how important popular and critical success in New York was to the company's future. Unlike the state-supported troupes of Europe and Russia, his was a commercial venture that survived on box office receipts, tour bookings, and the largesse of patrons of the arts. Poor reception in the lap of the nation's dance community would hurt future bookings and discourage existing and potential backers. Programming and casting decisions were crucial. The box office appeal of the company's veteran stars and proven ballets would carry the season, but without a good sampling of new works and fresh young talent, the company would be criticized for repeating itself. Competition for roles within the company reached fever pitch, and the pressure to succeed set everybody's teeth on edge.

During rehearsals for the New York season, Danilova and Mia Slavenska, Betty Marie's former teacher, worked with her before the opening night performance of *Chopin Concerto.* "It was a very difficult ballet and Nijinska had made several changes since I had performed it at the Hollywood Bowl. Between Danilova and Slavenska, I gained enough technical confidence to be able to concentrate on the nuances of style and presentation that Nijinska had intended to be part of the role." In his review of the performance, the *New York Times* dance critic John Martin applauded Betty Marie Tallchief's stunning debut in her first major role with the company.

At the conclusion of the season, Martin further clarified his opinion of Betty Marie in his overall summary published in the *Sunday New York Times*. He named her the season's most significant discovery in classical ballet. Crediting her with demonstrating effortless and brilliant technical authority as opposed to mere bravura in Nijinska's *Chopin Concerto,* he predicted she could not escape becoming ". . . somebody. She is well off the beaten track in ballerina types but she is a ballerina as surely as this is Sunday."

As great an impact as the praise of the esteemed dance critic and author had on her immediate future in Denham's company, Maria is adamant that his review accomplished what she had been unable to do—convince her mother that ballet was the right career choice. That Ruth Tall Chief would decide whether Betty Marie became a pianist or dancer did not come as a surprise. Maria had always known, in the end, her mother would make the final ruling between ballet and piano.

The problem was that Mother didn't know enough about ballet to understand how well my career was going. Her only exposure to ballet was through

Marjorie and me. She didn't understand the significance of succeeding in leading roles in Nijinska's *Ancient Russia* and *Snow Maiden,* performing the Waltz in *Les Sylphides,* or having Agnes de Mille create a small role for me in *Rodeo.* I wrote letters almost daily, describing my progress and life in the company, but Mother still wasn't satisfied that ballet was right for me.

With a second-year contract from Denham that she considered far more impressive than her first, Betty Marie headed home for the final showdown.

When Mother first saw me, she got very upset. I had left home a very healthy seventeen-year-old. In the year I was away, I had lost a lot of weight, become drawn, and picked up a terrible cough. Her first reaction was that the rigors of being a dancer and touring were too hard for me and the piano deserved serious consideration. Then David Lichine brought her a copy of John Martin's summary of the season to read. There was nothing she could say, and she agreed to let me return to the Ballet Russe.

Once the career issue was settled at home, Betty Marie returned to daily classes with Nijinska and Lichine. "We didn't have regular classes on tour and first-year corps girls spent a lot of time in boots doing *demi-caractère* or nonclassical roles. I had lost some technique and needed to work. Years later, I finally realized the only reason I was allowed to perform the Waltz in *Les Sylphides* was because it was so difficult, no one else wanted to do it. But I was just so glad to get out of my mazurka boots and into pointe shoes, it never occurred to me." Unlike her contemporaries, who made intricate schedules for their careers, she did not set goals. "I was never really striving for anything. I never had a timetable for when I would perform my first this or that. I just wanted to dance the best I could."

Well aware that her second year in Denham's company would offer greater opportunities to dance her best, Betty Marie embraced her classes with unbridled energy and pushed herself relentlessly. She had proven capable of surviving the grueling pace of touring, ignoring backstage politics, and coming through onstage regardless of the circumstances. And she had won a second-year contract and her mother's approval to pursue her career as a dancer.

Chapter Twelve

Balanchine's Muse

On signing her second contract with the Ballet Russe de Monte Carlo in 1943, Betty Marie officially became Maria Tallchief. The name change was suggested by Agnes de Mille. As Maria remembers it, "I created a small part in the original cast of her *Rodeo* during my first year with the company, and she said I should change my name because there were too many Bettys in the company." Although adding Russian-sounding endings to American dancers' names was all the rage in the early 1940s, Maria admits that she never gave any serious consideration to Denham's suggestion—Maria Tallchieva. While her parents had no objections to the name change, Ruth Tall Chief took issue with a second-year option included in her new contract. Concerned that her daughter was too young to make a two-year commitment, Ruth Tall Chief held her ground until Denham removed the clause from the contract. "Mother never had any qualms about approaching Mr. Denham," says Maria. "And it was always interesting because she always won!"

Reflecting on the reputation she had earned as a hard worker during her first year with the company, Maria shrugs.

For me, it was actually less work than what I had been doing before I joined the company. At home, I spent a minimum of two hours a day practicing the piano, went to school, took as many classes at Nijinska's studio I could, and made concert appearances as a pianist and dancer. Being able to concentrate totally on ballet and not touch the piano for a year was a new experience. There was so much to learn and such incredible artists to learn from, I couldn't get enough. Massine was there in the very beginning. He terrified me, but he was incredible. And I never took my eyes off Danilova. She was so special and different. She was the ideal role model, onstage and off. Any time she had to make a public appearance to promote the company or was interviewed, she presented herself as the most glamorous person in the world. She was constantly telling us we had to dress properly and maintain the same image we had onstage wherever we went.

Maria's meteoric rise through the company ranks was without precedent. Within a year of making her professional debut in the back line of the corps in Massine's *Gaîté Parisienne,* she was performing the lead Can-Can Girl on a regular basis and winning popular and critical acclaim. Although she was never to be welcomed with open arms by various factions within the company, the hostility toward her eased. She also gained an enviable reputation as a tough poker player.

Well, we didn't have anything to do on the train, so we played poker. The Russians always had a game going. Our manager, Jeannot Cerrone, and Leon Fokine, who taught class and had the most incredible whistle of any human being I have ever heard, always seemed to be in the middle of a game. We'd play for hours, starting with a penny a point, then we'd get up to a nickel and finally a quarter. It was great fun.

Always one to demand more of herself than anyone else did, Maria made progress faster than her peers and refused to acknowledge injury or illness.

I was either sick or injured my first few years in Denham's company. I developed infected soft corns between the toes of my feet that were absolutely excruciating. I remember not being able to sleep with even a sheet because the pain was so severe. But I split my pointe shoes so I could get my feet into them and danced anyway. Actually, it turned out to be a solution to my problems balancing on pointe. I had never had good, solid balances, but it hurt so much to come off pointe I discovered I could balance for extreme lengths of time. Nijinska had impressed on me the importance of never letting anything that bothered you show and I didn't.

Maria describes an incident in the beginning of her third year with the company that remains one of her fondest memories of her career in the Ballet Russe.

The company had started back to work in Los Angeles. I was in rehearsal, and all of a sudden I heard my mother's voice. Well, here was my tiny little mother and the very tall Mr. Denham discussing my third-year contract in the hallway. I think I had been making $37.50 and Denham had offered me $42 and Mother wasn't satisfied. She had a handful of reviews to back up her argument and somehow got Denham to agree to give me $45 a week and soloist billing! It was a very funny scene and really had an impact on my career.

No one, not even Ruth Tall Chief, could have predicted that during the course of that rehearsal period Maria would meet George Balanchine and, for the second time in her life, find herself learning to dance all over again. In 1944 Balanchine began a two-year association as resident choreographer of Denham's company and Maria Tallchief's destiny in the world of ballet began to take shape. When he joined the company in Los Angeles to choreograph and stage the Broadway-bound musical *Song of Norway*, Balanchine had already decided that Maria would understudy Danilova in Anitra's Dance. Maria says, "He must have seen me dance *Chopin Concerto* because he already knew about me. When he started rehearsing his ballets for our New York season, which was scheduled to open immediately after we left the show on Broadway, he gave me leading roles in *Danses Concertantes* and *Le Bourgeois Gentilhomme.*"

Maria's face lights up and her words tumble out enthusiastically as she describes her first impression of Balanchine.

Once I met Balanchine, there was no doubt in my mind that that was the way I wanted to dance. He was not demanding at all, but what he demonstrated was so exceptional you wanted to do exactly what he did. It's interesting because he was very different from Nijinska. They had both come from the same school, but because of the kind of work emanating from him he didn't have to be demanding. I don't mean to make Nijinska sound like the ogre, because her approach was crucial to my development, but Balanchine was never demanding. I could feel how he demonstrated with his arms and the breadth of his movement. As much as people always associate him with teaching feet and legs, he was a poet and very lyrical. He taught you to be an artist, to be able to interpret and go way beyond the feet and legs.

When Balanchine came to Denham's company, a small group of dancers who had been trained at his school and had been performing his works for several years joined him. Never having been exposed to Balanchine-trained dancers, Maria was taken aback. "After I saw Mary Ellen Moylan, I knew that that was the kind of technique I had to aspire to achieve. And because she had been trained at Balanchine's school, I knew that was where I needed to go to learn how to dance all over again." Maria did begin studying at the School of American Ballet as her Ballet Russe schedule permitted. Her primary teachers at the school, founded in 1934 by Balanchine, Lincoln Kirstein, Edward M. M. Warburg, and Vladimir Dimitriev in the style of the Russian Imperial Ballet School, were Pierre Vladimirov, Muriel Stuart, and Anatole Oboukhoff.

You know Balanchine never told me I had to go back to the beginning. He wasn't like that. He was very gentle. He was very Oriental, I think, because he just quietly saw everything and made things change. At that time, I was still a little pudgy, had awful feet and essentially no turnout, but all he ever said to me was that if I could learn to do battements tendus properly, I wouldn't have to learn anything else. We were performing in Baltimore and

I was hiding backstage doing my barre when he came by and told me that. I thought to myself, Oh no, that could take twenty years. So I didn't ask him to show me what he meant. I just said, "Thank you very much, Mr. Balanchine," and realized that if I wasn't executing the second exercise at the barre properly, everything I was doing was incorrect.

Eager to launch the relearning process and somewhat concerned by the fact that she was nineteen, Maria remembers being exasperated because Balanchine seemed to attach no urgency to the issue. "He kept saying, 'there will be time later,' and I kept wondering when 'later' was going to arrive." Meanwhile, Maria had her hands full learning the roles she had been given. Shortly after *Song of Norway* opened for a two-week run in Los Angeles, Danilova became ill and Maria took over her role in Anitra's Dance. Although she did not perform it on Broadway, her appearances in California prompted the show's producers to offer her a lucrative contract to remain after the Ballet Russe concluded its limited engagement on Broadway. "They made a very good offer, but I wanted to be a ballet dancer and my place was with the Ballet Russe. I thanked them for their interest and headed uptown with the rest of the company to begin our fall season in New York's City Center of Music and Drama."

Maria's "place" in the Ballet Russe de Monte Carlo was on the verge of entering a new dimension. For the first time in her career she would be presented in ballerina roles created for her. As impressive as her repertory of inherited and shared roles was, she had always been bound by the imprint of a predecessor and compared to everyone who had ever danced the role. The nuances of style, musicality, technical virtuosity, and timing, which shape a role from the first day of rehearsal to the first performance, would be hers. The short-cropped tutu she would wear in *Danses Concertantes* would have one name written neatly on the waistband—Tallchief.

Balanchine created wonderful roles for me, and he was the first choreographer I had worked with who approached the score like a musician. *Song of Norway* was a tribute to the Norwegian composer Edvard Grieg, and I was extremely familiar with his piano concerto. I had studied it and performed it in concert, so I was fascinated by the way Balanchine worked with the music. He put the accent at the *top* of the note, so you were always there by "one," which put the emphasis on the musical accent. He had the same steps or vocabulary of movement to work with as any other choreographer, but he broke down the inherent rhythm of the music to make the movement more exciting. It was phrasing, not timing, that allowed the speed of movement and translated the music into action. My music proved to be very valuable to me, and I think it was one of the things about me that intrigued Balanchine.

Cast in a pas de trois with Mary Ellen Moylan and Nicholas Magallanes in *Danses Concertantes* and performing a pas de deux with Yurek Lazowski in *Le Bourgeois Gentilhomme,* Maria had to work very hard.

Mary Ellen was technically much better than I was. She had been studying at Balanchine's school and performing his ballets while I had been touring with Denham's company dancing in mazurka boots and picking up bad habits. I had a lot to learn, but Balanchine was so intelligent and sensitive. He wouldn't say "horrible feet." On the contrary, he would quietly find a way to make you aware of them. You had to watch very carefully because he didn't explain, he showed.

Balanchine showed, Maria learned, and when the reviews were published Maria Tallchief was universally recognized as a star in the making.

During the final year of his association with Denham, Balanchine restaged Marius Petipa's three-act *Raymonda* in collaboration with Danilova and created *Night Shadow,* later renamed *La Sonnambula.* Maria was cast opposite Danilova in the new work and remembers being cast in the more technically demanding of the two leading roles.

Most people have forgotten that I did a tremendous number of dramatic roles during my early career with the Ballet Russe de Monte Carlo. It wasn't until much later that it changed. If Balanchine hadn't asked Danilova to choose which role she wanted in *Night Shadow,* I probably would have automatically been given the Sleepwalker. But he did, and she wanted to do that role, so I was cast as the Coquette.

At this point, Maria remembers that changes were beginning to show as she worked to master a new technique. "My muscles were stretching, my legs were changing shape, and I could see the turnout coming. Because it was a gradual process, I never lost what technical strength I had. It just improved, slowly. Ever so slowly." Onstage, Maria's personality gained sparkle as she gained technical strength, and a sense of artistry began to emerge. That she would become a ballerina was no longer a question. Exactly when and where, however, remained to be seen.

Maria laughs today that no one was more surprised than she when Balanchine asked her to marry him. A man of few words who reserved spectacle for the stage, Balanchine preceded his proposal without fanfare, courtship, or evidence of romantic interest. He simply asked Maria to marry him. She recalls, "Vida and I were still roommates and I remember going home and asking her what she thought about me marrying George. She looked at me and asked 'George who?' Well, I thought since he had asked me to marry him I could call him George, and we both had a good laugh."

Ruth Tall Chief did not find any humor in Balanchine's proposal. "Mother's reaction was not good. She didn't understand what Balanchine did. She had been impressed by Lichine, who was always so glamorous with his scarf around his neck. I don't think she had seen one of Balanchine's ballets, so all she knew about him was that he was a foreigner. That he had been married before. And that he was forty years old." Maria credits her mother's sister for enlightening Ruth and explaining why it would be very good for Maria to marry him. "She was more worldly than my mother, married to a doctor, and living in Colorado. I don't remember why, but she knew all about Balanchine and his family. She even knew his father's rank in the military. So that helped, but I don't think Mother ever really approved. Eventually my parents gave their consent, but it took a while." As soon as word got around that Maria and Balanchine were getting married, any doubts about what the future held for Maria were dispelled. The enigmatic choreographer had displayed an uncanny and consistent habit of marrying women bound for stardom. All of his former wives—Tamara Geva, Alexandra Danilova, and Vera Zorina—had become legends in their own time.

On August 16, 1946, Elizabeth Marie Tall Chief was married to Georgi Melitonovitch Balanchivadze in the Manhattan County Court House in New York City. Company Manager Cerrone and his wife served as witnesses, Maria remembers fondly. "I was staying with Jeannot and his wife in their apartment in New York at the time. He had been a very good friend the entire time I had been in Denham's company. In the beginning, when it was difficult, Jeannot always made sure I got flowers onstage when everyone else did and things like that. He was so sweet." Although the newlyweds were working and had little time to celebrate, they spent the weekend in a cabin near Jacob's Pillow in Lee, Massachusetts, owned by the Russian costume designer Barbara Karinska, before returning to rehearsals on Monday morning.

Chapter Thirteen

New Frontiers

Less than a month after their 1946 marriage, Balanchine left for Paris and Maria headed for California. "I had to finish my contract with Denham before I could join George at the Paris Opéra. He had signed a six-month contract as guest ballet master and I was engaged as guest ballerina." To her dismay, Maria suffered a serious ankle sprain during rehearsals. "I was staying with my parents in Beverly Hills and got stuck in traffic on the way to the studio. I was late for rehearsal, so I didn't warm up, and I was breaking in new pointe shoes. I came out of a lift wrong and my ankle went. It took forever to heal because I never took time off to give it a chance to mend. It was still bad when I got to Paris, so

Maria Tallchief and George Balanchine visit the Tall Chief home in Hollywood, California, 1948. (Personal collection.)

it must have been six or eight months before it felt like an ankle again."

The excitement of preparing to go to Europe for the first time to join her husband and assume her first position with ballerina billing eased the trauma of sustaining her first serious injury. "John Taras took me out to buy a hat before I left. Dressing properly was very important, and you did not arrive in Paris without a hat. So we looked and looked and finally found the right hat. I was so proud of that hat, and the first thing George said when he met me at the boat was, 'Where did you get that awful hat?' The hat was never seen again."

When she assumed her position as guest artist, Maria became the first American ballerina to appear with the Paris Opéra in more than a century. As the Opéra is considered the cradle of classical ballet, to be ranked as one of its ballerinas or étoiles was a very great honor. Even though Balanchine did not approve of titles, such as ballerina or choreographer, Maria says, "I was a ballerina because that is what he did for me. He gave me that and all the tradition that is part of it—the responsibility of knowing that if you didn't dance well the ballet would be no good and that if you didn't have the proper image offstage, you made a comment about the entire company. That is what Balanchine taught, the whole picture."

At the Opéra Maria did not carry the performing load she had become accustomed to in Denham's company, which left time to study with Balanchine.

He didn't really begin teaching me until after we were married. And still it was a very subtle, gentle process of reteaching and reshaping the muscles. Now it is very interesting to look back at old pictures and realize how much patience he had because it took so much time. I had to evolve. You just don't get the arches, the turnout, or the line you need overnight. We also spent a lot of time in Paris dedicated to finding the right pointe shoe for me. George believed that pointe shoes should fit like a glove and help your foot. After determining what I needed in a shoe, we ended up having them custom-made.

Although highly acclaimed for her technical and dramatic skills performing the Paris Opéra's standard classical repertoire and Balanchine's *Apollon Musagète,* Maria felt that her appearances as the Fairy in Balanchine's restaging of *Le Baiser de la Fée* were her greatest triumphs in Paris.

It was one of my favorite roles. The score had been composed in 1928 by Igor Stravinsky as a tribute to Tchaikovsky and was based on the Hans Christian Andersen fairy tale "The Ice Maiden." It was very dramatic and revolved around the story of the muse's fatal kiss. The costumes were gorgeous and the production was very elaborate, with a magical snow scene and fiery gypsy scene. It was very special. When Balanchine brought it back in 1950 as *The Fairy's Kiss,* it became one of my most famous roles.

Living in Paris afforded Maria the luxury of being able to see her sister on several occasions.

Shortly after I arrived, George and I went to Vichy for Marjorie's wedding to George Skibine. I'll never forget that trip. I had been very careful to drink only bottled water, but I made the mistake of drinking something with ice in it and spent most of the time in the bathroom. The hotel didn't have rooms with private baths, so I went back and forth to the bathroom all night. George was very sweet and about two o'clock in the morning he went out in search of a pharmacy. I don't know what he brought back, but whatever it was, it worked. I also went to Monte Carlo when George restaged *Concerto Barocco* and *Night Shadow* for the Marquis de Cuevas company and created *Pas de Trois Classique,* to a Minkus score, for Marjorie, Rosella [Hightower], and André Eglevsky. That time, I didn't get sick.

Adjusting to living in Europe and being married did not lessen the emphasis on work. Marie says, "Dance was Balanchine's life, but he never wanted to talk about dance. He talked about cooking or music, not dance. We played the piano a lot, and that was wonderful. But our existence revolved around ballet. And it should have. There was so much to be done. He was just starting to build a company." The company Balanchine was building had been established a month before he and Maria were married. Ballet Society, Inc., organized by Balanchine and Kirstein, was supported by subscriptions and promoted as a company dedicated to the production of new works in support of the advancement of lyric theater. Maria's career and the company developed simultaneously.

Between 1947 and 1957 Maria created leading roles in twenty-two ballets choreographed by Balanchine. Public recognition and respect were won concurrently. A combination of Balanchine's genius and Maria's aptitude created an alchemy that changed the tempo of classical ballet. The dynamics of this new, distinctly American style, Balanchine often said, reflected the pace of his adopted country and glorified the sleek, lean beauty of the American dancer. As his star pupil, Maria became the prototype for a new breed of classical dancers—the Balanchine ballerina.

Maria remembers it was a difficult period despite the great artistic progress.

Because the company didn't have any money, costumes were always a problem and never ready on time. Sometimes, they wouldn't arrive at the theater until a half-hour before curtain. And we never knew if any of the new ballets would be successful until we heard the audience. For several, including *Firebird,* the opening night audience did not respond until the end of the ballet, so we didn't know it was a success until the curtain came down! The other problem was that in the beginning we only performed three or four times a year. A dancer's life is very short, and at twenty or twenty-one, I had to perform. George knew how important it was and encouraged me to make guest appearances. When it was possible, he helped me get engagements.

For Ballet Society's first series of dance performances at New York's City Center Theatre, Balanchine choreographed *Symphonie Concertante.* Maria says, "He did that ballet for Tanaquil LeClercq and me. It was extremely interesting because he was really teaching both of us to dance through the choreography he was creating. Primarily, I think he was teaching me. She was five years younger and had come out of his school, so everything was already there."

The following year, 1948, the company unveiled *Orpheus,* a stunning artistic collaboration among Balanchine, Stravinsky, and sculptor-designer Isamu Noguchi. The work catapulted Ballet Society, Inc., into the mainstream of the ballet world. "Balanchine and Stravinsky had worked on the score, sending it back and forth between New York and Los Angeles, for at least a year before the ballet went into rehearsal. I remember Stravinsky would send pieces of the score in the mail and George would spend hours at the piano going over it note by note by note." Knowing full well that that was how her husband was going to work with the score until it was completed, Maria took up sewing again. "Mother had always insisted that my sister and I learn how to sew, and it came in very handy. I remember making a very complicated Indian skirt of some sort, while George played the same notes over and over and over."

When rehearsals started, Stravinsky came to New York and the collaboration moved to the studio. According to Maria, contrary to the popular myth that Balanchine worked out his ballets before he started working with the dancers, he and Stravinsky wanted the dancers' contribution very much. "I remember being asked how long it would take me to die, so the amount of music needed for the scene could be determined. It was an incredible collaborative artistic achievement, and because of it we became New York City Ballet."

As significant as the decision was to the future of Balanchine's company and American dance, it appeared to the dancers rehearsing onstage nothing more than an idle conversation between three men standing in the aisle of City Center Theatre. As Maria recalls,

It actually happened right under my nose, and I missed it! We were rehearsing *Orpheus* onstage and a man, who I don't think anyone knew except George and Kirstein, wandered in and sat down. As I soon found out, the man was Morton Baum, who was chairman of the theater's executive committee. He was so impressed with what he saw, he suddenly approached Balanchine and Kirstein with an invitation to rename the company New York City Ballet and become the resident company at City Center.

Under the terms of the agreement, Ballet Society, Inc., remained active as a sponsor for special projects, and the company assumed responsibility for providing opera ballets for the City Center–based New York City Opera and presenting repertory seasons independent of the Opera. Unfortunately, the company's new identity and home base had no immediate effect on its limited performing schedule.

Following the company's City Center debut as New York City Ballet in October 1948, Maria was engaged by Lucia Chase to appear as a guest artist with Ballet Theatre. During the company's Chicago engagement Maria performed her first *Swan Lake* opposite Igor Youskevitch with Erik Bruhn performing the role of the Prince's friend. She had never worked with Bruhn, and to her chagrin the experience was more embarrassing than inspiring.

I was terribly nervous. So when I went to step into the arabesque position on his thigh, I missed. Instead of his thigh, I stepped on the edge of his knee. Thankfully, he was such an incredible partner, he somehow managed to hold me up there. It wasn't exactly an auspicious note to begin what would become a lasting relationship as partners!

At the conclusion of her guest engagement with Ballet Theatre, Maria returned to New York and went into rehearsal for New York City Ballet's second City Center season. During the rehearsal period, Maria recalls an incident that took place at the Russian Tea Room.

George and I were having dinner and impresario Sol Hurok came over to the table and said, "Don't you want your wife to dance *Firebird*?" George didn't say anything and I thought to myself, Oh no. So many ballerinas of the Diaghilev era had made the role famous, I could envision being compared to all of them. Well, it turned out that Hurok owned the original Marc Chagall costumes and sets, which had been created for the 1945 Ballet Theatre production. He and George worked out some arrangement, Stravinsky was contacted to start making some revisions in the score, and we began working on the ballet.

It was put together very quickly. I had just had my tonsils out and was not well. The first thing Balanchine choreographed was the pas de deux, which I danced with Francisco Moncion. Then he did my variation. I remember he had been giving us very difficult combinations in class, and when he started my variation, I suddenly realized all the steps he had been giving us were going into my variation. It was very difficult and had a lot of turned in and turned out movements that had to be executed very fast. I had to build stamina for it because the variation went into the pas de deux without a stop. While George worked on the princesses' dance and the monsters section, I worked by myself. I had a record player and just kept doing the variation until I could get through it. For me, once that variation was over, the hardest part of the ballet was over. The pas de deux was my favorite part. It was very Russian, the music was wonderful, and the atmosphere was so beautiful.

With no time to spare, the dress rehearsal for *Firebird* started at eight o'clock on the morning of its premiere.

Starting that early didn't bother me because I was always a morning person, but Frank was not. His entrance followed my variation, and he had to step in and catch me in a turn. But the lighting for the end of my solo was a single spotlight and the rest of the stage was absolutely dark. So Frank really couldn't see me. Well, I came flying toward him out of the darkness and practically knocked him over. I remember feeling him groan and asking if we could take it a little easy because it was only eight in the morning.

Although it was customary to set bows for a new ballet, no one considered it necessary for *Firebird*. That night, however, the audience had a different opinion.

People started shouting bravo after the final curtain and stood up to applaud. We couldn't believe it. Nobody could believe it. There was complete pandemonium backstage, and someone took pictures showing George bowing in front of the curtain. I think I fainted after the bows. It was an incredible experience and the reviews were wonderful. *Firebird* was our first big popular success. We had to add performances of it because everyone wanted to see it and that was a first!

During the 1950 season New York City Ballet made its European debut, performing a three-week season at London's Royal Opera House, Covent Garden, prior to a three-week tour of England. With her performances in *Firebird, Orpheus,* and *Serenade,* Maria won acclaim as the epitome of the Balanchine ballerina. That same year Balanchine's *Prodigal Son*—a ballet Maria did not feel comfortable performing—entered the New York City Ballet repertoire.

Jerry Robbins and I did the leads. I wasn't tall enough to do the Siren and couldn't wrap my legs around him, which made it difficult. It didn't work at all, and opening night was a disaster. At one point, I completely forgot to get into my position on top of Jerry's shoulders and I can still remember hearing him hissing "Sit, sit, sit" onstage. One of the critics referred to my performance as a classic example of the age-old premise that if you make a mistake, make it again and maybe no one will notice. It was very funny but certainly not a great moment in my career.

Also that season, Balanchine and Robbins collaborated on their first ballet, *Jones Beach.* Maria thoroughly enjoyed it and relished having an opportunity to be funny. "Everyone was dressed in bathing suits and the scenes were set at the beach. Jerry and I led the 'Hot Dog' section and there was a scene titled 'War of the Mosquitos.'"

For the spring City Center season, Maria re-created her role as the Fairy in *The Fairy's Kiss,* dancing opposite Nicholas Magallanes. "Nicky always kidded me about looking like Dolores Del Rio in my gypsy costume, with my hair down and big gold earrings." Hesitating, she adds, "You know, Nicky was very special. And he never really got credit for his technical abilities because he was such an incredible partner. He had been with the original group that came to Denham's company with George in 1944, and we had worked together ever since." That season, Maria also made her debut in the most technically challenging role of her career, *Sylvia: Pas de Deux.*

Gradually, my ballets had been getting harder and harder. I had gone beyond the rebuilding stage, and the turnout, the feet, and the classical line were there. I was ready for new challenges. George created the pas de deux for me to dance with André Eglevsky, who was scheduled to join the company midway through the season, but André didn't arrive from Europe in time to do the premiere. So Herbert Bliss and I did it. Herb did *Sylvia* very well.

I will never forget the first time we rehearsed it onstage. The entire company was sitting out front to watch. All of a sudden they started to applaud. I couldn't believe it. It was very difficult and a technical tour de force, but to have my colleagues applaud was unbelievable to me.

The *New York Herald-Tribune* dance critic, Walter Terry, was equally impressed by Maria's performance in *Sylvia*. He wrote, "Not only did the ballerina accomplish the impossible multiple turns with nary a waver, and long sustained balances on pointe. She danced the incredible, which is quite different from merely executing the difficult."

In 1988, watching the sun bounce off the steel cars of the elevated train clattering past the spacious studios of her School of Chicago Ballet, Maria reminisced about the theater where New York City Ballet emerged. "We were very lucky at City Center," she remarks, leading the way to a narrow, well-lit office dominated by a handsomely carved grand piano. "We were like a big family and the theater was our home. The atmosphere was friendly and the stagehands, ushers, and box office people were very sweet and supportive. It was a wonderful place to build a company."

Chapter Fourteen

Just Rewards

In 1951, Maria Tallchief was named Woman of the Year by *Mademoiselle* magazine. Being recognized outside the realm of the dance world was a new experience. "I was deeply honored," she says. "You know, as a dancer you never think you're famous. You strive for perfection, never take any time off, and every time you step out onstage it's the same as the first time. You never stop learning, and you're only as good as your last performance."

Maria would have ample opportunity to exhibit her growing stature as a ballerina during the next twelve months. New York City Ballet expanded its performing schedule at City Center and made its American touring debut, presenting a two-week season at the Civic

Opera House in Chicago. A large number of new works were presented, including Balanchine's version of the Petipa-Ivanov *Swan Lake*. "George always wanted me to do the role. I loved the ballet, but I do not think I really danced it well until close to the time when I stopped dancing. George had been deeply impressed by Olga Spessivtzeva's Swan Queen, and I never thought I measured up to her."

As far as the reigning dance critics of the day were concerned, there were not enough adjectives to describe Maria Tallchief's Swan Queen. Martin of the *New York Times* commented that she was "a miracle of classical brilliance"; Terry of the *New York Herald-Tribune* credited her with "outdoing herself." Although *Swan Lake* drew the lion's share of popular and critical acclaim, Maria made her debut in several other important ballets during the company's 1951 City Center seasons. Among them, Balanchine restaged *Apollo, Leader of the Muses,* and *Pas de Trois.*

Eglevsky had been in the original *Pas de Trois Classique* George choreographed in 1948 for the Marquis de Cuevas company. My sister and Rosella [Hightower] created the roles with Eglevsky, and in our version I did Rosella's role and Nora Kaye danced Marjorie's. Nora wasn't really Balanchine's kind of dancer, but he did a wonderful variation for her in the pas de trois. That year, we also did *Capriccio Brillant* and a balletic comedy called *À la Françaix.* It was a spoof and I got to be the joke. It started out with a tennis player flirting with a girl. Then I appeared in a Romantic-length tutu, complete with sylph wings, and the tennis player runs after me. In the end, the tutu and wings came off to reveal a tennis outfit. I always got a laugh.

Maria's ability to pull off the tongue-in-cheek role prompted Terry to write, "Tallchief displayed a fine comic flair with her straight-faced (or almost) characterization of the elusive nineteenth-century ballerina."

By the conclusion of the 1951 New York City Ballet season at City Center, Maria and Balanchine had encountered a stumbling block in their marriage. She wanted to have children. He did not. Although they were not seeing eye to eye at home, they did not bring their personal lives to the studio.

At the time, the company was preparing to leave on a four-and-a-half month European tour immediately after the City Center season. Balanchine also was choreographing *Caracole* to Mozart's Divertimento No. 15, featuring Maria and Jerome Robbins.

That was the ballet that brought Jerry's performing career to an end. His mother came backstage on opening night right after the final bows and we were still in costume. She looked at Jerry, who had a little tam with a feather on it on his head, and very clearly suggested that he find a more practical career. He never thought he was a great classical dancer, so we laughed. But that was when he retired from performing.

Shortly after the company returned from its 1952 European tour, Maria filed for an annulment.

It didn't have any effect on our relationship in the company. In fact, after the annulment was granted I went straight from the courthouse to the theater to rehearse *Scotch Symphony*. Balanchine was so innately dignified and gracious, his marriages were always dissolved amicably. I think it was Bernard Taper, in his biography of Balanchine, who first noted that it was not uncommon to see Balanchine's wives, past and present, lined up at the barre in his class.

After finishing the 1952 City Center season, Maria headed to Hollywood to portray Anna Pavlova in MGM's full-length feature film *Million Dollar Mermaid*.

It was an Esther Williams extravaganza, and I even had lines that I had to speak with a Russian accent. Vida [Brown] and I used to sit in the coffee shop across from City Center practicing my Russian accent. It was quite funny. Anyway, they wanted me to do the *Dying Swan,* but with a few "flashy steps to liven it up." They asked to see something from *Firebird*. So I, like a dummy, showed them that very difficult turn at the end of my variation. I have no idea why I decided to show them that step because the floors on the set were heavily waxed and were so slippery you had to wear rubber on the bottom of your pointe shoes to dance. Of course, the weight of the rubber made everything very uncomfortable. George helped me figure something out and it worked, but it was an exhausting experience.

The glamor of having her own trailer and limousine on the set did not appeal to Maria.

One day I was darning a pair of regular pointe shoes on the set and someone came up to me and called wardrobe to relieve me of the chore. I explained that nobody else darns a ballet dancer's pointe shoes, but they didn't understand. It was interesting and certainly a completely different world.

On September 15, 1952, Maria added a new dimension to her private life. Following a whirlwind romance, she married Elmourza Natiroff, a Russian-born charter airline pilot. "He was very sweet," Maria says, "but he didn't understand the life of a dancer. It was fascinating and exciting to be married to a ballerina except when it meant I wasn't home for long periods of time." The marriage ended in divorce within a year.

Maria returned to New York City Ballet in 1953 for a cross-country American tour and performed on the eve of President Dwight Eisenhower's inauguration. Following the performance she was introduced to Eisenhower. "I thought I was going to faint when I shook his hand. He said that it was an honor to meet me and that he admired what I did, which was a complete shock."

As America's first and foremost ballerina, Maria had become a public figure. On May 2, 1953, she was presented her second Woman of the Year Award by the Women's National Press Club in Washington, D.C. Recognition from Oklahoma followed swiftly. With approval from the state senate, then-Governor Johnston Murray proclaimed June 29, 1953, Maria Tallchief Day in Oklahoma. In celebration of her Osage legacy, the Osage Tribal Council and Chief Paul Pitts named her Princess Wa-Xthe-Thonba (Two Standards) of the Osage Nation, in ceremonies held in the Tall Chief Theatre in Fairfax. She was also named an honorary colonel on Governor Murray's staff and given the title Commodore in the nonexistent navy of landlocked Oklahoma.

That same year, Balanchine created the company's first full-length ballet, *The Nutcracker*. His decision to produce the ballet, which would feature Maria as the Sugar Plum Fairy, was not greeted with pleasure.

Everyone in New York was against it, including the critics. The company was struggling financially and the comment was always "How can you spend so much money on a single production?" Well, thank God we did, because it saved the company. Despite the popular success of *Firebird* and other ballets, if we had not done *The Nutcracker* in 1954, New York City Ballet probably would have gone out of business.

It was a gorgeous production—and included a huge cast of children selected from the school. We rehearsed until the last minute, our costumes didn't arrive in time for the dress rehearsal, and everyone was completely exhausted. André [Eglevsky] was supposed to dance the Cavalier but injured his ankle, and Nicky [Magallanes] had to jump in at the last minute. Opening night I watched Tanaquil LeClercq in the Waltz of the Flowers from the wings. She was a brilliant dancer, and every time she exited the stage you could hear tremendous applause, which became screams of "Bravo" by the end. Then I had to make my entrance to this very grand but very slow music and do one of the most difficult pas de deux I had ever danced, including *Sylvia*.

I don't know if it's danced the same way today, but when Balanchine choreographed it for me, he said, "It must be like ballroom dancing." Of course he said ballroom dancing, but I had to do a double pirouette that started out unsupported and ended up in a fully supported backbend leaning on my partner's arm. If I didn't do the first pirouette right, it was disaster. There also was a very difficult lift to the shoulder, but Nicky was there and everything went like clockwork. I remember getting the chills, it worked so well. At the end of the pas de deux, there was an ovation. The audience went absolutely wild.

The popular appeal of Balanchine's *Nutcracker* in New York was only the beginning. Today the ballet has become as much a part of the American Christmas tradition as Santa Claus. Because of the ballet's staggering success at City Center, it was promptly added to the company's touring repertoire. Students from local schools in every city on the company's tour schedule flocked to auditions with hopes of being chosen to perform with New York City Ballet.

Vida was ballet mistress by then, and she went ahead of the company to audition and teach the children their roles before we arrived in each city. Usually, there were enough talented children at the auditions that she would end up with more than one cast. So when tickets went on sale, we would

Maria Tallchief as Zobeide in *Scheherazade*, 1954. (Personal collection.)

have people lined up around the block. Everybody related to any child in the production wanted to see it. And that was the beginning of the tradition that is still keeping ballet companies alive across America. Even people who don't know anything about ballet, know about *The Nutcracker*!

Among requests for personal appearances benefiting worthy causes, guest artist contracts, and offers to star in various productions, Maria was invited to return to Denham's Ballet Russe de Monte Carlo. The recently reorganized troupe was preparing to embark on a thirty-week cross-country tour under the aegis of Columbia Artists Management. As guest ballerina Maria was offered the unheard-of salary of $2,000 a week. "Well, Columbia had stipulated that they would not book the company if I wasn't signed," Maria says, "and they agreed to pay half my salary. Balanchine thought it would be good for me and money was somewhat of a concern. I hadn't taken anything as far as a settlement from the annulment. There wasn't anything to take. We had a house in Westport and that was it. My mother could never understand that."

Although prior to 1954 Maria had appeared in several touring summer musical productions, including a revival of *Song of Norway* in 1949, the addition of touring to the New York City Ballet schedule left little time for outside work. Although touring increased the number of weeks in her contract with New York City Ballet, her salary fell far short of the lucrative fees she earned for guest engagements. Immediately after Maria accepted the offer from Denham and her leave of absence from New York City Ballet became public knowledge, Columbia launched a major publicity campaign. *Newsweek* dedicated its October 1954 cover story to the world of ballet and America's first "homegrown" ballerina. A well-researched, in-depth profile of "the finest American-born ballerina the 20th century has produced" stirred tremendous interest in Maria, ballet, and the Ballet Russe de Monte Carlo.

"Unfortunately, I remember spending most of the tour in high heels and a harem hat, performing the lead in *Scheherezade,* Maria says. "Nina Novak was Denham's leading lady, and he wanted her to do all the good ballets." By the end of her engagement with Denham's Ballet Russe de Monte Carlo, Maria was ready to go home—to New York City Ballet.

Chapter Fifteen

Home, Sweet Home

A sold-out house and wildly enthusiastic applause greeted Maria's return to the City Center stage. There had never been any question that Maria would resume her position as leading ballerina of New York City Ballet and she was glad to be back. Although the Ballet Russe engagement had been a financial success and had won her significant acclaim for her performances in several roles, including *Swan Lake* opposite Frederic Franklin, it had not offered the grueling physical and mental challenges Maria thrived on. Returning to New York City Ballet in 1955, she created the leading role in Balanchine's very successful new virtuoso work *Pas de Dix*, quickly dispelling any fears that her technique had suffered during her absence.

During the company's subsequent engagement in Chicago, Maria was introduced to Henry Paschen, Jr., a successful Chicago contractor. Paschen, who was an avid social dancer and completely unaware of Maria's unparalleled fame in the world of classical ballet, remembers commenting to a friend that her skills on the dance floor had impressed him. Fortunately, the friend wasted no time explaining who Maria Tallchief was. The casual introduction led to romance, and on June 3, 1956, the couple was married in Chicago. Today Maria and Buzzy, as Paschen is known familiarly, laugh about spending their honeymoon in Europe on tour with New York City Ballet. Maria recalls, "He has always supported my career. Of course, in the beginning I thought he was going to move to New York and instead I ended up moving to Chicago. But he went to Europe with me after our wedding and I remember becoming quite ill, so it was good that he was there. That was the tour during which Tanaquil LeClercq contracted polio and everyone was completely devastated."

By 1956, New York City Ballet was recognized as the leading force in American ballet. Although the company would always have to struggle with limited budgets, survival from season to season was no longer in question. The company had gained a solid base of patrons, organized a powerful board of directors, and established effective fund-raising policies. That year, the company and its affiliated School of American Ballet relocated from Manhattan's East Side to larger studios at Eighty-second Street and Broadway. Shortly after the move, Balanchine created one of his most universally popular ballets, *Allegro Brillante*. Maria remembers, "That ballet was so enjoyable to dance! The Tchaikovsky score, of course, is absolutely wonderful. Nicky [Magallanes] and I did the leads, and it was very successful with audiences and the critics." Balanchine also spent five months away from the company, setting several works for the Royal Danish Ballet.

In 1956 the Canadian Broadcasting Corporation began filming New York City Ballet repertoire in Montreal for future telecasts, and the company presented seasons in Chicago and Philadelphia in addition to an eight-week season at City Center. In 1958 Balanchine choreographed *Gounod Symphony*. It would be the final ballet he would create featuring Maria. The ballet, set to a recently discovered Gounod composition, received only fair treatment by the critics, but

Maria Tallchief, her daughter Elise, and grandmother Eliza. Fairfax, Oklahoma, 1959. (Personal collection.)

Maria's performances were highly praised. In the spring of that year, New York City Ballet also made its first tour to the Far East, with engagements in Japan, Australia and the Philippines. "I didn't want to be away from Buzzy that long, so I was only scheduled to go with the company to Japan." The Japanese press was enthralled with Maria, and her performances were greeted with tremendous audience response.

On her return to Chicago Maria and Buzzy discovered they were expecting a child. Taking maternity leave from the company, Maria began preparing for motherhood. Although she stayed in shape throughout her pregnancy, she admits it was the longest time she had ever spent not performing. On January 3, 1959, Elise Paschen entered the world at six pounds, three and one-quarter ounces. Maria had no difficulty giving birth or adjusting to her new role. The Paschen clan, one of Chicago's leading families, celebrated the addition of its new member with enthusiasm.

Back home in Fairfax, Eliza Tall Chief waited to meet her great-granddaughter.

Grandmother did not travel well. And my father was ill at the time, which made it difficult for my mother to leave. So I asked for an extension of my maternity leave and Buzzy and I took Elise to Fairfax to meet my family in June. It was very important that my daughter meet my grandmother and see my father. I didn't realize how important it was at the time, but it will always be one of my most vivid memories of Fairfax.

In October, Alex Tall Chief died.

On her return to New York City Ballet for its 1959 winter season at City Center Maria was reunited with Erik Bruhn. A premier danseur with the Royal Danish Ballet, Bruhn had been a frequent guest artist with American Ballet Theatre (the name taken by Ballet Theatre in 1957), but the season marked his debut with Balanchine's company. Having forged a partnership to make guest appearances since meeting in Ballet Theatre in 1948, the two made a striking couple at New York City Ballet. According to reviews of their performances together during the season, the dance world had just gained a new and incredibly powerful team. Maria's jet black hair and striking angular features against Bruhn's blond hair and delicate Danish features created an extraordinary appearance. Commanding equal technical skills, the two were an ideal match and often gave the illusion of moving within the same breath.

The company also appeared on the "Bell Telephone Hour."

I performed the *Sylvia: Pas de Deux* and *Scotch Symphony*. It was very difficult. We had done marathon sessions in Canada and they had filmed practically the whole repertoire. But the Bell special was different, and it was very much a pioneer effort for all of us. There was no video equipment at that time, so everything was done on film with two stationary cameras. In those days, "live broadcast" meant they only filmed it once and there were no retakes no matter what happened! The studio wasn't suited for ballet, and we had those heavy rubber soles on our pointe shoes and danced in a space half the size of what we needed. But it was a major breakthrough for ballet on American television and very exciting because we knew we were making history.

By the end of the company's 1959 season, life became complicated again. American Ballet Theatre was invited to tour Russia under the auspices of the U.S. State Department. Terms of the invitation, extended as part of a cultural exchange program between the two nations, stipulated that Maria Tallchief appear as guest artist.

Bruhn, who had been a regular guest artist with the company before his brief departure to New York City Ballet, also was to rejoin the company. Maria remembers it as an incredible honor and opportunity, but also that it was very difficult for her to leave her family, but she had no choice.

Representing American ballet as its foremost ballerina was, in Maria's eyes, a tremendous responsibility. "Performing in Russia was very different. Their theaters had little or no heat. One night I performed the 'Black Swan' pas de deux and never felt my feet. They were still cold by the end of the pas de deux. Heaven only knows how I danced." Maria was extremely well received by the Russian audiences, press, and dance community. During the company's appearances in Tiflis, she was coached by the great Vakhtang Chabukiani. One of Russia's most celebrated male dancers before assuming his duties as ballet director and chief choreographer of the Tiflis State Theatre, Chabukiani freely admitted he considered Maria one of the greatest ballerinas of the time. In addition to teaching her a new variation using different music for the "Black Swan" pas de deux, he taught her parts of *Giselle*. "There wasn't time to learn the whole ballet, but I think we did everything but the Mad Scene. I had never experienced anything like that in my life. He was incredible and I learned so much."

Following the Russian tour, which included appearances in major European cities, Maria, along with Igor Moiseyev and Merce Cunningham, was presented the 1960 *Dance Magazine* Annual Award. The citation read in part, "Maria Tallchief. A star with truly American flavor, whose qualities of elegance, brilliance, and modesty enabled her to make a distinguished contribution to the recent cultural mission of American Ballet Theatre in Europe and Russia."

Her engagement with the troupe also resulted in an unprecedented contract, stipulating that she could appear with American Ballet Theatre as leading ballerina any time she wished in roles of her choice opposite any partner with whom she wanted to dance. Not prepared to resume her position with New York City Ballet, Maria's leave of absence was extended. "I had been invited to guest with the Royal Danish Ballet and I wanted to spend some time with my family at home—not on weekends or a few days here and there in New York."

Before going to Denmark to appear with Bruhn and become the first American ballerina to appear with the Danish company in its two-hundred-year history, Maria went home to Buzzy and Elise and made guest appearances with Ruth Page's Chicago Opera Ballet and the Chicago Lyric Opera. Prior to her return to New York City Ballet in 1963, Maria visited Oklahoma to receive the Indian of the Year Award in ceremonies closed to the press in Anadarko. She was the first ballerina to receive the highly coveted honor, and Maria recalls the invocation was presented in native tongue and followed by ceremonial dances.

During her absence from New York City Ballet, Maria's relationship with Balanchine had remained constant. "George was always like a father and brother to me, and it was the same with Buzzy and Elise. When I rejoined the company, there had been considerable changes. Erik came back to the company for one season and we did dance together. There was a lot going on and I remember that is when I started teaching at the school and performing." At the time, construction at New York's Lincoln Center complex was in its final stages and New York City Ballet was preparing to leave City Center for its new home in the State Theater.

Balanchine was involved in all stages of the design process and it was a very exciting moment. The only thing I never understood was how any of us were going to work in studios without windows. Since our first studios on Madison Avenue, we had always worked in studios with wonderful large windows and open airy spaces. At the State Theater, everything was climate controlled and artificially lit. But the stage was tremendous, and after the cramped wing space at City Center, it was a different world.

By that time, New York City Ballet had adopted an alphabetical listing for its featured artists. The company had increased in size and a great number of fresh, young talents from across the United States had been selected to participate in a Ford Foundation Scholarship program that provided a monthly stipend of $150 to offset the cost of living in New York City while studying at SAB. Among the first SAB Ford Scholarship recipients was Suzanne Farrell, who, according to Maria, was perfectly suited to Balanchine penchant for constantly changing, revising, and fine-tuning his ballets. "Suzanne was

Maria Tallchief and daughter Elise on stage before *Swan Lake,* Miami, Florida, 1961. (Photo © Jack Mitchell. Reprinted by permission.)

completely malleable and innately musical," Maria says. "Balanchine had gone on to a new phase and I was left with little to dance."

In early 1965 Maria announced that she would retire from the company at season's end. Her announcement stirred controversy and prompted editorial comments alluding to the fact that Maria was quitting because she was not interested in dancing without star billing. Maria says, however, "That was not the case. The only comment I ever made to the press was that I had no objection to the alphabetic listing of names. My objection was that when parts were distributed in alphabetical order, 'T' comes very near the end. There was no split between Balanchine and me. We remained very close

Maria, Buzzy, and Elise Paschen in a studio portrait, 1961. (Photo © Jack Mitchell. Reprinted by permission.)

until his death. It was simply time for me to leave New York City Ballet."

During her final season with the company, Maria received the highest honor bestowed within the American dance world, the Capezio Award.

It was a phenomenal tribute. I was so nervous at the awards ceremony, I thought I was going to faint. Sir John Gielgud made an eloquent speech before presenting me with the award. The audience was filled with my contemporaries and everyone I respected and revered in the dance world. Being honored by my peers had always been somewhat overwhelming to me and the Capezio Award was the ultimate recognition.

Inscribed on the Capezio Award plaque were these words:

"Her artistry which encompasses superb technical discipline, command of style and arresting individuality is admired, respected and applauded around the world. Thus, as an American ballerina, she has brought luster to American ballet itself, contributing immeasurably in placing it on equal esthetic footing with the ballet standards of those European cultures which first nurtured the art of ballet."

The first few months after her resignation Maria continued to make appearances in South America and Europe. During engagements with Peter van Dijk's fledgling Hamburg State Opera Ballet, she appeared in a number of European galas with Bruhn and Rudolf Nureyev, who had recently defected. In late 1965 she and van Dijk won the Best Lyrical Team Award during the Third International Dance Festival competition in Paris. Guesting, however, took its toll.

It wasn't working. I was constantly going from one engagement to another. Buzzy was in Chicago and Elise was traveling with me. Finally, after a performance in Caracas, I said "This is enough," and headed home. I had had a career that brought more than one life's share of achievement and I could take great pride in looking back. It was time to go on—my family was waiting.

Chapter Sixteen

Rosella Hightower
Professional Debut

In 1938 no one would have suggested that the slender young girl who arrived from Kansas City to join the newly formed Ballet Russe de Monte Carlo would some day become one of the world's most acclaimed ballerinas. At eighteen, the future of Charles Edgar and Eula May Hightower's only child did not look promising. Although Rosella could shake off the effects of sailing third-class on an overcrowded ship and spending a sleepless night aboard the train from Paris, youth, enthusiasm, and determination could not overcome the surprise waiting for her at the ballet office. Arriving for her first class with the company in a small studio facing the courtyard of the ornate Casino de Monte Carlo, Rosella was promptly informed that she did not have a job, that she had been invited to the tiny Mediterranean principality by Massine to compete against two hundred other promising young dancers for one of sixty openings in the troupe's corps de ballet. There would be no contract and no paycheck, and no assurances given that either would ever become a reality. Rosella had not expected a special welcome to the world of professional ballet, but she had not anticipated being told that she had traveled halfway around the world to compete in an audition.

Shaking her head, Rosella insists that Massine intended no malice by inviting every promising young dancer he had auditioned during his final touring season with the Blum–de Basil Ballets Russes to "join" the new company he was building in Monte Carlo.

It was the way he did things. There were no immigration quotas or unions to say he couldn't do things that way, so he did. Actually, it was quite funny. Here we all were, packed into the tiny Casino studio working as hard as we could, convinced that Massine had eyes for only "me." When, in fact, he was in the back of the room working on his own technique. I don't know if he ever watched any of us in class.

The situation put Rosella into an immediate financial bind, but she firmly believed it was only a temporary setback. "It never occurred to me that I might not get into the company. I was determined to stay on as long as it took, even if it meant following the company on tour across Europe. I knew how to live on a little bit of money and was prepared to wait it out." With no source of income to rely on except what her family could send, Rosella immediately rented a room with another American girl. "It was very small and the bathroom was down the hall. But it had a sink and a single Bunsen burner, and we could afford it." In her letters home, Rosella described her adventures getting to Monte Carlo and casually mentioned that her position with the company would not be official until after one more round of eliminations. "I may not have gone into great detail about the situation, but I let them know that I would need them to continue sending me money until the final elimination process had been resolved." Satisfied that she had taken care of her living costs for the time being, Rosella launched into the work at hand.

Massine had a three-month rehearsal period to set the repertoire for his new company. Following an inaugural season in Monte Carlo, the troupe was scheduled to embark on an extended tour that would include debut appearances in Paris, London, and New York. In addition to restaging existing ballets, Massine was creating new works, including *Gaîté Parisienne*. Rosella's former teacher, Michel Fokine, was on hand as well, staging his 1937 work *Les Éléments*. Between the number and variety of ballets to learn, Rosella was too busy to worry about anything else: "I knew it was up to me to stand out and make myself valuable. So I learned every role I possibly could." Rosella's penchant for hard work and determination to succeed did not alienate her from other company members. "There were a lot of Russians in the company, of course, but to them we were nobodies and they didn't pay much attention to us. It wasn't easy for any of the Americans. I don't think Massine was really interested in any of us, but there was American money involved, so we were somewhat of a necessity."

American money was more than involved in Massine's venture, it was the basis of his entire operation. During the latter months of his association with de Basil, Massine initiated negotiations with millionaire Julius Fleischmann of the Cincinnati-based Fleischmann Yeast Corporation and the New York financier Sergei Denham to establish a solid financial base for his new venture. His efforts resulted in the formation of World Art, Inc., later known as Universal Art. Once his financial backing was in place, Massine approached René Blum, who had resumed direction of the opera ballet in Monaco after disassociating himself from de Basil's operation. Convincing Blum to join forces with him in establishing a company capable of challenging de Basil's monopoly on Russian ballet, Massine gained the right to use the "Ballet Russe" name and inherited the dancers, sets, costumes, and repertoire of the existing company in Monte Carlo.

Although he was infuriated by Massine's shrewd business tactics, de Basil did not take Massine's challenge seriously until several of his leading stars, including Alexandra Danilova, Tamara Toumanova, George Zoritch, and Marc Platoff, defected to Monte Carlo and impresario Sol Hurok announced he was joining the Massine-Blum camp. Knowing full well that de Basil would attempt a counterattack, Massine worked quickly to sign Alicia Markova, Nathalie Krassovska, Mia Slavenska, Serge Lifar, Igor Youskevitch, Frederic Franklin, and other firmly established stars. When the dust settled, de Basil's star roster had been decimated. Undaunted, he regrouped the company around Tatiana Riabouchinska, Irina Baronova, David Lichine, and Anton Dolin, the latter signed as a guest artist following the disbanding of the Markova-Dolin Company.

Remembering the chaos, Rosella contends that the upshot of being in the midst of one of the most controversial and competitive periods in the history of ballet had tremendous benefits. "I was very fortunate, because I was exposed to so many great artists at a point when the ballet world was in a state of change. Taking class and watching Danilova, Toumanova and Markova in rehearsal was an invaluable experience. And because Perky had taught me so much about the history of dance, I knew how important it was at the time."

Consumed by the challenge of proving herself worthy of a contract, Rosella was usually one of the first to arrive at the studio in the morning and last to leave at the end of the day. Soon after rehearsals began, she became friendly with Frederic Franklin.

He was as determined as I was to learn as many roles as he could. When everyone else would go out to have something to eat during a break, we'd stay behind and work on a pas de deux from this ballet or that. But he was already a seasoned professional. He had worked in London musical reviews with Wendy Toye and been a soloist with the Markova-Dolin Ballet. He loved to teach and got a kick out of passing on to me what he knew. Every once in a while someone would ask us what we were doing and we always said, "Oh, just working."

Franklin takes equal delight in reminiscing about his first impressions of Rosella and recalling the obstacles she had to overcome during her first few months in Monte Carlo.

Ah, Rosella! Actually, I remember the day she arrived for class in Monte Carlo. She was very strong, and you couldn't help noticing her in class. But it was terribly difficult for her in the beginning. She worked harder than anyone I think I had ever met and learned very fast, but there were so many dancers, it was almost impossible to be noticed. Technically she could do anything, and when she couldn't, she pushed herself unmercifully until she mastered it. She was always very cheerful and had a smile for everyone, but there was a grim determination about her that you couldn't miss.

When she wasn't dancing, she watched everyone else and absorbed what she saw like a sponge. It was a very odd situation there in the very beginning for all of us. I felt more comfortable with the American dancers than the Russians and had a lot of affinity for Rosella. We were both sort of out of our element, I being British and she American. So we worked together quite a bit and became very good friends.

When she wasn't working with Franklin, Rosella worked on her own, and eventually the long hours she put in at the studio began to pay off.

I always stayed to work after rehearsals were over. The Russians left promptly, but Massine often stayed to work on his new ballets. Finally, after weeks of seeing me working on my own in the back of the studio, he asked me to try something for him. That was when he first saw what I could do and his attitude toward me began to change. And that's when I realized how important demonstrating for Perky had been. All he had to do was start a movement and I could finish it for him. Gradually, he started asking me to show the company what we had worked out and other people started to notice me.

Ultimately, Massine called Rosella aside to tell her that regardless of what happened when contracts were given out, she should stay on. Somehow, he said, he would see to it that she got into the company. Those words of encouragement proved invaluable when Rosella discovered that she was not among the dancers offered contracts at the conclusion of the rehearsal period. "What happened," she explains, "was that Massine went off to Paris and visited with the great Russian teachers Lubov Egorova and Olga Preobrajenska. Through them he was introduced to a group of fourteen-year-old White Russians, who were there with their mothers, and he felt that he had to make places for them in his company. Of course, that threw everything out of balance again because it left even fewer places for the rest of us."

Although many dancers had left Monte Carlo as soon as they realized they were there to audition, Rosella estimates Massine had the equivalent of two complete corps de ballets on hand by the time contracts were extended. Convinced that Massine's encouragement was genuine, she was in the process of figuring out a way to follow the company on tour after the conclusion of the Monte Carlo season when she was suddenly called to the ballet office. Straightening up in her chair, Rosella says, "For some reason, one of the dancers dropped out and they gave me her spot. It happened at the very last second, but all I cared about was that I had finally made it!"

For the first time since she had left Kansas City Rosella wrote letters to her parents and Perky that were completely dedicated to her career, the roles she was and would be performing, and her absolute elation at having made it into the company. Although she had told them of Massine's interest in her and repeated his words of encouragement, most of her letters had focused on the luxurious environment in Monte Carlo. She had sent postcards showing the gold and velvet interior of the diminutive Casino opera house and described the exclusive shops flanking the palm–tree-lined street winding up the steep hill to the Casino. She had even written about the primitive plumbing, unadorned cement walls, and low ceilings in the basement practice room the company used in addition to its ground-floor studio overlooking the glimmering blue and purple waters of the Mediterranean.

Everyone was beside themselves at home. And surprised. It was the first time they realized that it was all going to come true and I was finally on my way. They were very relieved because they could stop sending me money and saving up to buy my passage home. I'm still convinced they started putting money away to bring me home before I ever left Kansas City. So it was very, very exciting.

Chapter Seventeen

The War Years

Having prepared for an eleventh-hour opportunity since discovering that Massine's invitation to Monte Carlo was not a job offer, Rosella jumped at the chance to fit into the corps de ballet with little or no re-hearsal. In fact, she made her debut in Fokine's *Les Éléments* in Monte Carlo, before the company left on an eight-month European tour after its debut season in Monte Carlo. Rosella's ability to step into roles proved invaluable. Intent on gaining the same notice onstage as she had in the studio, Rosella turned her energies to developing her performing skills.

Markova and Danilova became my primary role models. I admired them equally. They were so fabulous, each in her own way, and so very different.

Being able to watch them onstage every night was incredible. Their contrasting styles and perfection made a great impression on me. To me, dance has always been an adventure. To have limited myself to what I could learn from one person would have been less of an adventure.

Rosella had the same attitude about working with choreographers.

Since it was always easy for me to follow, I enjoyed switching from one to another and being able to say, "Oh, that works too." Massine was the first choreographer I worked with as a professional. Later, when Balanchine came to work with the company, I was fascinated by the tremendous differences between them. Massine brought such striking avant-garde qualities to his works for that time and used such different elements of style. He concentrated more in the demi-caractère idiom and creating fantastic group compositions. With Balanchine, it was a musical story. He demanded great speed, which I enjoyed thoroughly, and I deeply appreciated his musicality. I always loved to dance his ballets more than watch them. Even today, I do not enjoy watching them as much as I had enjoyed dancing them.

The scene at the railroad station the day the company left on tour was Rosella's first exposure to the organized chaos that was part of life on the road with the Ballet Russe de Monte Carlo. Counting dancers, stagehands, wardrobe, management, support staff, and assorted family members the company numbered well over one hundred people. Rosella recalls, "We rode in reserved cars on the train and were shepherded from destination to destination as a group. We had to pay for our own food and lodging, but the company manager reserved our rooms, handled whatever papers we needed to go from country to country, and took care of booking and paying for all our travel expenses."

Not having to worry about anything except showing up at the appointed time on travel days was a new experience and one Rosella fully appreciated. "The company was like one big family on tour. There was a sincere sense of camaraderie and a wonderful feeling that everyone was watching out for everyone else." En route to London, Rosella wasted no time catching up on the status of the battle between Massine and de Basil. Despite her lack of interest in company politics and power struggles, she was aware that the stage was set for a showdown between the rival companies in London.

An attempt to merge both troupes under the Universal Art banner had failed, and de Basil had booked his company's annual season at Covent Garden to run through the first week of Massine's Ballet Russe de Monte Carlo's debut at the Drury Lane. To complicate matters further, both companies would be performing ballets created by Massine during his tenure with the rival company. "Everyone was in an uproar," Rosella says, "and the public and the press were having a great time. Except for the fact that it put management on edge, it was exciting to be dancing practically across the street from each other. There were dancers all over the place, and everyone did their best to see what the other company was doing. As I remember it, the whole mess ended up in court."

A court battle did ensue and resulted in de Basil being forced to resign his post as director to allow the company to continue its season under a new name, Covent Garden Ballets Russes. Universal Art, however, pressed for the removal of "Ballet Russe" and the company became known as Educational Ballets, Ltd. Rosella explains, "Of course, what de Basil did was arrange for his company to go to Australia for an extended residency. Once there, he regained control, and that's when he changed the name to the Original Ballet Russe."

Although the war between the two companies would continue through 1947, Massine won the battle in 1938. In the midst of all the controversy, the Ballet Russe de Monte Carlo was such a box office success at the Drury Lane that the management at Covent Garden immediately engaged the troupe to make its debut there before departing for America. A new full-length production of *Coppélia* featuring Danilova during its first season engagement at Covent Garden drew further popular and critical acclaim—and an invitation to present a longer season at the same theater the following year.

The company was expected to remain in London for several weeks following its appearances at Covent Garden, but management suddenly announced the company would set sail for New York within a few days of its final performance. The threat of war in Europe was increasing daily, and mounting apprehension over whether the company's large contingent of non-Americans would be allowed to travel freely prompted the change in schedule. The company remained intact, however, and made its long-awaited debut at New York's Metropolitan Opera House on October 12, 1939. The season was an unmitigated success. Stunning praise from the New York critics fueled ticket sales, and box office receipts turned a handsome profit. Hurok could not have had better notices to send across the country to stir tickets sales if he had written them himself.

Although the Met season had been a sensational success, Toumanova and Lifar resigned and Markova was injured. Having been so excited after seeing her parents and making her debut at the Met less than a year after going off to Europe on her own, nothing fazed Rosella. Despite the grueling itinerary of the tour, the perpetual internal turmoil, and the constant challenge of dancing in new theaters with little or no rehearsal, the multitude of opportunities to excel more than compensated for the discomforts. Rosella recalls, "Markova and Danilova became my mentors. So when Markova did not dance, I performed her role in *Pas de Quatre*. Because of that, I was promoted to soloist during my second year. And when Danilova would stay behind or go ahead to the next city to make personal appearances, I would dance for her. That was how I came to dance with Massine."

Dancing with different partners was part of the challenge of being thrust onstage as a last-minute replacement. Being able to hold her own opposite Massine had a significant impact on Rosella's immediate future in the company. At the same time, she was beginning to dance on a fairly regular basis with André Eglevsky.

He joined the company roster during our Covent Garden season. I remember he was quite young and a very big boy. He had been dancing professionally since thirteen or fourteen and had to support his family. His mother didn't go on tour with us as many of the other "Russian mamas" did. She wouldn't leave her small, very modest house between Cannes and Cagne sur Mer.

Rising to let her German Shepherd, Baptiste, in the front door of her spacious villa perched high above the sun-drenched beaches of Cannes and adorned with fragrant tropical vines cascading into flower beds brimming with colorful blooms, Rosella pauses. "I'm convinced that the heart problems he developed later all started because he had to do the work of a man at too young an age. Technically, he was outstanding and competitive in the best way. He liked me very much and we enjoyed working together. I was about the only one he partnered well in the company. Otherwise he was a bit lazy about lifting most of the girls."

Life on tour, Rosella found, did allow time for personal relationships to emerge. Midway through the tour, she announced she was marrying one of the young Russians in the company, Mischa Resnikov. Raising her hand to her forehead, she says, "I still remember Eglevsky's reaction. He was so furious he would not speak to me or look at me for weeks. It was quite serious because we danced together almost every night. I can't explain how difficult it is to dance with someone who insists on looking in the opposite direction! He had a very protective attitude toward me and did not approve of Mischa."

Eglevsky was not the only person who was against Rosella's marriage. "Mother was absolutely against it, and my father didn't approve but as usual went along with it figuring it would work out for the best in the long run. Of course, everyone was right. Mischa was not an ambitious boy, so it didn't work at all and we were divorced within a year." With the exception of her mother, no one ever made an issue of the episode again. Eglevsky got over his anger, and he and Rosella forged a dancing partnership that remained a significant element in both their careers for many years.

By the conclusion of her first contract with the Ballet Russe de Monte Carlo, Rosella had gained soloist status. Her success in the company, which she had had to wait in the wings to join, did not surprise anyone—least of all Franklin. "Watching her work her way up the ladder was exciting. She never let up, and it seemed as though every step up the ladder she made, she added another rung at the top. She had had very good training, she knew what she needed to work on, and she did." Franklin also remembers that once Rosella took on a new challenge, it wasn't a case of *if* she would master it but *when*. Pointing out that at that time there weren't any major reviews written outside the large cities, audience response was the only measure of success any of the dancers had. "Well," Franklin says, "Rosella developed a charming presence onstage that made her an audience favorite."

For Rosella the first cross-country American tour proved that the harder she worked, the more opportunities she was given to work harder. On her own, she focused her attention on what she perceived as her major shortcomings.

I always had trouble with my extremities. The upper body and legs were fine, but my feet and hands needed work. I remember having horrid problems with pointe shoes until I discovered a shoe made by Mendola. After we returned to Monte Carlo, an Italian shoemaker came to visit the company to introduce us to them and I wore them from that moment on. Actually, the same man made my shoes for the rest of my career. They were wonderful and made a tremendous difference for me.

The company's decision to return to Monte Carlo in March 1939 was not well thought out. Returning to Europe after completing a second New York season, which was booked around a special appearance in Cincinnati hosted by Universal Art's president, Julius Fleischmann, Rosella recalls, "We practically had the whole ship to ourselves. There were very few passengers other than us. So we did barre on deck and had a wonderful time." Unfortunately, the lack of other passengers was a sign that the threat of war, which had prompted the company's hasty departure from London six months earlier, had not diminished. The potential dimensions of the conflict had in fact increased, and there were strong indications that Hitler's forces were mobilizing along the Polish border. Despite mounting tensions throughout Europe, life in Monaco remained unchanged. The affluent who sought respite from the dreary signs of approaching war at the gambling tables of the Casino in Monte Carlo showed little concern that the 370-acre Riviera resort intersects the Mediterranean coastline between France and Italy and the upper section of Monte Carlo is behind the French border. Arriving "back home" with less than a week to prepare for the first performance of its second Monaco season, the company had enough on its hands without worrying about the threat of military aggression in Europe. During the rehearsal period following the season, rumors began circulating that the company's engagement at Covent Garden, scheduled to open September 4, would never be presented.

Despite the rumors, no changes were made in the touring schedule and the company headed for Florence, Italy, in May and on to

Paris from there. After the season in Paris, the company returned to Monte Carlo and the dancers were given a monthlong vacation period before rehearsals were scheduled to resume in Paris in preparation for the Covent Garden season, a second engagement at the Met in New York, and a subsequent American tour. Rosella says, "That was when I first spent time in Cannes. Eleonora Marra, Marc Platoff, Freddie, myself, and two other Americans went to stay in the *pension de famille* of a Russian family in Cannes." The shadow of war and growing concerns over the possibility of being trapped in Europe cast a pall over holiday relaxation. Although company members returned to Paris following their layoff, as scheduled, there were no rehearsals. "We were told to await word concerning our future and then chaos broke out," Rosella recalls.

On September 1, Germany unleashed the full power and might of the infamous Blitzkrieg on Poland, casting the gauntlet of World War II. Within forty-eight hours of Germany's brutal invasion, France and England issued a declaration of war. "All of a sudden the company disbanded and everyone was on their own," Rosella says, "The Russians dispersed in all directions, Massine left for New York by plane, and we Americans were stranded in Paris." Franklin ultimately made his way safely back to England, but he stayed to help the Americans.

Of course, none of us had any money. But the American Embassy sent us home on the last boat to leave. Le Havre already had been mined, so we got out just in time.

None of us had any idea of what to expect when we reached New York, but when we arrived at the pier Massine was waiting for us with the money to pay for our passage! He never explained how he knew which boat we were on or when we were arriving, but there he was. He was very excited and barely waited until we got off the boat to explain that we had to immediately begin rehearsals with the American dancers he had hired for the season at the Met.

In typical Massine style, the indomitable choreographer had succeeded in having the originally scheduled season at the Met postponed for several weeks to allow time to train an entire new company.

That meant, of course, that we had to teach the repertoire to the new company in less than a month. We worked like dogs and did exactly what he had said we would. Freddie arrived from England, and a few stragglers from the old company found us, but it was still an incredibly difficult experience.

Then the day we moved into the Metropolitan Opera to begin dress rehearsals, all the Russians showed up. So Massine had two companies again and we alternated casts for the entire New York season.

With the company scheduled to embark on a cross-country tour immediately following the season at the Met, Massine had to pare the company down to a reasonable size. "This time, all of us who had helped put the new company together felt safe. Since we had done all the work, Massine could not get rid of us."

Chapter Eighteen

Changing Directions

As difficult as her second cross-country tour turned out to be, Rosella found it very exciting because she had so much to dance. Unfortunately, by the time the company arrived in California a new problem developed. With a slight edge to her voice, Rosella explains, "Massine got all mixed up with films and temporarily lost interest in the company. It was very difficult because quite a few of us were not interested in working in films. So we were left not really knowing what to think about the future." With the exception of those few who shared Massine's infatuation with Hollywood, his lack of interest in the company succeeded in costing him several of his best dancers.

"I remember Eglevsky calling me," Rosella says. "He was all ex-

135

cited about a new company being organized by Lucia Chase and Richard Pleasant and said, 'Let's go.' Dolin was already there, Markova and Baronova were going, and they encouraged me to go with them. So I did." The company Eglevsky described as "being organized" had made its official debut as Ballet Theatre in 1940, following the expansion of the Mordkin Ballet into a fully professional operation. Chase, an American dancer who controlled a considerable fortune, was responsible for providing primary funding and artistic direction.

Joining Ballet Theatre as a soloist in late 1941 was the beginning of a new phase in Rosella's career: "I always had a strong sense of where my career was going and when it was time to change direction. And I made the right decisions." The company was preparing to launch its first major tour of North America and take its chances in the arena of major ballet companies. There had been a changing of the guard within management and the company was pursuing a more Russian-European image to compete at the box office. Chase had turned the reins of daily artistic management over to Baronova's husband, German Sevastianov, and Dolin had been instrumental in bringing Hurok onboard to present the company and contribute artistic guidance. The nucleus of the company's principal and soloist roster spent the summer of 1941 at Jacob's Pillow in the New England Berkshires preparing for the tour.

"It was very exciting," Rosella recalls. "Antony Tudor, Jerome Robbins, Hugh Laing, Maria Karnilova, Nora Kaye, and all sorts of people were there. I shared a cabin with Nora, and that's when we became very good friends."

In addition to rehearsing, the dancers performed on weekends as part of a dance festival cosponsored by Markova and Dolin that essentially relieved Ballet Theatre from the financial burden of a summer-long rehearsal period. Although the rough-hewn barn converted into a theater by Ted Shawn in 1930 for his legendary all-male dance troupe provided a setting that was completely different from the opulent splendor of European opera houses, little else was different. Rosella explains, "We had to learn an entire repertoire and become a company by the end of the summer. It was wonderful. There were so many choreographers to work with and new ballets to learn and very few distractions."

In addition to performing essentially the same roles in Ballet

Theatre's productions of the standard classical repertoire, Rosella danced an expanding array of bravura pas de deux. The "Bluebird" pas de deux in Dolin's staging of *Princess Aurora* proved to be one of the most successful roles of her first season with the company. Dancing opposite Eglevsky, Rosella won both popular and critical acclaim for her virtuoso technical skills. As much as Rosella admits enjoying the challenge of her roles, she remembers becoming aware that she was being typecast.

The tendency to categorize dancers in Ballet Theatre was very strong. Nora did dramatic roles, I did the technical ones, and when Alicia Alonso returned the following season, she also did dramatic roles. I never liked that. Once you were thought of as a certain kind of dancer it was very difficult to change. And to cross back and forth would have created problems because everyone had their own repertoire.

Although responsible for an extensive repertoire of her own, Rosella continued her practice of learning other roles. "I didn't just learn roles I thought I might have the opportunity to perform. It was my way of learning how new choreographers and other dancers worked."

Despite her obvious dedication to hard work, Rosella had no difficulty making friends or adjusting to the environment of a new company. "The company was different, and on tour the atmosphere was completely different. With all the Russians in the Ballet Russe it was more of a family affair and a lot of the families traveled with the company. Ballet Theatre was a group of young New Yorkers out on tour and it was party time—inside and outside the Pullman cars."

Another significant difference between the two companies was the fact that Ballet Theatre's primary backer also served as one of the company's ballerinas. Although Chase remained actively involved in major artistic decisions and continued to provide the lion's share of the company's funding, Sevastianov handled day-to-day operations to allow her to perform with the company until he was drafted into the army in 1943. As much as Chase wanted to be treated as just another dancer in the company, her presence was at best odd. "She could be very exasperating at times. Lucia was a quirky kind of person. I remember she watched everybody backstage and was always making little comments, here and there. But, actually, for all she went through to make the company work, her interference was minimal and often positive."

Between 1941 and 1944, Ballet Theatre continued to fortify its Russian image. Hurok's promotional claim, "The Greatest in Russian Ballet by Ballet Theatre," was supported by the repertoire Sevastianov built. Fokine continued to mount new productions until his death in 1942, Nijinska resumed her association with the company, and both Balanchine and Massine appeared on the scene. Despite an infusion of Russian and Slavic choreographers brought in by Sevastianov, the company maintained an extremely diversified repertoire, with Tudor creating some of his most significant works, Dolin continuing to mount one-act versions of various classics, and the Americans Eugene Loring, Agnes de Mille, and Jerome Robbins contributing major new works.

As stimulating as Rosella found working with Massine again and being exposed to so many new choreographers, Nijinska made the greatest impression.

She was a true genius and all-around artist. She had never been a great, great dancer, but she was a great musician. Massine was a good musician and Balanchine the greatest of all, but in the same sense Nijinska had learned fantastic formation from the conservatory in Russia. She went further musically and realized, what I eventually learned the hard way, that much of technique and virtuosity is rhythm. When she choreographed or taught, it was often from a rhythmical approach. She liked me and cast me as Markova's understudy in one of the ballets she did for us, which gave me a good deal of time to work with her.

By the conclusion of her first year with Ballet Theatre, Rosella was recognized as one of the company's most impressive young soloists and had proven herself capable of even greater challenges. In addition to her classical repertoire, Rosella was cast in Tudor's *Lilac Garden* and *Dim Lustre*. "I enjoyed working with Tudor," Rosella recalls, "but essentially those were Nora's ballets and I only performed secondary roles. Agnes also liked me, and I danced *Tally-Ho* and *Three Virgins and a Devil*. She was very interesting to work with, and her approach to movement was, again, quite different. I always felt that her tendencies and heritage stemmed from her uncle, Cecil B. DeMille."

Massine's arrival in the Ballet Theatre camp in late 1941 marked the end of his association with the Ballet Russe de Monte Carlo and left Denham to reorganize that company without a resident choreographer. The temporary artistic incapacitation of the Ballet Russe de Monte Carlo succeeded in removing Ballet Theatre's only potential competitor for the duration of World War II. Colonel de Basil's Original Ballet Russe had run afoul of wartime immigration regulations while trying to leave South America and would remain there until 1946. Closer to home, Balanchine had been forced to suspend the joint operations of Ballet Caravan and American Ballet after Lincoln Kirstein was inducted into the U.S. Army.

While Ballet Theatre endured more than its share of hardship and inconvenience during the course of both its North and Central American tours during the war, the company never encountered any insurmountable setbacks. For Rosella, the abundance of new ballets being produced and the high energy level within the company more than made up for the discomforts imposed by the war. Considering her appetite for learning new idioms of movement, her stunning command of the classical technique, and her dauntless stamina, the environment was ideal for the next step up the ladder to the status of ballerina.

By mid-1943, Rosella's promotion to ballerina was imminent. She had won popular and critical acclaim performing a full complement of ballerina roles on tour and was to make her debut in Dolin's restaging of the Grand Pas de Deux from *The Nutcracker* during the company's October season at the Met. Reviewing the debut, the *New York Times* dance critic John Martin cited Rosella as "one of the finest of young ballerinas of inherent brilliance and fluency." He also credited her with offsetting her technical prowess with unusual softness. He wrote, "Here assuredly, is an American ballerina in the full sense of the term." Following her subsequent promotion to ballerina, Rosella performed her first Swan Queen with Dimitri Romanoff, took over the role of Myrtha in *Giselle* on a first cast basis, and continued to win accolades for her stunning command of the "Black Swan," "Don Quixote," "Bluebird," and "Nutcracker" pas de deux. When the company was not on tour, she took advantage of being able to study with Anatole Vilzak, Madame Fedorova, and the Russian-born Elizabeth Anderson.

Fedorova prepared me for Black Swan and Madame Anderson coached me in the Swan Queen. In the beginning, Edward Caton taught company class, which was wonderful. Then he decided he was "allergic" to the company and posted a notice on the board saying he would teach class for anyone not in the company. He liked me, though, so I usually got away with taking class at his studio.

Despite her swift rise through company ranks, Rosella was well liked.

I had a lot of "severe" friends, who criticized me because they liked me and could see that I was going to have a career. It was constructive criticism, mostly because they were so much more experienced and had been in the company longer. In some ways, they adopted me and were very supportive of my progress. That was important and very valuable to me.

One of the most unusual experiences of Rosella's career with Ballet Theatre has since been memorialized in the 20th Century Fox feature film *The Turning Point,* starring Anne Bancroft, Shirley MacLaine, Mikhail Baryshnikov, and Leslie Browne. The late Nora Kaye served as executive producer of the film, and her husband, Herbert Ross, in association with Arthur Laurents, produced and directed. "Nora called me to ask permission to use an incident she had never forgotten from one of our seasons at the Met. We had a good laugh remembering the details," Rosella says, referring to a scene in the movie showing Browne being put onstage in an inebriated state.

Nora, Alonso, and I were sharing a dressing room and Nora witnessed the entire episode. Anyway, I had been given a free night and some friends threw a party for me in Greenwich Village. The party was in full swing when someone said that Hurok was on the phone and wanted to talk to me. At first, I thought it was a joke. Then I got on the phone. He told me I had to come to the theater immediately because whoever was scheduled to dance the pas de deux had suddenly been injured. I remember saying "But Papa Hurok," which is what we used to call him, "you can tell by listening to me on the phone what state I'm in. You certainly can't be serious." Of course, he wouldn't listen to me and kept saying, "Don't worry, I'm sending a car. Get in it, come to the theater, and we'll fix everything." So I went to the theater.

The minute I arrived at the theater they grabbed me, stuck me in the shower, poured coffee down my throat, and put me into a costume. I remember being told I would be dancing with George Skibine and thinking Thank God, it's Skibine, because he was very good at improvising. I went along with everything until I looked down and saw they had put me in the Black Swan tutu. Then I said, "No! I won't do it. I've come this far, but I will not do Black Swan. It has to be 'Don Quixote,' because we can somehow get through that." Without any argument, they said, "Go ahead and dance whatever you want!"

So Skibine and I went out on stage and did some semblance of "Don Quixote" in our Black Swan costumes. God only knows how we got through it, but we did.

Whether Hurok alerted the critics to the situation is unknown, but the performance was not reviewed the next day. Rosella adds, "Since the incident became one of those no one ever forgot, the Hurok people didn't object to it being in the movie either."

Rosella's progress as a ballerina was well noted by the leading critics of the day. Reviewing one of her first performances of *Swan Lake* in 1944, Edwin Denby of the *New York Herald-Tribune* praised her ability to make "perfectly clear the very interesting three-dimensional values" of the solo variations. Martin expressed a similiar opinion of her New York debut in the role of Myrtha in *Giselle,* writing, "It is a delight to see a ballerina with so instinctive a realization that it is the arms and upper body, and not mere extensions, turns and beats that exhibit the true aristocrat of her calling."

By the close of Ballet Theatre's 1945 New York season, major changes were under way in the ballet world. The war had ended, Denham had signed Balanchine to a two-year contract as resident choreographer for the Ballet Russe de Monte Carlo, de Basil's Original Ballet Russe was preparing to make its first appearance in New York in four years, and Hurok had renegotiated his contract with Ballet Theatre to resume his prewar post as impresario of dance at the Metropolitan Opera House. Leading dancers were being lured from one company to another at an alarming rate and several new groups were emerging on the horizon. Eglevsky had left Ballet Theatre to appear as a guest artist with several companies including Massine's newly organized Ballet Russe Highlights.

Before Rosella's contract with Ballet Theatre expired, she was approached by Massine and accepted his offer to join his company.

It didn't turn out to be much of a company. And then Hurok called me with an offer to join de Basil's Original Ballet Russe as a ballerina. Markova and Dolin had signed as guest artists for the New York season and cross-country tour and Hurok was gathering a group of principals and soloists from Ballet Theatre to join the company in South America. Marjorie [Tallchief] and Eglevsky went with us, and Skibine and a few others joined us when we arrived back in New York. We didn't know what to expect. But because Hurok was involved we knew it was secure.

Chapter Nineteen

The Marquis de Cuevas

On her arrival in South America in 1946, Rosella encountered hostility from other dancers for the first time in her life. "It was completely understandable," Rosella explains. "Hurok had sent us down to take over specific roles. For me, it wasn't that difficult because I came in as a ballerina and knew several dancers from the early Ballet Russe de Monte Carlo days. There was a tremendous amount of work to be done and ballets to learn in a very short period of time, so I really didn't have time to get involved." Returning to New York by boat from South America within a few days of opening a fall season at the Metropolitan Opera House in 1946 was not, according to Rosella, a brilliant move. "Everyone still had sea legs, and the first few performances did not go well."

143

After a less than sensational response in New York, the company embarked on a cross-country tour that would conclude with a second New York season at the Met in the spring. By the time the troupe arrived back in New York, everyone was exhausted.

Most of us were sick and there was tremendous chaos. But as sick as some of us were, we were more concerned because Markova was ill. She and Dolin were scheduled to perform *Giselle* on opening night, and Hurok, of course, had promoted it as the major event of the 1946–47 dance season. None of us knew what was going to happen when we arrived for rehearsals the day we were scheduled to open.

Suddenly, Dolin and Hurok appeared in my dressing room and told me I was going to replace Markova. I remember standing there, realizing that it was one of those opportunities that usually comes once in the life of a dancer and that I was very fortunate it had happened to me. I considered it a turning point in my career and wished that I was not sick as well. But my first concern was how Dolin felt about it. I wasn't sure he was happy about the situation and thought maybe he would have preferred to cancel the performance, rather than open the season with someone who had never danced the role.

On the contrary, Rosella discovered that Dolin and Markova had complete confidence in her and that Dolin was only concerned that she grasp how much her success meant to him. He made it very clear that he was eager to introduce a new ballerina.

Having less than six hours to prepare for the most significant role in her career was hardly ideal. "But," Rosella remembers, "I had learned the role by watching it. Of course, watching it and doing it are entirely different, and there was the question of learning it with Dolin, who had his way of doing it with Markova." In consideration of the fact that Rosella was sick and running a fever, Dolin encouraged her to mark or walk through as much of the choreography as possible. "Because it was a two-act ballet, we needed a full day's rehearsal to get through it and he tried to keep me in check by not doing anything full out, unless it was absolutely necessary." Falling back into a mix of French and English, Rosella continues rapidly,

He was so much with me and considered it his idea, I could feel him making it happen for me. Up until that point, essentially I had been doing vir-

Rosella Hightower backstage at the Metropolitan Opera House before a performance of *Giselle,* 1947. (Personal collection.)

tuoso pas de deux and suddenly to be thrust into the pinnacle of dramatic roles made it more complicated than getting the steps and placement into my head. I was not as concerned about the second act because it was more technical, but I had to find time to think about the character, the first act Mad Scene, and pacing myself. Dolin was totally confident in me, so that gave me strength.

As swiftly as everything had come together since being told she would perform the role that morning in her dressing room, Rosella remembers that the wait in the wings to go onstage seemed like an eternity. Describing those moments the following day in the *New York Herald-Tribune,* Walter Terry wrote, "As the lights were dimmed Anton Dolin stepped forward to announce that Miss Markova was ill and that Rosella Hightower, following a few hours of coaching by Mr. Dolin, would dance the role of Giselle for the first time." There was a general groan when Markova's illness was announced and then cheers at the mention of Miss Hightower's assignment, and the performance was on.

"Of course, all I heard," Rosella says,

was the famous groan. The one that destroys your knees and then you have to pull yourself back together before the curtain opens. That was the worst part. Once I got onstage and began to dance, my confidence started to come back. I was extremely nervous and had to calm myself down. I really was not distracted about whether the audience would like me or not because I was so worried about what I was doing. I could feel the memory coming, beginning to work, and finally I began to relax. Dolin kept saying little things to me, and that carried me through the first act. Then we started the second act. Because there is not much room for audience reaction or applause in the second act and it is more what you are giving out onstage, I suddenly began to realize the audience was working with me. I could feel their presence and that they were part of it.

Closing her eyes tightly, she recalls that when the curtain lowered at the end of the ballet there was absolute silence in the theater, followed by a thunderous roar of applause.

It was incredible, and I could feel it inside. I knew, because of certain sensations I had had with Dolin onstage and some of the exchanges between us, that it had been a great success. I was completely exhilarated and Dolin gave me a kiss during bows. The response from the audience was so powerful, it was almost overwhelming. I was exhausted, but I didn't suffer that tremendous fatigue immediately afterward that can easily turn into depression because you are so empty. I was totally happy about the situation. And because I had been so well received, several things happened that made it a complete celebration.

Before the final curtain calls had been taken and the ovation subsided, dancers and others gathered behind the curtain to congratulate her. The jubilation continued all the way to her dressing room. Among the steady stream of people who flocked to her dressing room the remainder of the evening was a gentleman whom Rosella had not met before.

He was extremely distinguished and presented himself graciously as the Marquis de Cuevas. He was very excited and told me how impressed he was with my performance. Then he offered me a contract to join his company as leading ballerina, right there in my dressing room! I had no idea who he was until that moment and didn't quite know what to do. But he was very polite and said that he would contact me to work out the details.

De Cuevas, born the eighth Marquis de Piedrablanca de Guana de Cuevas in Chile in 1886, was raised in the strict traditions of Spanish royalty. Following his marriage to Margaret Strong, granddaughter of John D. Rockefeller, the Marquis's already substantial fortune expanded to mammoth proportions. A great lover of the arts, he established his presence in America as an art patron of significant means and controversial taste by sponsoring the Masterpieces of Art Exhibition at the 1939–40 New York World's Fair. In 1940, he became an American citizen and within three years established a ballet school and began building his first company under the name Ballet International. Although the troupe was a complete financial disaster, it succeeded in winning a respectable artistic reputation.

Sitting back in her chair, Rosella says,

Of course, Eglevsky was the first person I talked to about my visit from de Cuevas, known familiarly as the Marquis. He had performed as a guest artist in the Marquis's first venture, Ballet International, before he went with Massine's Ballet Russe Highlights and knew all about the Marquis's plans for a new company. He also had been invited to join the company, initially known as the Nouveau Ballet de Monte Carlo, so his reaction was instant. He just said, "It is the opportunity of a lifetime. We can call the shots and control what we dance. It will be our company." He made sense, because I knew that as much as I had succeeded in *Giselle,* to have been allowed to shift into more dramatic roles would have been almost impossible. I wanted to change direction very much, and then Eglevsky said something that touched a nerve, "No more one-night stands."

After close to ten years of going from one marathon cross-country tour to another, Rosella had come to dread the thought of going back on the road: "I remember waking up one morning a few days after our conversation and saying 'That's it, I've had enough touring.'

And that was when I decided to accept the Marquis's offer. But first, I had to finish the season at the Met." With Markova out indefinitely Rosella had little time to contemplate the future. In addition to her own roles, she replaced Markova in several other ballets including the premiere of *Pas de Trois,* a new work created by Robbins for Markova, Dolin, and Eglevsky.

When the reviews of the company's opening night performance appeared in the next day's papers, Rosella was proclaimed a star by the *New York Times, New York Herald-Tribune,* and the *New York Sun.* Hurok's staff busily dispatched mimeographed copies of the unanimous reviews by Martin, Terry, and Irving Kolodin to theater managers, the news media, and booking agents around the world. Arriving at the theater the morning after her sensational debut in *Giselle* to prepare for her New York debut in Edward Caton's *Sebastian* and William Dollar's *Constantia,* Rosella was greeted with congratulations and extra copies of all the reviews. In addition to hailing Rosella as a star, all three critics had noted that despite the appearance being an emergency replacement, she had given a performance superior to many veteran ballerinas in the role.

More important, as far as the international dance world was concerned, Martin summarized the impact of Rosella's emergence as a star in the *New York Times* at the conclusion of the company's first week of performances: "With considerable trepidation, some of us went back the next night to see if perhaps it had been a fluke. But Miss Hightower lost no time in dispelling such a possibility." Martin's opinion of her performance of the lyrical *Constantia* and the melodramatic *Sebastian* equaled his praise of her *Giselle.* Noting that she sustained her technical and dramatic prowess throughout the week's performances, he called her "a star of considerable magnitude." And after calling her soft presentation of tremendous technical strength "the proverbial steel in velvet of the classic style," he praised her ability to carry her movements through to complete fulfillment. He was also impressed by her use of the arms and superior carriage of the upper body, declaring them the difference between "the ballerina to the manner born and the mere executor of prescribed acrobatics of the feet and legs." Although it is unknown whether Martin was aware that Rosella was joining the de Cuevas company, his final comment was completely apropos: "She has won the accolade of ballerinahood. Gentlemen, La Hightower!"

Martin's words literally echoed across the ocean to Europe, preceding Rosella's arrival there in 1948, and set the stage for the sensation that followed her debut at the Alhambra Theatre in Paris as the leading ballerina of the de Cuevas company, which had been renamed the Grand Ballet de Monte Carlo. "The press swarmed her, the public adored her and she appeared technically capable of anything. A fascinating, extraordinary virtuoso, Mme. Hightower exhibits rare fluid style, musicality and secure balance," wrote the French dance critic Irenè Lidova. She went on to praise Eglevsky's performance opposite Rosella in the "Black Swan" pas de deux: "dynamic, electrifying and magnificent double turns in the air, incredible batterie and dazzling multiple turns."

André-Philippe Heresin, founding editor and publisher of the French equivalent of *Dance Magazine, Les Saisons de la Danse,* remembers the event vividly. Sitting behind a massive rolltop desk piled high with a chaotic array of photos, press proofs, and notepads in a windowed corner of the publication's headquarters located in the midst of one of Paris's busiest market areas, Heresin speaks rapidly in a mixture of French and English. "The public fell in love with Rosella. No one [in Paris] had ever seen a ballerina of such strength and force with the classical port de bras, presence, and charm that she had. Maybe they had seen one without the other. But not all together in one ballerina. Her debut here with the Marquis's company was a shock for the public and created a huge success."

Having won unprecedented acclaim during its initial season in Vichy and Paris, the troupe's arrival in Monte Carlo to prepare for its first season as the resident ballet company of Monaco was greeted with tremendous celebration. A manifestation of the Marquis's eclectic vision, the company possessed a fusion of various elements. In addition to combining his Ballet International with the existing company in Monte Carlo, the Marquis engaged Nijinska and Dollar as ballet masters, extended top billing to Rosella and Eglevsky, and signed Marjorie Tallchief and George Skibine to head an impressive roster of leading American and European dancers. The only professional American ballet company based in Europe at the time, the troupe had been incorporated in the state of New York and all financial matters were handled by a New York law firm.

Serge Lifar, who had been in charge of the Monaco company

since resigning his post as director of the Paris Opéra amid controversy over his political allegiance during the war, delayed his return to the Paris Opéra until after the Marquis arrived on the scene. Lifar's reinstatement at the Paris Opéra created somewhat of a stir and immediately resulted in the exodus of a large number of company dancers, most of whom had followed Lifar from Paris in the first place.

Rosella recalls, "Lifar was in Vichy when I arrived, and dancers were coming and going. It was very hectic. I had just come from Mexico after performing with Markova and Dolin and I went right into rehearsals for the gala premiere in Vichy before going on to Paris." The volatile emotional atmosphere and exhausting pace, however, quickly subsided after the company began rehearsals for its debut seasons in Monte Carlo and London. "By then," says Rosella, "we had established ourselves in the eyes of the public and press. And the company had started to gain a sense of identity."

Chapter Twenty

A Company, a Home, and a Family

During the Paris debut of the de Cuevas company, Rosella performed the standard classical repertoire, virtuoso pas de deux, Caton's *Sebastian,* Nijinska's *Brahms Variations,* and Dollar's *Constantia.* In Monte Carlo, she began learning Lifar's *Suite en Blanc* and was cast in a pas de deux Eglevsky was creating in collaboration with Salvador Dali, *Colloque Sentimental.* Shortly after rehearsals started John Taras joined the company as ballet master and Balanchine arrived to restage *Concerto Barocco* and create *Pas de Trois Classique* to a Minkus score. Most of Rosella's attention, however, was focused on working with Nijinska.

151

Rosella Hightower and Bronislava Nijinska backstage during a
dress rehearsal of *Rondo Capriccioso,* 1952. (Personal collection.)

Because I had worked with her before and she had liked me, I knew how
much there was to learn and how to approach working with her. By that
time she was a little deaf, and although she understood French and English
she always limited herself to Russian. It was a bit of a cat-and-mouse game,
but it didn't bother me. She would always touch me on the shoulder with a
little rhythmic tapping of the fingers or flick of the wrist, and I could figure
out what she was getting at.

Of all the choreographers Rosella worked with during her career,
Nijinska remained her favorite.

Massine would be second, then Balanchine and Caton. Nijinska set a tremendous number of ballets for us. Some were restagings of the classics,
some revivals of her own works, and some new creations. To me, her *Coppélia* was the work of a genius, and I will always feel very fortunate to have
worked so closely with her.

Once the company had settled into a daily pattern of classes and
rehearsals in Monte Carlo, Rosella became aware of a young French
designer working with the company, Jean Robier. "I had asked someone who he was the first time I saw him backstage in Vichy. But it
wasn't until the rehearsal period in Monte Carlo that we actually had

time to see each other outside the theater." Sitting in front of a mural painted by Robier in their spacious living room in Cannes depicting scenes from ballets created for Rosella and several of her famous canine companions through the years, the two share a laugh. "It was a long courtship. We actually met in 1947 and were married in Paris at Saint Sulpice in 1951. There was no reason to hurry. We were very busy with the company, so we took our time."

As leading or prima ballerina, Rosella's responsibilities exceeded those of a dancer, which ultimately proved very good training for everything she went on to do. Making personal appearances and being interviewed with or without the Marquis were part of her job that she relished. "The Marquis loved speaking to the press, and when he did, he usually said more than he should. Before we opened in London, we all could have killed him because he made a statement to the press that his ballerinas were better than the British. But we were very successful in London and the company continued to grow at a very fast pace."

By 1949, the company had added works by Massine, Lichine, Dolin, and Taras, and Skibine and Ana Ricarda had emerged as significant choreographic talents. The company's popularity in Europe continued to grow, and appearances in the Far East and South America under the auspices of the U.S. State Department brought greater acclaim.

Satisfied that the company was ready for New York, the Marquis initiated negotiations in late 1949 for its American debut the following year. Rosella returned home for a visit for the first time in two years. After a brief vacation in Kansas City, she returned to New York to represent the company at a variety of publicity events. On the eve of her departure for Paris to rejoin the company, she was feted at a gala party hosted by the New York press agent Marjorie Barkentin. Rosella remembers, "Danilova, Franklin, Balanchine, and most of the significant people in the dance world were there. It was a major social event and was covered by the press. And my mother was there because she was going to Europe with me for the first time. I was very happy that she could see all of the excitement firsthand."

Prior to making its New York debut in October 1950, the company changed its name to the Grand Ballet du Marquis de Cuevas and announced it would be moving its home base to Cannes. Roughly forty miles east of Monte Carlo, the city had its share of expensive hotels and shops but offered a more affordable lifestyle to accommodate its predominantly resident rather than tourist population. And the Municipal Casino Theatre in Cannes provided comparable splendor and more gracious rehearsal space than the theater in Monte Carlo.

Compared to the pressure mounting over the company's New York debut, the relocation to Cannes seemed inconsequential. "The New York season was not well thought out," Rosella says. "There were sixty dancers in the company, we were accustomed to performing in the big opera houses in Europe, and our productions were designed for those theaters. The Century Theatre in New York was much too small, and that created tremendous problems." Individually, Rosella, Eglevsky, Tallchief, Skibine, and most of the company's leading dancers won high praise. John Martin went so far as to say that "if the Marquis had done nothing more than to restore Rosella Hightower to us in all her glory, we would have ample cause to be grateful to him."

The consensus among the New York critics, however, pointed to inconsistencies in artistic direction and production quality and a lack of uniformity in style. To further complicate matters, Rosella was injured during a performance of Dolin's *Pas de Quatre*. "It was a superficial muscle tear and I was able to perform the next night. But the season was a fiasco." Despite the disappointments of the New York engagement, it had no serious effect on the company or its popularity in Europe.

In mid-1951, Eglevsky resigned to assume a position as principal dancer with New York City Ballet. Rosella says, "He had a wonderful opportunity and as much as I didn't want to see him leave, it was a good move for him. I was happy for him, and since I was dancing with Skibine, George Zoritch, and Serge Golovine on a regular basis, it didn't create a problem for me."

The following year, the company encountered an unusual situation.

The lawyers handling the company's finances in New York informed the Marquis that to protect the nonprofit tax-exempt status of the company, he had to terminate his financial involvement. I have no idea what the actual tax problem was, but it put the company in a position of having to be self-supporting for a period of five years. The Marquis was terribly hurt and felt left out because everything was handled during that period by lawyers and a typical New York accountant.

For us, it was a challenge and a lot of good things came out of it. We had such popular appeal we decided to try something in Paris that had never been done. Tickets to the ballet were too expensive for the average working person so we started selling "Standing Room" tickets. We were performing in the Empire Theatre, which had room to accommodate a standing room crowd, and we filled it. The response was phenomenal. We brought in a totally new audience and the company made money. When they finally closed the Empire to make it a cinema, we moved to the Champs-Élysées and continued offering popular prices. What we started still goes on today and makes it possible for anyone to go to the ballet.

For Rosella, 1952 proved to be a year of tremendous artistic development. Of the five ballets created for her, three proved to be significant additions to her repertoire. Dancing opposite Skibine, she gained tremendous acclaim as a dramatic ballerina in Ana Ricarda's *Doña Ines de Castro* and won even greater accolades for her virtuosic skills in Nijinska's *Rondo Capriccioso*. The premiere of Taras's *Piège de Lumière* at the Empire Theatre on December 23, 1952, remains one of her most treasured memories. "If it is possible to say that I had a favorite ballet, it is *Piège*," she says, pointing to the wrought iron gate outside her villa bearing the name of the ballet.

After her tremendous success in Taras's ballet, Rosella began working with Harald Lander on a new production of the Bournonville masterpiece, *La Sylphide*. "That was an incredible experience. We worked very slowly for several months, and he taught me the role by having me follow him step-by-step, arm-by-arm, and hand-by-hand through the entire ballet. As we worked, he explained each movement, what it meant and how it logically led to the next. Putting the ballet together that way taught me the intricacy of the Bournonville quality and style of movement." Rosella won instant acclaim in the role of the Sylph, and her portrayal remains legendary in the history of contemporary ballet.

In 1954 Rosella discovered a new role in life—motherhood. To make an appearance with Massine in the film *Neapolitan Carousel,* she temporarily resigned from the Marquis's company and returned to Kansas City with her husband. "We decided our child should be born

Rosella Hightower in *La Sylphide*, circa 1953. (Personal collection.)

in America to allow dual citizenship until the age of eighteen, and we decided to make a go of it in America. We moved—lock, stock, and barrel." Rosella took classes and taught at Perky's studio, and Robier, who had begun his career as a painter, had little difficulty establishing himself in Kansas City as a portrait artist. "Jean had more work than he could handle. His portraits became somewhat of a status symbol, and I think he must have painted every woman involved in the social circles in Kansas City with or without her children. It was very good for him."

On February 18, 1955, Rosella gave birth to a healthy baby girl. "We named her Dominique, but from the beginning, we called her Monet. She was so small for such a big name." Shortly after her daughter was born, Rosella accepted an offer to return to Ballet Theatre. Although not looking forward to leaving her husband and daughter to go on tour, she welcomed the excellent opportunity to resume her professional career.

When she rejoined the company for a fall tour beginning in Mexico, Rosella's repertoire included *Swan Lake, Giselle,* and Balanchine's *Theme and Variations.* The most significant element of her return to the company was the opportunity to develop a partnership with Erik Bruhn. "He had appeared with us in Europe as guest artist and I always liked working with him. He had such a fantastic lyrical quality and brought so much to everything he did. Erik was such a perfectionist, it was wonderful." Following a New York season at the Metropolitan Opera House and a series of performances in Brooklyn, the company had a brief layoff before embarking on an extended tour of Europe.

By that point Rosella and Robier were giving serious consideration to returning to Europe. "It had become obvious that to live in the style we were accustomed to in Europe, we would have to join a country club, own a large home and all of those things which required a greater income than we were earning as artists. Before I left on tour we made arrangements for Jean to return to France with Monet and stay near his family outside Lyons until I was free to join them." During Ballet Theatre's engagement in The Hague, Rosella announced she was returning to the Marquis's company as leading ballerina and artistic consultant.

The Marquis insisted that I have the liberty of choice in my repertoire and he made me promise to never the leave the company again. He had had difficulties after I had left and told me that I was the backbone of the company. He gave me that responsibility, and he wanted it to be that way. Jean resumed his association with the company as well, and Cannes became home base once again. And we've been here ever since.

Rosella Hightower's husband, Jean Robier, in his studio, Cannes, France, 1957.
(Personal collection.)

Making her first appearance with the Marquis's company in two years, Rosella was greeted by a fifteen-minute standing ovation in Paris.

I performed *Piège de Lumière* and the audience was so demonstrative I could not hear the music above the applause for the first five minutes after I made my entrance! It was very good to be back. Going to America had been a good experience for us and I had enjoyed working with Ballet Theatre again, but the future was limited there. Plus, it meant being away from my family.

In addition to her existing repertoire in the company, Rosella continued to be featured in new works.

David Lichine did *Corrida* for Nicholas Polajenko and me. It was a very disturbing, complicated story involving a bullfighter with a split personality who commits suicide after discovering one of the young toreros is actually a girl. I was dressed as a boy and did a male variation, on pointe, with double tours and big jumps. It was a fabulous role and very difficult technically and dramatically. Nick was wonderful in it.

Rosella also re-created her role as the Glove Seller in Massine's *Gaîté Parisienne* and performed the leading role in Caton's *Triptyque*.

In 1959 Nijinska arrived to stage a new production of *The Sleeping Beauty.*

Sadly, the Marquis was not well, and he wanted very much to see the ballet done. His nephew, Raymondo de Larrain, was responsible for designing the entire production, and it became a huge, complicated, expensive, and emotionally unsettling undertaking. Unfortunately, Nijinska suffered terribly. I could see what was happening, but there was nothing I could do to stop it. Suddenly, Robert Helpmann arrived and Nijinska immediately walked out. It was a very difficult time. Helpmann came to me for help and I did what I could. He was very upset and rightfully so, because he had no idea Nijinska was still involved until he arrived. Eventually, she did come to see the production on tour and seemed pleased with the way it had come out. But it was a horrible experience.

A few months after the company returned to the Champs-Élysées to present a second six-month season of *The Sleeping Beauty,* the Marquis died. The responsibility of keeping the company together to fulfill existing contractual obligations fell on Rosella's shoulders. Working with longtime company manager Claude Giraud, Rosella succeeded in handling the troupe until the Marquise de Cuevas and Larrain took over as directors. Withdrawing from the company, Rosella turned her energies as quickly as possible to making guest appearances and completing plans inspired by the Marquis to create a school in Cannes modeled after her own ideas of multidisciplinary training reminiscent of the traditional conservatories of Europe and Russia. With Robier, former company music director, Claude Pothier, and dancers Arlette Castanier and José Ferran, the school became a reality in 1962. Ironically, that year the Marquise de Cuevas and de Larrain dissolved the company they had taken over.

Establishing the school was very difficult for us. There was no money, but we managed to secure a loan and slowly the school began to pay for itself. In addition to the children, we also attracted a lot of professional dancers. Bruhn came and Sonia Arova and then after Rudolph Nureyev defected in

From left to right: Rudolph Nureyev, Sonia Arova, Erik Bruhn, and Rosella Hightower in a publicity photo taken in the main studio of Rosella's school. Cannes, France, 1962. (Personal collection.)

1962, he joined us and we formed a concert group of our own. I liked working with Nureyev, he was so open to everything and had such a dynamic quality. The four of us did a series of galas through 1963. After Bruhn left in 1964 to assume his duties as guest artist with the new Harkness Ballet, directed by Skibine, the foursome dissolved. The Harkness, however, came to Cannes to make its official debut in February 1964 and used our studios to rehearse. Shortly after the company departed for its debut in Paris, Nureyev left to join the Royal Ballet.

160

Within a year, Rosella brought her performing career to an end after a guest appearance in China with the Grand Ballet Classique de France, a group loosely affiliated with the school and organized by Giraud. "I performed for some time after that," she says, "but it wasn't the same thing after 1964. To me, my career ended in China. And the adventure continues today, here at the school with my students."

Maria Tallchief before she began working with George Balanchine, 1942. (Photo © Jack Mitchell. Reprinted by permission.)

Maria Tallchief in her most famous role, George Balanchine's *Firebird.* (Photo © Jack Mitchell. Reprinted by permission.)

Rosella Hightower and Leonide Massine performing *Gaîté Parisienne*, Paris, 1939. (Photo © Serge Lido, Paris. Reprinted by permission.)

Yvonne Chouteau as a young dancer, 1943. (Personal collection.)

Right, Yvonne Chouteau performing her most memorable role, Prayer, in *Coppélia,* 1945. (Personal collection.)

Below, Dancers in the Ballet Russe de Monte Carlo, 1946. *Back row, from left to right,* Alexandra Danilova, Nicholas Magallenes, Casimir Kokitch; *front row, from left to right,* Frank Hobi, Yvonne Chouteau, Shirley Weaver. (Personal collection.)

Left, Maria Tallchief and Michel Renault performing *Apollon Musagète* during Maria's guest engagement with the Paris Opéra, 1947. (Photo © Serge Lido, Paris. Reprinted by permission.)

Below, David Lichine rehearses Rosella Hightower and André Eglevsky in the basement studio of the Casino Opera House, Monte Carlo, Monaco, 1948. (Photo © Serge Lido, Paris. Reprinted by permission.)

Marjorie Tallchief and George Skibine in *Real Jewels,* Paris, 1949. (Personal collection.)

The Marquis de Cuevas congratulates Rosella Hightower in her dressing room, circa 1949. (Photo © Serge Lido, Paris. Reprinted by permission.)

Above, Yvonne Chouteau performing the Glove Seller in *Gaîté Parisienne,* 1950. (Personal collection.)

Left, Rosella Hightower in *Rondo Capriccioso,* 1952. (Photo © Serge Lido, Paris. Reprinted by permission.)

Above, Marjorie Tallchief and George Skibine performing *Idylle,* 1954. (Photo © Serge Lido, Paris. Reprinted by permission.)

Right, Marjorie Tallchief performing *Giselle* at the Paris Opéra, 1957. (Personal collection.)

Maria Tallchief and Erik Bruhn in a studio portrait of *Giselle,* a ballet they never performed together. Jacob's Pillow, 1958. (Photo © Jack Mitchell. Reprinted by permission.)

Chapter Twenty-One

Marjorie Tallchief
Professional Debut

On September 26, 1944, Marjorie Tallchief made her debut in the world of professional ballet in Montreal, Canada, as a soloist in Lucia Chase and Richard Pleasant's Ballet Theatre. Executing the virtuoso Competition Dance in David Lichine's *Graduation Ball* with uncommon speed and technical security, she drew an enthusiastic audience reaction. A glowing mention in the *Montreal Gazette* the following day enhanced the triumph. Although Marjorie would perform her share of ensemble roles as a first-year soloist, Ruth and Alex Tall Chief's youngest child would never be a member of the corps de ballet.

A combination of her stunning technical skills, ebullient stage presence, pretty feet, and elongated classical line continued to bring

171

favorable popular and critical reaction throughout the Canadian tour. By the conclusion of the company's October season in New York's Metropolitan Opera House, the dance world was aware that Ballet Theatre had its own Tallchief. Establishing an individual identity in the ballet world was crucial to Marjorie's future, and she wasted no time making her presence known.

Settled comfortably in an ornately carved, high-backed parlor chair, Marjorie says, "I never auditioned. Mr. Denham invited me to join Maria in the Ballet Russe de Monte Carlo and impresario Sol Hurok offered me a soloist contract with Ballet Theatre." As Bronislava Nijinska and David Lichine's star pupil, Marjorie was steered in Hurok's direction. Unlike her sister, Marjorie did not encounter antagonism because of her American heritage.

Because of Lucia, it was an asset to be American in Ballet Theatre. But everyone hated me anyway because I had been hired by Hurok and was receiving a stipend from him, in addition to my salary from Ballet Theatre. It was not comfortable, and I did not like being in that position.

Plus, the company was in the midst of union problems when I joined, and there was talk of a possible strike. The first time I met Rosella Hightower she was on the union side and not pleased to see me. Later we became very good friends, but in the beginning I was not one of her personal favorites. None of the dancers under contract with Hurok were very popular though, so I wasn't alone.

Marjorie spent neither time nor energy worrying about who did and who did not like her. Although outwardly the more carefree, happy-go-lucky of the Tall Chief girls, she harbored no illusions that her first year in a professional company would be easy under any circumstances. While starting out as a soloist gave her a definitive edge, she knew it did not ensure a second-year contract. That would have to be earned.

As a first-year soloist with responsibilities in the ensemble, Marjorie had a large repertoire of roles to learn. "The opportunities were unlimited. I had learned *Graduation Ball* and worked on it with Lichine, but the rest of the repertoire was new for me. I learned as many roles as I could, as quickly as I could, because I knew that was how you moved up faster. I was always going on for someone else at the last minute, and glad to have the chance." Being surrounded by a dazzling array of legendary and emerging stars also proved fascinating.

When I entered the company, Alicia Markova and Anton Dolin were featured artists, Tamara Toumanova was there, and Lichine and Riabouchinska were guests for our New York season. There was so much to learn by watching them work. I also watched Rosella, Nora Kaye, and Alicia Alonso, who were veteran soloists at that point. Of all of them, Markova and Toumanova were my favorites.

Markova made a tremendous impression on me and I learned a lot from her. Evidently, I went too far. I didn't think I was starting to emulate her, but Nijinska felt otherwise. She called me out of class one day to say "You are dancing like Markova, and it is ridiculous. You can't look like her, so you must stop." Nijinska adored Markova and she was absolutely correct, of course.

Shooing her Yorkshire terrier, Fifi, from beneath the legs of her chair, Marjorie laughs. "I was very upset when I went back into class, but I got over it. Markova was so special and so unique, it must have been quite funny. I was not at all like her and could never have been."

Determined to make the most of her first exposure to the legendary dance studios in New York, Marjorie ultimately discovered it was possible to take too many classes.

There were so many incredible teachers to study with, I was taking as many classes as I could between rehearsals and performing at night. Finally, my knee gave out. They were never sure what I did to it, but I had to stay off it for several days. It seemed to heal fine, but it bothered me off and on for years afterward. Of course I was devastated because I had to miss a performance of *Graduation Ball*.

Marjorie admits having been appalled that Ballet Theatre was going through a period without regular company classes.

Edward Caton was supposed to teach a daily class for the company, but ultimately he refused. One morning, he walked into the studio to start class as usual, looked around the room at all of us, and turned around and left.

Nothing was ever said, but that was the end of company classes for a long time. So I studied with Caton at his studio, took classes with Anatole Vilzak and Ludmila Shollar, and studied at the School of American Ballet. After the injury, though, I never took more than two classes a day.

Despite the knee incident, Marjorie's debut New York season was a resounding success. As Ballet Theatre depended just as much on a good showing in New York as did its rival, the Ballet Russe de Monte Carlo, gaining acclaim as a bright new soloist put Marjorie in good stead with management. Marjorie was ideally suited for Chase's vision for Ballet Theatre. She had been trained in the uncompromising tradition of the Russian Imperial School by Nijinska, her technical prowess was exceptional, and she brought an unmistakably American exuberance to the stage.

Shortly after the company concluded its New York season, Ruth Tall Chief headed back to the family home in California. Marjorie had been accepted as part of the team and held a secure position within the hierarchy of the company.

It was hard for Mother. All of a sudden the entire focus of her life changed. My parents and Gerry stayed in California about two more years and then returned to Fairfax. Mother immersed herself in all kinds of community projects and always made sure everyone knew how well Maria and I were doing. She always found a way to stay busy, but the central focus of her life had come to an end.

Touring appealed to Marjorie's natural curiosity. "I never minded traveling. It was always a challenge getting used to a new stage every night and holding on to your technique without regular classes. But it was part of being a dancer. Touring kept ballet companies in business, and if you didn't tour, you didn't dance." It also provided opportunities to perform new roles. Among them, Marjorie recalls her most significant and difficult assignment was learning the demanding role of Myrtha, Queen of the Wilis, in *Giselle*. A test of technical skill and stamina for a classical ballerina, the role contains an unsupported promenade in the arabesque position followed by an excessive number of jumps and long passages of sweeping movements across the stage.

Marjorie Tallchief: Professional Debut

Preparing for my debut performance in Boston was the most difficult period for me during my first season. I had done movies and light operas and I could do fouettés standing on my head, but Myrtha was different.

It was the first role I performed since joining the company that put me onstage alone. It was the only time I can remember ever being scared in front of an audience. I stepped into the arabesque position, and all of a sudden I felt my supporting knee start to quiver. I didn't know if I would be able to get around in the promenade! I did, but it was a completely new experience.

The reviews reflected none of the fear she had experienced. Her interpretation of Myrtha was praised as "stately and formidable," and she was described as a dancer of "remarkable grace and assurance with the grandest of grand jetés."

Marjorie says,

It was a wonderful but very difficult role that took many years to fully develop. And it was always a challenge. But that was what I liked about being a dancer. I always enjoyed the physical challenge of trying to jump higher or turn faster or balance longer than anyone else. When I was a child, and first learned to do thirty-two fouettés, the first thing I did was start working on doing sixty-four. That never changed for me. Every time I mastered something difficult, I would discover something new to replace it. It was a never-ending process that always fascinated me.

Marjorie also received a fair share of favorable mentions for her sensitive portrayal of the Nurse in *Romeo and Juliet*.

I was Lucia's understudy, and I never understood the logic behind casting a seventeen-year-old in that role. It always surprised me when I got mentioned for it because I was convinced you could see right through the costume and makeup. Actually the one role I always wanted to do, but never got the chance, was one of the four little swans. I performed so many wonderful roles, but no one ever let me do that variation. I had loved it as a child and set my heart on someday having the opportunity to perform it. I always thought that the day I performed that variation would be the greatest day in my life. But they said I was too tall, and I never had the opportunity.

Among her numerous understudy assignments, Marjorie was cast as Nana Gollner's understudy in the role of Medusa in Antony Tudor's 1945 work, *Undertow.* Eager to explore her dramatic as well as technical potential, Marjorie was delighted to have the opportunity. "It was a very valuable experience for me. And shortly after its New York premiere during our spring season at the Metropolitan Opera House, Gollner left the company, so I took over the role. I was fascinated by the way Tudor worked. He was completely different from anyone I had ever encountered, and working with him really prepared me for later in my career, when I would work with so many different choreographers."

Her success in Tudor's ballet added depth to her growing recognition as a technical powerhouse. Writing for the *New York Herald-Tribune,* Walter Terry called her debut in a dramatic role "outstanding." That season, Marjorie also made her New York debut as Myrtha in *Giselle,* prompting John Martin of the *New York Times* to write, "Playing her first important role hereabouts, there is no doubt Miss Tallchief can dance rings around the role."

Emphasizing that she enjoyed the challenge of mastering technical and dramatic roles equally, Marjorie explains she did not prefer to dance one style over the other. "I loved to dance and it didn't matter to me if the challenge was technical or dramatic. All that mattered, as far as I was concerned, was that I had roles to perform." By the conclusion of her second New York season, Marjorie's impressive talents had earned her a sizable repertoire, the respect of her peers, and a second-year contract far more generous than her first. More important, Marjorie had revealed the artistic and technical versatility needed to set her on a distinctly individual path to stardom.

Chapter Twenty-Two

Opportunity Knocks

Within six months of signing her second-year contract with Ballet Theatre for the 1945–46 season, Marjorie received an invitation from Sol Hurok to join Colonel de Basil's Original Ballet Russe as a leading soloist. Despite the progress she had made in Ballet Theatre, the de Basil offer was an undeniable step up the ladder. Marjorie says, "When opportunity knocks, you take it! The whole thing came as a complete surprise. It was Hurok's idea and somehow part of his arrangement with de Basil to bring the company back to America after the war." In anticipation of the easing of stringent immigration codes following the end of World War II, Hurok had resigned from Ballet Theatre management to resume his position as impresario of the

Metropolitan Opera House. His first dance season at the Met would be highlighted by the long-awaited return of the Original Ballet Russe from its wartime exile in South America.

According to a complicated agreement between Hurok and de Basil, the impresario agreed to engage the company for a fall season at the Met, assist in promoting a subsequent cross-country tour, and book the company for a return engagement at the Met in the spring of 1947. In return, Hurok was to select the troupe's featured guest artists and expand the company's roster of soloists. After signing Markova and Dolin as guest artists, Hurok began assembling a cadre of soloists to send to South America. Keeping his recruiting efforts focused primarily on current and former members of Ballet Theatre, Hurok extended Marjorie a leading or first soloist contract. The artistic validity of the offer was never in question.

Besides Markova and Dolin, he had signed Rosella and André Eglevksy. And you could trust Hurok. He knew what he was doing and he took care of you. After all, he had brought me into Ballet Theatre.

Of course, it meant going to South America by boat, but we survived. It took three weeks to get to Rio de Janeiro. And when we arrived no one was glad to see us. Obviously, the dancers who had been stuck in South America all that time were not very happy about Hurok bringing us in to take over the best parts. But I had been through the cold shoulder treatment before, so it didn't bother me.

With performing in the corps de ballet eliminated from her life, Marjorie was free to concentrate on soloist and leading roles. In addition to retaining the roles she had performed in Ballet Theatre, she was cast in the company's repertoire of virtuoso pas de deux. The challenge of learning new roles, adjusting to a new company, and adapting to less than ideal conditions suited Marjorie well. In fact, she admits, the South American excursion held more than its share of unexpected challenges. "The trip back to New York was another disaster. That time it took only two weeks, but the company was booked to open at the Metropolitan Opera House the day after we arrived. No one had their legs back. So the opening night performance wasn't very good at all."

The New York season was further confused by the addition of a second contingent of dancers hired by Hurok. Among them, George

Skibine received the warmest welcome. He was the son of a Russian dancer engaged in Serge Diaghilev's legendary Ballets Russes, and in true Russian tradition, he toured with his parents and grew up backstage. A student of Olga Preobrajenska and Lubov Egorova, he joined Leonide Massine's newly formed Ballet Russe de Monte Carlo in 1938, shortly after making his professional debut in Paris. His tall, aristocratic bearing, superior partnering skills, and lyrical style rapidly won acclaim. He was also noted for his dramatic as well as his technical abilities. Skibine had performed with de Basil's Original Ballet Russe during its inaugural Australian tour before joining Ballet Theatre as a soloist in 1940. Two years later, he resigned from the company to serve with distinction in the U.S. Army.

Rising to the rank of top sergeant during his tour of duty in the First U.S. Combat Intelligence Unit, he was the recipient of a Bronze Star, five campaign medals, and two Bronze Arrowheads. On his return to civilian life, he essentially abandoned plans to resume his career as a dancer. He was working as an interpreter and secretary for a New York art dealer when Hurok intervened. Renowned for his powers of persuasion, particularly in dealings with fellow Russians, Hurok promptly brought Skibine back to the ballet world. After close to a three-year hiatus from the stage, Skibine appeared with the temporarily active Markova-Dolin Ballet to regain his technique and partnering skills before resuming his association with de Basil's troupe. In addition to reestablishing his frequent and much-celebrated Ballet Theatre partnership with Rosella Hightower, he and Marjorie were cast as the troupe's up-and-coming pas de deux team. Well matched onstage, the pair rapidly gained popular and critical acclaim. The attraction between them onstage, to no one's surprise, did not end in the wings.

Sitting with her back to a wall filled with handsomely framed, signed renderings of costumes and sets created for many of her late husband's ballets, Marjorie refers to Skibine by his familiar name. "Of all the partners I ever danced with, Youra was the best. When he stopped dancing, I missed him terribly because we worked together like one person. We moved so well together and our timing was always perfect." Stopping to laugh, she adds, "Of course, that was not how it was when we first started working together. It was anything but easy. I remember we worked together for a very long time before everything fell into place."

Between Skibine's gracious, outgoing nature and Marjorie's bountiful good humor, the relationship flourished despite the unrelenting pace of the company's subsequent cross-country tour. "I was thrilled about the tour because it gave me the chance to introduce Youra to my family. My parents liked him from the beginning. And he got along very well with my grandmother." With the remainder of the tour to complete and a second New York season ahead of them, the couple was not prepared to make definite plans. There was, however, little question where their relationship was headed.

As the company worked its way eastward to New York, flu began taking its toll on the dancers. "By the time we arrived in New York, no one was in good shape. And Markova was ill. She was scheduled to perform *Giselle* opening night and we had no idea what was going to happen." Arching her neck and looking toward the ceiling, Marjorie retraces the events leading up to the company's opening night performance in New York's Metropolitan Opera House. "The day we arrived in New York, the entire company was told there would be an early rehearsal at the theater the next morning. When we arrived, we were told that Markova was seriously ill and would not be able to perform. Then they announced that Rosella would replace Markova, I would replace Rosella as Myrtha, and Tatiana Stepanova would perform the "Black Swan" pas de deux with Eglevsky. No one was expecting it to turn out that way. And, of course, it meant a tremendous amount of work to prepare Rosella for the role.

Although she had learned it on her own, she had never been an understudy and had never rehearsed it. Working her into the second act wasn't that difficult, but the first act was very complicated. She interacted with almost all of the dancers onstage and had to learn all the spacing and her relationship to everyone else. It took tremendous concentration, but it was one of those incredible opportunities and everyone knew it. It was a phenomenal experience and brought Rosella recognition as a ballerina overnight. I remember she was sick too, but she gave an incredible performance. It was a complete triumph.

Reviews of the unexpected opening night victory brought Marjorie a good measure of praise as well. Martin of the *New York Times* gave Marjorie's performance high marks and Terry of the *New York*

Herald-Tribune cited her performance as "regal, intense and implacable to just the right degree." Kolodin of the *New York Sun* concurred, writing, "Also sharing in the bravos of a large audience was Marjorie Tallchief who took over as Queen of the Wilis and danced splendidly."

Markova's illness persisted throughout the first week of the season, necessitating further cast changes and giving Marjorie even greater exposure in leading roles. By season's end, she had proven more than worthy of immediate promotion to the status of ballerina.

Unfortunately, the future of de Basil's Original Ballet Russe did not look as brilliant. Colonel de Basil had succeeded in showing the darker side of his personality more frequently than was wise in front of Hurok, and their relationship was rapidly deteriorating. Despite sensational personal victories achieved during the season, the company itself had gained little ground in the eyes of the dance world. By the conclusion of the season, Markova and Dolin had launched plans to revive their own company, and Rosella and Eglevsky announced their plans to join a new company being formed by the Marquis de Cuevas.

For Marjorie and Skibine, it was time to make some serious decisions. They had decided to get married but wanted to settle the issue of their immediate future before setting a date. "Youra and I had both received offers from other companies. But Youra favored accepting a contract extended by the Marquis to join Rosella and Eglevsky in the Nouveau Ballet de Monte Carlo." The Marquis's offer, however, was not given a warm welcome by all members of the Tallchief family.

Maria was furious. And said "No" to the whole idea. She didn't think the Marquis was secure. A lot of people disliked him and thought he was completely mad. But Youra was convinced that because Nijinska was there, and also William Dollar and Caton, the venture was secure. Rosella and Eglevsky had signed as the featured stars and we were offered second billing. For us, it really was an incredible opportunity. Youra's family was living in Paris, so it wasn't as though we'd be stranded in Europe if everything collapsed. And I trusted Youra's judgment. So we accepted.

With the vigorous blessings of Alex and Ruth Tall Chief, the couple headed off to Europe following the completion of their contracts with the Original Ballet Russe.

My parents approved of our decision and gave us their permission to get married in Vichy. You couldn't get my father on a boat or an airplane, so they made no plans to attend the wedding, but they were completely behind it. We didn't plan on staying in Europe for more than a few months, and except for the fact that we were going to be married, it didn't seem any different from going off on another tour. We honestly had no intention of staying longer than the summer, but somehow, it turned into close to twenty years!

On August 5, 1947, Marjorie and Skibine were married in the Saint Sauveur Church in Vichy. With the gaiety of her words reflected in her eyes, Marjorie says, "Maria and Balanchine were engaged as guest artists at the Paris Opéra and came down for the wedding. Youra's family was there, and Nijinska and friends from the company." Getting married before the company's scheduled debut in late August became somewhat complex as everything had to be planned around the rehearsal schedule. "We were dancers and had almost an entire repertoire to learn. The company was on a very tight schedule and we both had a lot of work ahead of us. But in spite of everything that was going on, it turned out to be a lovely ceremony."

With the exception of a smattering of standard classics and virtuoso pas de deux, Marjorie once again faced the physical and mental challenge of learning an extensive new repertoire. Reveling in the severe regimen of Nijinska's tutelage and coaching, she immersed herself in the task. Among the eclectic array of roles Marjorie was to perform during her first season as a ballerina were Nijinska's *Brahms Variations* and *Les Biches* and Serge Lifar's *Aubade*.

It was very hectic in the beginning. The transition of power from Lifar, who had been director, to the Marquis was not smooth. At least it didn't take very long. By the time we left Vichy, Lifar had resigned to resume his position as ballet master of the Paris Opéra Ballet and most of the French dancers went with him. The Marquis immediately changed the company's name to the Grand Ballet de Monte Carlo and somehow managed to have that name in place before we arrived in Paris. A lot of things were happening at the same time and we had our hands full keeping up with everything.

Chapter Twenty-Three

Victorious in Europe

Fascinated by new surroundings and endowed with a vivacious personality representative more of the French than of her Osage heritage, Marjorie found adjusting to life in Europe fun. Owing to her husband's impressive command of Russian, French, and English, she encountered no language barrier and rapidly became fluent in French. "For Youra, it was home. He knew everyone and had friends throughout the arts community in Paris. From his exposure to artists from the Diaghilev era, he had a completely renaissance approach. To him, painters, writers, composers, designers, and artists outside the dance community were part of the total vision." Marjorie takes pride in Skibine's invaluable influence on her artistic development. "Because of his interests, I gained insight and knowledge that would have been beyond my reach. He gave me an education in the arts, as a whole, that I would never have received. And it had tremendous impact on my perspective as a dancer."

Although the Marquis's company drew enthusiastic popular and critical acclaim during its debut season in Vichy, Marjorie was not prepared for the sensation created by opening night at the Alhambra Theatre in Paris. "I never expected the audience to go completely wild. Obviously, I had seen my share of standing ovations, but they paled in the face of what we encountered in Paris. I still remember people waiting at the stage door to cheer us as we left the theater. I was amazed. I had never experienced anything like it, and that was my introduction to the Paris audience!" Reviews of the company's opening night performance echoed the sentiments of the wildly enthusiastic audience. "Marjorie Tallchief," wrote Iréne Lidova, "was immediately noticed for the assurance of her technique and for her great personality underlined by a strong dynamism. She is a marvelous dark and slender creature gifted with soft yet nervous movements of great stage effect. Her head has a royal carriage and her hands and arms are of a delicate and exquisite finesse."

Marjorie's popularity in Paris brought overnight celebrity status and drew tremendous attention from the Parisian press. Expanding on his earlier recollections of the de Cuevas company's inaugural season at the Alhambra Theatre, *Saisons de la Danse*'s Heresin remarks, "Marjorie was an instant success. The audiences went wild. She had an astonishing technique and magnetic electricity on stage. And she was beautiful, with very long legs and lovely feet. Her personality was so bubbly, the French immediately fell in love with her." Heresin also recalls that Skibine's return to the European stage drew high praise from the audiences and critics. "Skibine was already very popular in Europe. And the combination of the two of them onstage was magnificent. Marjorie also was new to us in Europe, which made it more exciting."

A good showing in Paris for the Marquis's company was equivalent to a good showing in New York for Denham's Ballet Russe de Monte Carlo or Chase's Ballet Theatre. Making a sweeping gesture with her delicate hands, Marjorie concedes that there was little doubt in her mind, or Skibine's, that remaining with the company would be in their best interest. "It was very exciting. Everyone was exhausted by the time we left Paris for Monte Carlo, but we were also very happy." Getting settled in Monte Carlo allowed a brief respite from the grueling pace of company life. The fairy-tale atmosphere of the tiny principality of Monaco appealed to Marjorie. She was fascinated by the quaint adobe and white stone buildings with red tile roofs rising from the hillside facing the mammoth Casino de Monte Carlo and by the luxurious shops lining the main avenue. Her penchant for temperate climates and unobstructed views of the horizon also was graciously served.

The beaches were absolutely fabulous. And the tiny medieval villages built into the cliffs were intriguing. The horizon disappeared into the sea, and there were always twinkling lights on the boats in the harbor. Monte Carlo and the entire Côte d'Azur was very beautiful. It was ideal for the Marquis, and he enjoyed being surrounded by the people who were drawn there.

Among the many contemporary artists who chose to live and work in the area, Marjorie mentions Picasso, Joan Miró, and Dali. She continues, "The Marquis encouraged collaboration among leading contemporary artists outside the field of dance, so the level of creativity was intense. And no matter how hard we worked, the environment generated its own energy and inspiration."

Describing the Marquis in a whimsical tone, Marjorie says,

He was a very eccentric person. And he was a member of royalty. Every time we visited him in Paris, he spoke to us from his bed with all of his Pekingese surrounding him. He was famous for his collection of Pekingese and had a very rare, solid black one. Once I said something about the black one, whose name was Monsieur. After that, Monsieur was never there when we went to see him. All the other dogs were in sight, but not Monsieur. I don't know if the Marquis was afraid I was going to put Monsieur in my ballet bag and take him home with me or what, but I never saw the dog again! The Marquis was very odd in ways like that, but he was fascinating. He loved to make great spectacles and stage balls with the company appearing in costume. A lot of people were against him, and I'm not saying that he was perfect, but he was the one supporting all of his ventures. Since it was his money, I think he had the right to decide how he spent it.

The Marquis's flamboyant style of entertaining succeeded in winning him the nickname "the Kissing Marquis" in the American press, but his commitment to building a ballet company was far removed from the eccentricities he chose to exhibit on the social circuit. Assuming control of the opera ballet of Monte Carlo in 1947, the Marquis combined the best of his existing own company with that of the opera organization to launch a company that would remain at the forefront of the European dance scene until his death in 1961. His innate sense of theatricality was evidenced by his acquisition of a repertoire that rejuvenated interest in dance in postwar Europe.

Marjorie was thrilled by the variety of choreographers, teachers, and coaches engaged to work with the company during its inaugural residency in Monte Carlo. "It was very stimulating and challenging. Balanchine and Massine came, and John Taras joined as ballet master and choreographer. Nijinska and Dollar returned to their posts, and Caton and Lifar were in and out." Among her most significant new roles, Marjorie was cast opposite Eglevsky in Dollar's *Five Gifts,* assumed leading roles in Balanchine's *Concerto Barocco* and *Night Shadow,* and was featured with Rosella and Eglevsky in Balanchine's new work, *Pas de Trois Classique.* The latter, she points out, was restaged by Balanchine under the title *Pas de Trois* for her sister, Eglevsky, and Nora Kaye during New York City Ballet's 1951 season. Of working with Balanchine, Marjorie says, "I was astounded by his musicality. That's why today, I can still remember *Concerto Barocco* step-by-step, just by hearing the score."

Immediately following a triumphant inaugural season in Monte Carlo, the company headed for London. Making a good impression on the British public and press also was important to the future of the company. "The Covent Garden audiences were much less emotional than those at the Paris Opéra, but the season was a complete success." Drawing impressive critical acclaim for her performance of Nijinska's *Les Biches* and Lifar's *Aubade* in London, Marjorie gained new stature as a ballerina. Fresh from their victorious engagement in London, Marjorie and Skibine welcomed Ruth Tall Chief to Paris. "By then, it was evident we were going to be in Europe for quite some time, so Mother decided she would come to see us. It was her first trip to Europe, and she thoroughly enjoyed it. We all had a good time. And, of course, Youra gave her a gracious introduction to Paris.

She visited us several times after that, but to see my father, we had to go to Fairfax."

Celebrating the conclusion of their first year in the Marquis's company, the couple was excited by the prospect of Skibine's upcoming debut as a choreographer. "Youra had been interested in doing a ballet for a long time and the Marquis was very supportive. It was the Marquis who gave him the opportunity to do his first ballet." Before the troupe launched into rehearsals for its second season, Marjorie and Skibine took advantage of a brief layoff to enjoy the splendid surroundings of the Riviera. "We developed an interest in vintage automobiles. And my car took second prize in the 1948 Grand Prix d'Élégance de Monte Carlo. It was great fun. We had lots of friends and enjoyed ourselves."

Skibine's first work, *Tragedy in Verona,* a romantic pas de deux set to music from Prokofiev's *Romeo and Juliet,* proved to be a popular and critical success. "It was quite lovely, and because the Marquis was pleased, Youra knew he would get the opportunity to do another ballet and that's what mattered. He wanted his career to go in that direction, and it was on its way." Although Skibine's prominence as a leading dancer would take precedence over his emerging choreographic talents for some time, he began devoting more and more time to his new role. Marjorie says, "I was never interested in choreographing. I enjoyed dancing. Youra was the choreographer."

The 1949–50 de Cuevas season was a never-ending succession of engagements stretching across Europe to Egypt and, ultimately, New York. Marjorie reaches deftly between a cluster of framed snapshots and retrieves a black-and-white photograph of Felia Doubrovska. "I remember Egypt because Mme Doubrovska was there. She was very grand with all of her scarves and chiffon skirts." Doubrovska's penchant for chiffon and making grand entrances into the studios at the School of American Ballet, where she taught until her death in 1981, were legendary. A product of the Russian Imperial School of Ballet, Doubrovska left Russia with her husband, Pierre Vladimirov, in 1920 to join Diaghilev's Ballets Russes. Although her most celebrated roles were the Bride in Nijinska's *Les Noces* and the Siren in Balanchine's 1929 *Prodigal Son,* she also had created the leading role in Nijinska's *Les Biches.* "The Marquis always brought guest teachers to work with us and Doubrovska came to help polish *Les Biches* for our New York debut."

In the process of preparing for the New York season, the company terminated its association with the opera in Monte Carlo. The Municipal Casino Theatre in Cannes became its home base, and the name of the company was changed to the Grand Ballet du Marquis de Cuevas before the troupe's arrival in New York. On October 30, 1950, the company made its American debut in New York's Century Theater. Neither the opening night audience nor the critics were impressed. Summarizing his opinion of the company midway through the season, Martin wrote, "It has become a weary platitude that no ballet company can be a good ballet company, no matter how great or gifted its stars may be, unless it has strong direction and a strong ensemble." Casting her eyes downward, Marjorie remarks, "It was an unfortunate situation. The theater was too small for our productions, so it was very difficult." Reminiscent of the bittersweet victories of their New York seasons with de Basil's Original Ballet Russe, Marjorie and Skibine won exceptional praise. In his review of opening night, Martin wrote, "Marjorie Tallchief has a warm and lyric quality that supplements admirably her technical facility, and makes of her, indeed, a most ingratiating artist." Of Skibine he noted, "George Skibine is handsome, gracious and theatrically gifted." Their performance of Balanchine's *Night Shadow* won high marks, as did their performance of the "Don Quixote" pas de deux and Marjorie's technical virtuosity in Balanchine's *Pas de Trois Classique*. Terry reserved his praise of the troupe's production of Balanchine's *Concerto Barocco* for Marjorie and Skibine and applauded Marjorie's performances in Dolin's *Pas de Quatre*. Skibine's *Tragedy in Verona* also won excellent audience response, and his potential as a choreographer was acknowledged without reserve by the reigning New York critics.

Chapter Twenty-Four

A Decade of Triumph

Working with Skibine as a choreographer did not present any new challenges for Marjorie. "Of course, we talked about his work at home, and I wanted his ballets to be a success for him. But as far as working with him in the studio, it was no different from working with anyone else." Skibine launched into rehearsals for his second ballet on his return to France after the company's New York season. Veering away from an existing theme and score, he commissioned Byron Schiffmann to compose a score for a work based on Edgar Allen Poe's poem *Annabel Lee*. He cast himself and Marjorie in the leads, and used three male figures clad in black to symbolize the dark undertones of the poem and create a recurring image of a tomb. The haunting, al-

189

legoric qualities of *Annabel Lee* sparked exceptional popular and critical acclaim and succeeded in winning new accolades for Marjorie's dramatic powers as well as Skibine's depth as a choreographer.

During the same season Skibine unveiled his third and most ambitious work to date, *Prisoner of the Caucasus.* "It was our first big popular success," Marjorie says, gesturing toward a handsomely framed artist's rendering of the costumes. "It was a wonderful ballet and great to dance. He used Aram Khachaturian's score for the ballet *Gayané* and it was very exciting. Youra was very good at creating a mood in his ballets and he always used the men in the company magnificently. It was a great hit. We had twenty curtain calls. It brought him tremendous recognition, and will always be one of my favorite ballets."

By mid-1951, Marjorie and Skibine discovered a new challenge—parenting. "Not long after we found out that I was expecting, they told us it would be twins! Youra swore there was no history of twins in his family, and since there was none in mine, we never figured out which side of the family was responsible." The news was received with great jubilation by the Tall Chief and Skibine families.

Everyone was thrilled. And I had no problems at all. I think it was harder on the wardrobe department than anyone else because they had to keep letting my costumes out. I danced quite late and performed until it became too obvious. I was doing the Sleepwalker in *Night Shadow* and thinking no one could tell because the costume was a flowing nightgown. But John Taras came backstage one night and said, "With the lights, when you turn sideways you are really starting to show." That's when I stopped.

In the early hours of the morning on July 3, 1952, Marjorie gave birth, five minutes apart, to healthy twin boys in Paris. George weighed six pounds, three ounces, and Alex, six pounds, six ounces. With Skibine's family to help, adjusting to life with twins was a pleasant experience. "We were trying to find a nurse so that the boys could travel with us, but Youra's family was there in the beginning." Within six months of the boys' birth, the couple hired Saruth, a young Swiss nurse.

She was wonderful with the boys and later with Maria's daughter, Elise. Shortly after she came to Chicago, to take care of Elise, she met a man from

Switzerland who worked in the construction business. After they were married, she decided to stay on as Maria's housekeeper. Alex and George always called her 'Sou' and used to see her when they visited Maria and Buzzy in Chicago. And she stayed on with them [until they retired and moved East].

Three months after Alex and George arrived on the scene, Marjorie returned to the stage. "I did the Mazurka in *Les Sylphides* and thought I was going to die. I was sure I was ready for it because I had always thought it was such a breeze. With all the jumps, once I lost my legs, it was horrible. I got through it, but how I don't remember." However, she notes, working her way back into performing shape through a more judicious selection of repertoire did not take long.

On January 2, 1954, Marjorie made her debut in what would become one of her most cherished and acclaimed roles, the White Filly in Skibine's *Idylle.* Set to a François Serette score, the ballet was based on a parable of human frailty manifested in a romantic tale of three horses. Skibine performed the role of the plain black horse who temporarily loses the heart of the filly, performed by Marjorie, to an elaborately festooned circus horse, performed by Vladimir Skouratoff. A tour de force for the ballerina as well as the male dancers, *Idylle* provided an ideal showcase for Marjorie's technical virtuosity.

As much as she enjoyed *Idylle,* she maintains her position that she has never had a favorite role.

I really liked different ballets at different times. I enjoyed changing from year to year. It wasn't that I did just one thing like Markova, who performed only certain kinds of roles and was magnificent at them. I liked to change. Some years I loved doing *Idylle,* and later, I didn't because it was so hard. I also went through periods of preferring softer, more romantic roles, but essentially I enjoyed doing different things.

Skibine's talents as a choreographer proved to be equally versatile. Within a few months of the successful premiere of *Idylle,* he unveiled a new production of *Romeo and Juliet* set to the Hector Berlioz score featuring Marjorie in the title role. "It was created for special performances in 1955 at the Cour Carrée at the Louvre. It was delightful and completely different from *Idylle,*" Marjorie says.

As significant an impact as Skibine's emergence as a choreogra-

191

pher had on Marjorie's career, it had little effect on life at home. "We had no difficulty living and working together. And it was nice to share the triumphs." Marjorie and Skibine also experienced minimal difficulty balancing the demands of their professional and family lives. The twins adopted their parents' ebullient approach to life and developed manners to fit their well-traveled existence. Quite content to adapt to the rules of their environment, Alex and George made friends easily on both sides of the Atlantic.

Despite maintaining completely different schedules, Marjorie and her sister remained close, and both Thanksgiving and Christmas holidays were generally spent with the entire family in Fairfax. "We always took Alex and George home for the holidays. They seemed to like Oklahoma and my husband loved it. We both loved to watch the sunset, which you could see forever because our house was right on top of a hill. I like Fairfax. I always have a good time there. And I like Indians. They are nice people and very friendly and peaceful."

In early 1956, Marjorie and Skibine joined luminaries of the dance world for a commemorative performance in London's Stoll Theatre honoring Anna Pavlova. Among the prominent stars appearing with the Covent Garden Sadler's Wells Ballet were Alicia Markova, Margot Fonteyn, Yvette Chauviré, Anton Dolin, John Gilpin, and Michael Somes. The guest appearance was the harbinger of a new phase in Marjorie's career. Nine years after making her debut as a ballerina in the Marquis's company, Marjorie had taken her place among Europe's most prominent artists. She had set new standards of technical and dramatic excellence and had won a strong, loyal following. From her perspective, she was driven to dance, not driven to succeed. "I never set goals for myself. I loved to dance, and I was very lucky that people let me. I didn't have any blinding ambition or burning desire to get ahead. I always seized the opportunities that came my way, but I never had a plan." Since making her professional debut as a soloist in Ballet Theatre, Marjorie really hadn't needed a plan. Her career had advanced swiftly and steadily through offers received, not solicited. Less than seven months after her victorious guest appearance in London, another such offer emerged on the horizon. Marjorie was invited to join the Paris Opéra Ballet as a leading ballerina with the title of Étoile.

Although her position in the Marquis's company left little to be desired, she could not refuse the opportunity to take her place in the history of ballet as the first American ballerina to join the Paris Opéra Ballet as *première danseuse étoile*. The invitation was a complete surprise—and a complete departure from precedent for the company that had given birth to classical dance in 1671. An outgrowth of the Académie Royale de Musique, founded in 1661 by order of Louis XIV, the Paris Opéra Ballet had had its share of guest ballerinas, including Maria Tallchief, who in 1947 became the first American guest artist engaged by the troupe in more than a century. None, however, had been invited to join the troupe's illustrious roster of leading stars.

Although a handful of dance historians have argued that an engagement of the Philadelphia-born Augusta Maywood in 1838 marked the Opéra's first American appointment, the brevity of Maywood's tenure precludes comparison. Only thirteen at the time, Maywood vanished from Paris and the Opéra in the midst of the 1838 season, following a performance of Joseph Mazilier's *Le Diable Amoureux*. She had, it was later discovered, run away to the south of France with her partner and future husband, Charles Mabille.

News of Marjorie's impending appointment as a permanent member of the Paris Opéra's star roster stirred mixed emotions. The public and press applauded, the dancers of the all-French company raised their eyebrows, and the Skibine household celebrated.

Youra also was invited to join the company as an étoile and choreographer. Of course, his appointment was not as controversial because he had been born in Russia and raised in Paris. It was an incredible honor for me, but most of all, I was thrilled because of Alex and George. As much as it meant for our careers, we welcomed the opportunity because it made life easier with the boys. It was a very hectic time for us, and we had to start thinking about the future.

Alex and George were almost four, and we knew that once they started school we weren't going to be able to take them on tour with us. Essentially, the Opéra Ballet didn't tour, so we could live in our house outside Paris and lead a much less complicated life. Because the company is completely subsidized by the government, the dancers have the equivalent of a civil service job in America. You work normal hours and receive all the benefits and protection of having a regular job. I remember when we joined,

Marjorie Tallchief and George Skibine with their twin sons Alex and George in Paris. (Photo © Serge Lido, Paris. Reprinted by permission.)

you were lucky if you performed once a week. That changed while we were there, but most of the time we finished at five o'clock. It was completely different from anything we had ever experienced.

In the midst of celebrating the opportunity awaiting them at the Paris Opéra, Marjorie and Skibine received an offer from Ruth Page to join her Chicago Opera Ballet for a five-month American tour. "It was a very good offer, and we knew Ruth. She had become very popular in France and had a place in Paris and St. Tropez. The tour began in November, when we usually took the boys home to Fairfax for the holidays, and didn't conflict with our schedule to begin at the Opéra in April. It seemed a bit like a vacation to us, so we accepted it." Leaving the Grand Ballet du Marquis de Cuevas to join the Paris Opéra did not create any bad feelings and the couple maintained their relationship with the Marquis.

Shortly after signing their contracts with the Opéra in late October, Maria joined the Skibines for the trip to New York aboard the *Liberté*. "Maria had just completed an engagement in Europe and it worked out for all of us to sail together." The prospect of spending five months in Oklahoma held tremendous fascination for the four-year-old twins. "It was the first time they had an opportunity to spend a serious length of time with my family. And, of course, they thought it was a great idea. In all fairness, I think my parents were just as excited as the boys, so everyone was happy. Plus, the tour included stops in Oklahoma, which really made it a homecoming."

Performing in America for the first time in five years, Marjorie and Skibine received an enthusiastic popular and critical reception dancing Page's *The Merry Widow* and *Revanche* (Revenge). Unfortunately, Skibine suffered a torn Achilles tendon during the tour. "I remember it was cold and the company bus was late getting to the theater. There wasn't time to warm up and it just snapped." Considering the seriousness of the injury, it mended well and had little impact on Skibine's immediate future. "It was never the same after that," Marjorie says, "but he was able to work on it by the time we started at the Opéra."

Returning to Paris in April, Marjorie encountered the same antagonism from the company's dancers that she had faced in every company she had joined.

We were not given a warm welcome. I didn't blame the dancers, especially at the Opéra. To begin with, they were very good dancers. And they had had to go through yearly exams since they had been accepted into the School of the Paris Opéra Ballet. To have someone who hadn't been through any of that brought in and put ahead of them wasn't pleasant. But my attitude always was that if people didn't like me, there wasn't much I could do about it. So I concentrated on my work.

Marjorie and Skibine's arrival also was viewed with displeasure by Serge Lifar. "As much as he liked Americans, Lifar was not glad to see us." Personal feelings aside, as ballet master of the Opéra, Lifar did work with Marjorie and she ultimately performed many of his works.

I did his *Firebird* and took over the lead in his *Les Noces Fantastiques*. Actually, I think *Les Noces* made him dislike me even more. He had created the ballet for Nina Vyroubova, whom he liked very much. For reasons I never knew she was let go, and I took over most of her roles. Because Lifar was very sensitive, my success in her roles made matters worse. He was strange. He was always getting involved in politics and had problems left over from the war that he could never shake.

During her first year at the Opéra, Marjorie made her debut in *Giselle*. "I had seen a lot of Giselles during my career, but it was my first opportunity to do the role. I remember performing it with Youra and with Peter van Dijk, whom I danced with frequently at the Opéra. I enjoyed the role and the challenge of its dramatic and technical demands." When pushed to agree or deny that she attained the pinnacle of her technical and dramatic abilities during her tenure with the Paris Opéra, Marjorie replies, "I would have to say that I reached my full potential there."

Chapter Twenty-Five

Homeward Bound

On signing their second-year contracts with the Opéra, Skibine's position as an étoile and choreographer changed dramatically. "Lifar resigned and Youra assumed his position as ballet master. It was a wonderful opportunity for him because it gave him a chance to develop as a director. At the Opéra, the role of ballet master is comparable to that of an artistic director in America." Wistfully, Marjorie adds, "Unfortunately for me, it essentially brought his performing career to an end. I worked with excellent partners at the Opéra and enjoyed dancing with Peter and Attilio Labis. But no one could ever replace Youra."

When he took over Lifar's post in 1958 Skibine immediately assumed responsibility for completing preparations for the company's landmark engagement at the Bolshoi Theatre in Moscow. "We were the first company to perform in Russia after the war, which made it a little bit scary and increased the pressure on everyone to make a good showing. But it was an incredibly successful engagement, and extremely interesting for Youra. We only went to Moscow, but I liked it and we had wonderful audiences."

After the company's triumphant return to Paris Skibine turned his attention to expanding the troupe's repertoire, which already included his wildly successful production of *Prisoner of the Caucasus*. He created *Isoline, Atlantide,* and *Concerto* in 1958. *Concerto,* set to a score by André Jolivet, proved the most noteworthy. Skibine also introduced a new element to the Opéra's repertoire by inviting guest choreographers to mount new productions of existing works or to create new ballets for the troupe.

Despite the rigors of their second year with the Opéra, and Skibine's first as ballet master, the couple accepted a return engagement with Page's Chicago Opera Ballet. "That's when Ruth did *Camille* for me. It was a very good experience and worked out well for the whole family." At the beginning of their third season at the Opéra, the post of general administrator of the French National Lyric Theatres changed hands. "What happens at the Opéra depends on the general administrator. When that person changes, everything does, because he can do whatever he wants. We had come in under Georges Hirsch's administration, and when he left in 1959, Youra started to have problems. The new man, of course, favored his own people."

Although Skibine's problems did not hamper his ability to create new works, an undercurrent of resistance to his direction of the company gradually took its toll. In 1961 Skibine created *Pastorale* for a gala performance in Versailles in honor of the official state visit of President and Mrs. John F. Kennedy to Paris.

That was the last ballet Youra created for the Opéra as ballet master. Shortly after the Versailles performance, we went to Buenos Aires as guest artists and Youra restaged *Concerto* and created *Metamorphoses* to Paul Hindemith's "Symphonic Metamorphoses on Themes of Weber." When we returned to Paris, both of us resigned from the Opéra. It was an amicable parting though, and Youra maintained his association as a guest choreographer.

The couple now turned their full attention to guest engagements, staging Skibine's ballets for various companies and developing a small concert group of their own. In 1963 Marjorie accepted an invitation from Serge Golovine to join his company as guest artist after his partner suddenly became ill. "He was a good friend and we had danced together in the Marquis's company. I always enjoyed dancing with him, and I was delighted to accept the offer." Not long after her return from touring with Golovine, Marjorie remembers, Skibine was approached by the couple's longtime friend Jeannot Cerrone to take the helm of a new American company being formed by the American art patroness Rebekah Harkness. Having observed her husband's impressive directorial strengths during his tenure as ballet master at the Opéra, Marjorie supported the move wholeheartedly. "I have always disagreed with people who don't believe they have a chance. Everyone has a chance. At some point, the chance will be there. You just have to take it. Accepting the offer from Harkness was one of those points for Youra."

Harkness, a woman of great wealth, was an aspiring composer and devotee of dance. In 1961, she established the Rebekah W. Harkness Foundation to dedicate her largesse to building the first major American ballet company in twenty years. Initially, the foundation sponsored a variety of contemporary dance endeavors, including Jerome Robbins's Ballets: U.S.A. and the establishment of an annual summer dance festival at the outdoor Delacorte Theater in New York's Central Park. In 1962 the foundation adopted the fledgling Robert Joffrey Ballet Company, under the artistic direction of Joffrey and Gerald Arpino. The troupe expanded rapidly. Touring, once confined to the limitations of a donated station wagon, moved into the international arena. With foundation support the company made two successful European tours and a visit to the Far East and appeared in Russia under the auspices of the U.S. State Department.

In 1964 Joffrey and Harkness parted ways under extremely volatile circumstances. Fueled by an overzealous dance press, the situation exploded into a battle reminiscent of the ballet wars of Massine and de Basil. Never having met Mrs. Harkness, and living an ocean away from the eye of the storm, Skibine and Marjorie turned to Cerrone for the truth. As Harkness's artistic adviser since the establishment of the foundation, Cerrone had been on the front lines of the ensuing melee. His explanation of the situation proved acceptable to Skibine and Marjorie. Skibine accepted the post as artistic director and Marjorie signed as featured ballerina.

Prior to his death on April 24, 1991, Cerrone served as general manager of the Houston Ballet and founding director of the Harid Conservatory in Boca Raton, Florida. In 1982, shortly after having open heart surgery in Houston, Cerrone, who never accepted the negative image unfairly imposed on Mrs. Harkness as a result of the Joffrey-Harkness split, requested a personal interview to "clear Mrs. Harkness's name." His explanation of the situation has been corroborated by Marjorie, former Joffrey dancers, and others close to Mrs. Harkness at the time.

"The whole truth has never been reported about the circumstances of the Joffrey termination," Cerrone said.

And I want it to some day be made public. The situation was a case of misguided artistic judgment. The problem we had was with the charter of the nonprofit foundation supporting the company. Because of increases in the size of the budget, we were forced to make changes in the charter or it would lose its nonprofit status. Among the changes was a requirement that the foundation had to be identified in the name of the company. Joffrey and Arpino could not accept that. Instead, they viewed the name change as an attempt by Mrs. Harkness to take greater artistic control. They became unreachable. Nothing could be done to alter the fact that the charter had to be revised or the foundation would lose its ability to continue functioning as a nonprofit. Mrs. Harkness was not prepared to give up her goal and took the only option open to her—to establish a new company.

Unfortunately, Cerrone was not allowed to refute either Joffrey's or Arpino's claims that Mrs. Harkness was attempting to increase her artistic control over the company. "Mrs. Harkness refused to confront the press with her side of the story because she was convinced anything she said would simply make matters worse," Cerrone noted. He also explained that she had attempted to deny members of Joffrey's company at the time from auditioning for the company established under Skibine's direction. "A group, representing the Joffrey dancers, appealed to the American Guild of Musical Artists to insist that the union's open audition policy was enforced. As a result, many of Joffrey's leading dancers were hired by Skibine. And once again Mrs. Harkness was falsely accused. This time, for stealing Joffrey's dancers."

Far removed from the political maneuvering of Joffrey and Arpino, Skibine and Marjorie prepared for their return to America. The move, Marjorie recalls, "was a lot more complicated than going to Europe had been in 1947. And, of course, everything happened very quickly. Youra went ahead to hold auditions and get the company started. I followed with Alex and George as soon as school was out, and we joined the company at its summer home in Watch Hill, Rhode Island." Situated on a thin strip of coastline cutting a jagged wedge between Block Island and the Fishers Island Sound, Watch Hill is a tranquil summer haven for some of the nation's most prominent families and enjoys little intrusion from the annual migration of tourists to New England's picturesque coastline communities. Watch Hill's tranquil setting and lack of outside diversions was an ideal environment for concentrating on dance. "We worked in a fire station that had been converted into studios for the Joffrey company. Most of the dancers lived in a boardinghouse adjacent to the studio and everything centered around the studio."

A combination of Harkness's circle of contemporary artists and Skibine's extensive connections in the art world drew a stellar group of artists to the company.

The level of creativity was very high. And, initially, the company was very strong. It was rich in the sense of what was being created, and the people who were part of it. Mrs. Harkness didn't pay her dancers fabulous salaries or anything like that, but she did provide an incredible environment to work in and insisted that productions be executed by only the finest costume and scenic houses in the business. She wanted the best, and she had the financial resources to have the best.

Erik Bruhn was engaged as featured guest artist for the company's first season and former Grand Ballet du Marquis de Cuevas stars Nicholas Polajenko and Daphne Dale signed as leading soloists. With less than eight months to pull the company together and build a repertoire before its scheduled debut in Cannes in February 1965, the summer proved to be an exhausting experience. Among the guest teachers and choreographers on hand were the Royal Danish Ballet's Vera Volkova, Alexandra Danilova, Valentina Pereyaslavec, Alvin Ailey, Stuart Hodes, Brian MacDonald, Norman Walker, Michael Smuin, Thomas Andrew, and company member Richard Wagner.

As leading ballerina, Marjorie's repertoire consisted of the standard classical pas de deux, Skibine's *Idylle* and *Annabel Lee,* and leading roles in several repertoire works including Ailey's new work, *Ariadne.*

It was the most diverse repertoire I ever had. I liked Alvin very much and loved working with him, but when we started working on *Ariadne,* I thought I was going to die. It was a very difficult ballet and the first time I had done anything modern. The positions were so different that every muscle in my body ached the entire summer. It was hard mentally, too. I had trouble remembering the choreography. In the classical repertoire you have thirty-two fouettés and patterns of turns and jumps, or whatever, that follow the music a certain way. With Alvin, there was none of that. I'm sure it wasn't easy for Alvin either. *Ariadne* was only his second work for a ballet company, and it was the first time he was using pointe work.

That is why, later, when he asked me to appear with his company as a guest artist, I considered it a great honor. He cast me in a leading role in his *El Amor Brujo,* which he created for his company to the Manuel de Falla score. It was a wonderful ballet, and I enjoyed working with his dancers very much. It was one of the ballets I performed during my farewell performances with the company at the Marais Festival in Paris in 1966.

On October 5, 1964, the Harkness Ballet presented a gala performance at the White House to christen the new stage installed in the Blue Room that had been underwritten by Mrs. Harkness. "We performed during ceremonies honoring the president of the Republic of the Philippines, Diosdado Macapagal, and his wife. I had never danced at the White House before, and it was a tremendous honor. President and Mrs. Johnson were very gracious and it was very exciting. We returned to perform at the White House a second time during the Johnson administration, and again, it was a delightful experience."

The company returned to New York to resume rehearsals before leaving for Cannes in January. "We spent the first six weeks in Cannes rehearsing in the theater and at Rosella's studio. She taught company class, and Youra also brought Marika Bessobrasova from Monte Carlo to teach."

On February 24, 1965, the company made its official debut in Cannes before an audience brimming with celebrated members of the international dance community and an impressive assemblage of major American and European critics. The reviews concurred with the enthusiastic response of the opening night audience and set the mood for a triumphant three-week season in Cannes. From there, the company headed to Paris and the gala premiere of Ailey's *Ariadne* at the Opéra-Comique.

Marjorie won new accolades as a ballerina of unlimited versatility and technical facility in her debut in a modern work. Although the diversity of the company's repertoire drew some criticism, popular and critical acclaim followed the troupe across Europe to Romania and the final stop on the tour, Portugal. There, a quirk of fate put Marjorie onstage with her husband again in Lisbon. "I was scheduled to perform *Annabel Lee* with Nick [Polajenko] and he hurt his back. No one else knew the role, so rather than change the program, Youra decided to go on. The entire company gathered in the wings to watch him perform. It was a wonderful experience."

Returning triumphant from Europe, the company headed for Watch Hill to begin preparations for its inaugural American tour in the fall. The absence of a featured male guest artist had little effect on Marjorie. In addition to working with Polajenko, with whom she had danced extensively in the Marquis's company, Marjorie had developed a comfortable partnership with company soloist Ali Pourfarrokh.

The American tour proved exhausting. Marjorie recalls, "Youra and I traveled with the company on the bus, and we crisscrossed the country for thirteen weeks. But the company was well received and we had decent houses." The acclaim garnered during the company's inaugural European and American tours fueled great expectations for the future of the company. "There was a constant tug-of-war on the management side, but it never bothered my husband. He was a firm believer in the theory that strong, creative people were worth the complications they caused."

On November 15, 1965, the Harkness House for Ballet Arts on

New York City's posh Upper East Side opened its doors. The mansion had been renovated to serve as headquarters for the company and its affiliated school. "According to Marjorie, the facility was without equal in the world of dance." Taking up residence in its new home, the company began preparing for its second season in Cannes and appearances in Tunisia, Morocco, Egypt, Greece, Germany, France, Italy, Sicily, and Spain under the auspices of the U.S. State Department.

Paris Opéra star Attilio Labis was engaged as guest artist for the European leg of the tour, and Skibine was busy choreographing *La Venta Quemada* featuring Marjorie, Pourfarrokh, and company principal dancer Brunilda Ruiz. It would be the final ballet Skibine would create for his wife. Ironically, the ballet premiered during the company's May 1966 engagement at the Gran Teatro de Liceo in Barcelona, Spain, shortly after the Alvin Ailey American Dance Theater joined the Harkness Ballet for the remainder of the Harkness European tour. Unexpected financial problems that arose during the Ailey company's concurrent African and Near East tour sponsored by the U.S. State Department with assistance from the Rebekah Harkness Foundation had left the company stranded in Africa. Because Ailey was due to join the Harkness Ballet in Barcelona for the premiere of his latest work for the company, *Macumba*, Harkness arranged for him and his dancers to finish the tour under the umbrella of the company.

For Marjorie, who would make her debut in Ailey's *El Amor Brujo* during the company's final engagement of the tour at the Marais Festival in Paris, the situation allowed additional rehearsals with his company. As a result of the two companies joining forces for a brief period, Judith Jamison, Miguel Godreau, and Morton (Tubby) Winston were invited to join the Harkness Ballet. Although Jamison and Godreau returned to Ailey's company after its financial difficulties were resolved, Winston remained through 1967.

Although Marjorie had been weighing the pros and cons of retiring for some time, she decided to end her performing career during the Paris engagement that included her debut as a guest artist with Ailey's company. With a gracious smile, Marjorie admits having decided to retire well before this.

"Alex and George were teenagers, and I really needed to be with them. And it was time to start bringing my career to an end. Youra signed with the company for another season, but I stayed in New York with the boys." Accepting only a fraction of the offers she received to appear as a guest artist, Marjorie remembers gradually adjusting to a light performing schedule. Raising her shoulders slightly, she adds softly, "It wasn't easy to retire."

Chapter Twenty-Six

Yvonne Chouteau
Professional Debut

Taking her first class as a member of the corps de ballet of Sergei Denham's Ballet Russe de Monte Carlo in 1943 was everything that Lucy and C.E. Chouteau's only child had hoped it would be. The soft-spoken, unassuming fourteen-year-old from Oklahoma was delighted to see that company members took their places at barre according to rank. "No one had to tell me that my place was last," Yvonne recalls. "I wasn't the only new corps girl, but I was the only fourteen-year-old." Remembering his first impression of Yvonne, Frederic Franklin remarks,

She and her mother lived a few blocks from my apartment, and I used to see them walking their little white dog. Yvonne was a tiny wisp of a thing and was terribly polite. She always curtsied and said "Good day, Mr. Franklin" when she saw me. And her mother would nod but never try to start a conversation. Then all of a sudden here she is in the company! Denham was very impressed by her potential, and Danilova was thrilled. She had kept an eye on Yvonne since the annual SAB scholarship competition and adopted her the minute she came to the company. I was surprised because Yvonne seemed so terribly young, and looked even younger. But she was very talented and had an ethereal quality that was unique.

Yvonne's age drew some raised eyebrows, but essentially it served only as an excuse to stir up new objections to American dancers. The clamor for younger dancers had diminished in the decade since de Basil had marketed the thirteen-, fourteen-, and fifteen-year-old prodigies Irina Baronova, Tamara Toumanova, and Tatiana Riabouchinska as the "baby ballerinas of Russian ballet" to boost box office appeal for the 1932–33 season of his Ballets Russes. Although American dance audiences would once again show an interest in youth on the ballet stage during the mid-1960s, in 1943 the issue was moot. Ironically, the Ballets Russes performance that inspired Yvonne to become a dancer featured the "baby ballerinas" performing *Les Sylphides* with Danilova.

There was no issue over age when I joined the company, but I was constantly under supervision. Mme Danilova's secretary, Elizabeth Twysden, was my chaperone on tour, and we would stay in the YWCA while the rest of the company stayed in a hotel. I will always remember, no matter where we were, she would leave one window open at night, and we had to be up early enough to attend 6:00 A.M. Mass. So once again I was drawn to Catholicism. I wasn't baptized in the Church until years later, but I never missed Mass!

Danilova wasted no time making it obvious that Yvonne was in her charge.

She took me under her wing and called me "Evonchiks," which means "little Yvonne" in Russian. That's what everyone always called me then, and my husband still calls me that, or "Chiksy." So I guess I'm stuck with it forever.

It was all for my own good in the beginning. But, unfortunately, I was treated that way my entire career. Later, after I was grown, married, and ranked as a ballerina, I was still "little Yvonne." It became infuriating, but there was nothing I could do to convince anyone that I had grown up!

When it came to breaking in new dancers, the troupe's Russian corps mistress didn't care how old anyone was or wasn't. "Tatiana Semyonova was a tough, unrelenting taskmaster. She always stood next to me, watching everything I did. And she'd hiss, 'Get down on your knee, what was that?' She gave us the real old-fashioned Russian treatment."

Semyonova's vigilance aside, Yvonne learned quickly. Having first encountered the mental and physical discipline of learning choreography at an age when most toddlers are learning to walk, Yvonne did not chafe under the demand to grasp roles quickly. "The challenge was invigorating. Learning roles came so naturally to me, I never thought much about it. When I realized it wasn't easy for everyone, I knew it would help me prove myself in the company. I adored the repertoire, so learning roles on my own was a joy. When I wasn't onstage, I watched from the wings, and I never took my eyes off what everyone else was doing in rehearsal."

To Yvonne's dismay, Miss Twysden arrived promptly every day to make sure she did not rehearse a minute longer than her contract allowed.

Of course, she always came on time. And that meant I had to leave and go back to whatever YWCA we were staying at that night. I was taking correspondence courses through the Professional Children's School to earn my high school diploma. After doing my assignment for the day, I would take a nap, sew my shoes, or soak in the tub. Then we would eat dinner in the YWCA cafeteria and return to the theater with plenty of time for me to warm up and get ready for performance.

On matinee days, Miss Twysden worked overtime. There was no time for schoolwork or a nap, and any rehearsals fell under an "unusual or emergency clause." Although praising Miss Twysden for being very sweet and completely dedicated to taking care of her, Yvonne admits she always considered her an obstacle when it came to learning as many ballets as she could and fitting in with everyone

209

else. "I always felt that I was missing out on things when she would come for me. And, in some ways, I was."

Despite all the performing experience Yvonne had acquired since making her first major public appearance at the 1933 Century of Progress World's Fair in Chicago, life in a professional ballet company was more than just performing. There was learning to put on makeup, mastering the mandatory classical and Romantic hairstyles, figuring out how to rotate a spartan allotment of pointe shoes to get the most life out of each pair, and learning to lay out what was needed for the second ballet before leaving the dressing room for the first. "Mme Danilova made sure I was taught to prepare myself for performance. And she was very clear that it was up to me to learn to take care of myself by watching how the other dancers in my dressing room took care of themselves. So there was no real problem with all of that."

Learning to cope with backstage politics and take insidious remarks with a grain of salt was not so easy.

What was difficult in the beginning had nothing to do with practical skills. A lot of the problems I had were just part of what everyone goes through during their first year in a ballet company. Obviously, because I was "little Yvonne," and Mme Danilova paid special attention to me, I attracted more than the usual amount of resentment. As unpleasant as it was, it was part of being a dancer. And, naturally, the more progress I made, the worse it got. Then there was Mr. Denham, who made a habit of keeping everyone in the company on edge. I had seen him do it to others, so I was prepared for my turn. One night he came up to me backstage and said, "I hear you are not working hard enough!" It was his way of preventing anyone from feeling secure.

With the exception of being allowed to join her parents at the launching of the Liberty vessel USS *Jean P. Chouteau* in Richmond, California, during her first tour, Yvonne did not continue her activities as a representative of Oklahoma. Yvonne says, "Denham downplayed anything that brought individual recognition. Heaven forbid that any of us should get a swollen head!" Although constantly under fire from various factions within the company, Yvonne won the friendship of the company's resident miracle worker, head wardrobe mistress Sophie Pourmel. A veteran of the crisis-ridden backstage world of ballet, the diminutive Mme Pourmel enforced the strictest costume rules in the business, but she was never too busy to sense the need for a kind word, a consoling glance, or a reassuring tap on the shoulder. Until her recent retirement from New York City Ballet, Mme Pourmel remained as adept at mending bruised egos as broken zippers and calming nervous understudies unexpectedly thrust on stage in the time it took her to sew them into costume. In 1943 Mme Pourmel was one of the few people Yvonne Chouteau knew she could trust without fear of reprisal. "Of course, no matter how much she liked you, if you didn't hang your costume up properly, she would see to it that you were fined. But she was always there when you needed her and made life so much easier."

Yvonne wrote to her parents daily but admits that she rarely told them of the problems she was facing. That was saved for her diary.

I didn't want to concern my parents, especially since there was nothing they could do about things. And besides, as young and naive as I was, being in the midst of people who were so much more worldly would have been uncomfortable no matter what. But it made me feel better to be able to put my feelings in writing. Even as discouraged and insecure as I sometimes felt, I could see that I was making good progress. Really, that was all that mattered.

Everyone was driven by the same commitment to dance. It was just that everything wasn't a completely new experience for them. Things they took in stride were new to me. By that I mean things like learning how to pack a suitcase so you didn't have to unpack it completely to get what you needed every night. I had to learn the little things that become second nature after you have done them a few times.

Grappling with the realities of touring did not take Yvonne's focus away from her work. Her dedication to the opportunities at hand did not win any compliments, but it was duly noted. Treating her understudy assignments with as much fervor as she approached the roles she performed ultimately proved beneficial. "I loved to step in at the last minute. And on tour there were always plenty of opportunities to do that. I loved to perform. And it never mattered to me what I was performing. As long as I was onstage, I was happy." Yvonne's innate ability to illuminate the stage also distinguished her from the sea of corps de ballet dancers. The radiant presence and delicate lyricism she evidenced as a fourteen-year-old caught the eye not only of company management but also of guest choreographers.

Looking back on her early career, Yvonne remembers Bronislava Nijinska giving her the opportunity to understudy a soloist role in *Snow Maiden* after seeing her perform in the work's corps de ballet. "Nijinska was very particular, and it mattered a great deal to me that I had caught her attention. I was fascinated by her approach to ballet. She was very musical and very strict about technique, but she paid so much attention to detail. There always was more than the steps, and every movement meant something." Agnes de Mille also was impressed with Yvonne's distinct personality on stage and cast her as the understudy for the small role created for Maria Tallchief in *Rodeo*. It was Massine, however, whose influence would remain with Yvonne forever.

He was a very interesting man. And so intense. No one ever knew him. Late during my second year with the company, after I had been given the ingenue role in *Le Beau Danube,* I had my first experience working with him.

He came to rehearse the ballet in Detroit, taking the role of the Hussar himself, with me doing the Young Girl. I think I was all of sixteen by then. It was a lesson I will never forget as long as I live. It wasn't my first hard lesson, but it happened in rehearsal, not class. The Mazurka is beautiful, but very fast, and the Hussar pulls the Young Girl through a series of traveling turns. He must have thought I needed to be put in my place or taken down a peg because when we got to that part, he dragged me down to my knees. He went so fast I couldn't believe it, much less keep up with him. I had never danced with anyone so fast or agile in my life. I felt like I was on a roller coaster, and he kept pulling faster and harder each time. I felt myself losing my feet, and then he yelled as loud as he could in Russian, "Who is this young child?"

Of course, I was completely humiliated and didn't know where to turn. It was the first time I had ever been put down like that, and at sixteen I didn't know how to handle it.

With a wry look crossing her face, she quips, "Then I found out he did it because he liked me! And forever after, I was a Massine dancer. He wanted me to do everything. I never understood it and just accepted it as the Russian way of keeping a young dancer in line.

Yvonne Chouteau and Leonide Massine performing Massine's
Le Beau Danube, 1950. (Personal collection.)

If I had had a big head it would have made sense, but I was so shy
and insecure, it seemed awfully harsh."

As she describes the enigmatic Massine, Yvonne sinks back into
the pillows of the couch.

He was a complex, wonderful man. I actually got as close to him as I felt anyone could get to someone like that. He was very evasive and kept a distance
between himself and everyone. But the very last time he came to the company, during our 1950 engagement in Chicago, I danced opposite him in
Capriccio Espagnol and performed the ingenue roles in *Le Beau Danube* and
Gaîté Parisienne with him. He was retiring from the stage and had come to
make his farewell performances with us. He also was more elusive than ever
before. When I went to his dressing room to say good-bye, his dresser an-

213

swered the door and announced who it was. Massine asked for me to come in. I was a little surprised because he was lying almost motionless on the couch in semidarkness, mentally getting ready for *Capriccio Espagnol.* I gave him a tiny gold Saint Christopher's medal to show my gratitude for everything he had done for me and all the coaching he had given me in his ballets and other roles. He thanked me and said he appreciated it very much.

Leaning forward, her eyes brightening, she adds,

Years later, I was told that Massine always carried that medal in his wallet and that he said he kept it "there forever." I also received a letter from a dance scholar in San Francisco not long after Massine passed away. She wanted me to know that Massine had told her he wanted to come to Oklahoma to do an Indian ballet and have me help him!

Massine was my choreographer. I was totally enamored with his work. It was not so much strictly classical but plastique, which suited me so well. I was groomed, from my first encounter with him at sixteen, to perform Lady Poverty in *St. Francis.* But that was just one of the many ballets Denham always promised to do for me and never came through on.

It is always so hard to know what someone like Massine really thinks about you. He was so full of contradictions, like so many geniuses are. You can say the same thing about Tudor and Balanchine. The only word that comes to mind to describe Massine is *austere,* in the positive sense of the word. Massine was of a different world, in another orbit, and it showed, in his eyes.

Chapter Twenty-Seven

A Child in an Adult World

Yvonne's second year in the Ballet Russe de Monte Carlo got off to a late start. While the rest of the company began rehearsals in Los Angeles for the Broadway musical *Song of Norway,* Yvonne stayed home in Oklahoma. "Mr. Denham insisted that Broadway was not a suitable environment for a fifteen-year-old. So I didn't go back to rehearsal until the company came back to New York."

Although her father had been reassigned to the Bureau of Indian Affairs office in Muskogee, roughly twenty-five miles southwest of Tahlequah, Yvonne spent most of her time visiting friends and relatives in Oklahoma City. Despite being swamped with invitations to parties held in her honor and requests for interviews with newspapers big and small, she reserved the time and energy to return to Fronnie Asher's studio. The luxury of taking class far from the roving eye of the professional dance community was invigorating. "It was wonderful," she says. "And it gave me a chance to think about everything I had learned."

To her dismay, her father insisted that after Yvonne left to go on her next tour his wife should come back home for good.

Momma had stayed in New York with Fluffy during my first year in the company. She had a really good job at Bergdorf Goodman's, and everyone adored her. Momma was such a beautiful woman and completely devoted to my father and his goals. She never questioned anything he said and would tell me "Listen to your father, he knows what's best." She came from a long line of Southern statesmen, including Alexander Hamilton and Benjamin Rush, but gave all the attention to the Chouteau family legacy. I see some of her in me, but my independence is very dear to me.

Returning to New York well before the company was due back, Yvonne went straight to classes with her favorite teachers, Anatole Vilzak, Pierre Vladimirov, and Anatole Oboukhoff. Although Yvonne's departure from SAB had not been greeted warmly, it was not held against her.

The school had put some high values on my potential and wanted to develop it. Mr. Balanchine had insisted that I needed more training before joining a company, and he was right. But it hadn't been my decision to make. Daddy had said, "You must go to the Ballet Russe." Everyone knew I hadn't acted on my own, so when I came back to study with Mr. Vladimirov and Mr. Oboukhoff it wasn't an issue at SAB or with Mr. Balanchine. It was always interesting to me that even though I was not Balanchine's kind of dancer, he always gave me a soloist role in his ballets when he came to the Ballet Russe.

Balanchine's engagement as resident choreographer for Denham's Ballet Russe began in 1944 with rehearsals for *Song of Norway*. When he and the company returned from Los Angeles, Yvonne was delighted to find that the lion's share of rehearsal time in California had been dedicated to the musical and that Nicholas Magallanes and several other dancers she had met at SAB had joined the company.

It was a madhouse. Mr. Balanchine was creating *Danses Concertantes* and setting *Le Bourgeois Gentilhomme* for our season at City Center and *Ballet Imperial* for our October performances in Chicago. The company was doing eight shows a week on Broadway and rehearsing in different studios around the city all hours of the day and night. Because I wasn't in the show, I had the advantage of being able to fill in at rehearsals for people who couldn't be in two places at the same time.

In addition to being assigned to understudy several demi-solo roles in the existing repertoire, she was cast in a variation for six women in Balanchine's revival of *Le Bourgeois Gentilhomme*. "It was quite odd. We wore giant feather plumes on our heads. I also had a demi-soloist role in *Ballet Imperial* and understudied a soloist role in *Danses Concertantes*."

With her repertoire expanding, Yvonne was not surprised to find herself once again the target of snide remarks and disapproving glances. She was, however, better equipped to deal with it. While she is endowed with a gentle nature, Yvonne possesses extraordinary stubbornness in the face of adversity. Aware that at fifteen she was no match for her veteran antagonists, she took the track of passive resistance. "Plus, it was such an exciting time to be in the company, I wouldn't let little digs distract me. I knew who my friends were by then and there was so much to learn and so many talented dancers to watch."

In addition to Danilova and a few other company ballerinas, Yvonne learned a great deal from Maria Tallchief and Mary Ellen Moylan. "If I had any doubts that I should have stayed at SAB, instead of joining the company, all I had to do was look at Mary Ellen. She had such exquisite technique. She helped me a lot and often joined Miss Twysden and me at Mass on tour. Maria and I also had a closeness because we were both from Oklahoma. No matter how busy she was, she always had a smile or encouraging word for me."

During the company's 1944 fall season at City Center, concerns were voiced over the continuing escalation of World War II. The dancers were told before leaving on tour to expect problems owing to food and fuel rationing and to be prepared to make unscheduled appearances at military bases. Having survived her first tour under wartime conditions and familiar with the idiosyncrasies of the ever-present Miss Twysden, Yvonne saw the tour as an opportunity to extend her realm beyond the corps de ballet. "It was quite a tour! Mr. Balanchine was mounting a new production of *Mozartiana* and creating a new pas de deux for Danilova and Franklin to premiere during our February season at City Center. So things never slowed down."

For Yvonne, the tour brought performances of the demi-soloist roles she understudied in *Danses Concertantes* and *Snow Maiden* and a "trial" performance of her first major role, the Prayer solo in the third act of *Coppélia*.

Unless there was a catastrophe, the first performance in a major role always happened in a small town, far from the view of knowledgeable critics. If the performance met with management's approval, you would be given additional performances before making your official debut in a major city. Of course, management never gave any indication whether you passed muster or not, so you had to watch the performance schedule to find out.

Returning to City Center for the 1945 spring season, Yvonne discovered she was scheduled to make her "official" debut as Prayer on her sixteenth birthday. Swamped with notes, flowers, and knick-knacks known in the dance world as "merdes"—which, rather than the literal French translation, means good luck—Yvonne spent the day on which most American teenage girls worry about getting their first kiss preparing to dance her first major role in the professional world of ballet.

The *New York Herald-Tribune* dance critic, Edwin Denby, noted that Yvonne's debut in Prayer also was her sixteenth birthday and her performance was "lovely in every way." His review of the March 7, 1945, *Coppélia* also included praise for the eight friends of Swanhilda and singled out Ruthanna Boris, Pauline Goddard, Yvonne Chouteau, and Lillian Lanese. "Never has such a chorus been seen here before," he wrote. Yvonne's favorable mentions from the New York critics and solid audience response for the remainder of the season prompted rumors that she would be named a soloist. Yvonne recalls, "Management never gave compliments or acknowledged your progress, but when casting for the tour went on the board, I was scheduled to perform Prayer more than I expected."

The five-week jaunt across Canada to the West Coast proved a triumph for the company and for Yvonne personally. The Los Angeles critic Isabel Morse Jones praised her ethereal qualities, writing, "If she sang she would be a Melisande." Having learned not to get excited about anything in the Ballet Russe until it happened, Yvonne was ecstatic when Denham offered her a soloist contract at season's end. Exhausted but elated, she returned to Oklahoma for a brief respite before heading back to New York to study under Danilova.

With little time to prepare for the company's fall season at City Center, Danilova coached her protégée in the traditions of the Russian Imperial School with relentless attention to detail, nuances of style, and dramatic finesse. Having waited patiently to see if the winsome twelve-year-old student who had stood before her four years earlier at the School of American Ballet scholarship auditions would have the tenacity to prevail in the world of ballet, Danilova welcomed the opportunity to pass her legacy on to one who exhibited talent, respect for tradition, and artistic integrity worthy of carrying the treasure to future generations.

When rehearsals resumed, Yvonne's second cast assignments included Preghiera in Balanchine's *Mozartiana,* the Flower Girl in Massine's *Gaîté Parisienne,* and the Young Girl in his *Le Beau Danube.* While both assignments in Massine's ballets were ingenue roles, the latter was considered the domain of ballerina Nathalie Krassovska. "Krassovska was very kind and taught me the role very carefully," Yvonne comments warmly. Not expecting to appear in any new roles during the upcoming season at City Center, Yvonne was given ample performances of Prayer in *Coppélia* as well as Balanchine's *Danses Concertantes* and *Ballet Imperial.*

In the wake of preparing for the New York season the company found itself caught up in the jubilation that erupted following the resolution of World War II. Within days of the Ballet Russe de Monte Carlo's September 9, 1945, opening at City Center, Japan formally surrendered to Allied Forces aboard the USS *Missouri,* anchored in Tokyo Bay. The world was officially at peace. With a rosy glow rising to her cheeks, Yvonne recalls the joyous abandon that seemed to permeate the air. "There were no more blackouts or dreary faces in the grocery store as people waited to buy rationed goods. Strangers smiled at each other, and the city came alive." The usual tensions associated with a New York season eased, and there was a genuine sense of camaraderie backstage. Sergei Denham celebrated the Allied victory with unabashed enthusiasm. As infamous for manipulating people and events to serve his goals as Denham was, there was a fervently patriotic side to the Russian-born financier. With the same fervor that he had delivered his company to perform at military bases with no attempt to gain publicity, he rejected taking advantage of the phenomenal turn of events to promote his company's New York season.

As it turned out, it was an emotional opening night. Good luck telegrams arrived from rival companies, and as the dancers took their places onstage, the excited chattering of the audience filtered through the curtain. It would be the first time in six years that no war headlines would be blazoned across the front pages of the morning papers to erase the fleeting images of beauty seen the night before. With a grin, Yvonne admits the last thing on her mind was that she was making her New York debut as a soloist.

The company successfully maintained the electricity generated on opening night to complete one of its most triumphant engagements in New York. Audiences and critics responded enthusiastically, and the two-week season proved to be as notable artistically as it was financially. Summing up the troupe's high-powered season for the *New York Herald-Tribune*, Denby wrote, "Clear and fresh, the dancing of the company as a whole has been this season, but I have had little space till now to speak of the fine moments of individual dancers." Among veteran soloists he praised Maria Tallchief and Dorothy Etheridge. And he cited Yvonne "for a shining animation and precision."

For the first time since Yvonne had joined the company she saw the eager anticipation she had always felt at the launching of a cross-country tour reflected in the eyes of her colleagues. "It was wonderful. We got our Pullman cars back, and the only soldiers we saw were on their way back home!"

Although she was a ranked soloist, entrusted with roles reflecting her status, the agreement signed by her parents and Denham when she joined the company at fourteen remained in effect—with one exception. The restrictions placed on the number of hours she was allowed to work to protect her muscles from injury or improper development were lifted. She was, however, to remain under the supervision of a chaperone until she completed high school.

Chaperones and restrictions aside, Yvonne also was going through the physical and emotional changes normal for her age. Shortly after leaving on tour she began having problems with her skin, which prompted what she lightheartedly refers to as her "pure period." "Momma always told me, 'You aren't a beautiful girl, Yvonne, but you have a perfect complexion.' So when I began breaking out with blemishes, I was horrified. I also was going through an intensely religious stage and decided it was time to go on a cleansing diet. I fasted, ate only natural grains and vegetables, and promptly lost weight." Thin to start with, losing ten pounds gave Yvonne a gaunt look that drew raised eyebrows. Readily admitting that she *looked* too thin, Yvonne says, "If it had affected my health, Miss Twysden would have put a stop to it. My skin was clearing up, and I was thoroughly enjoying a feeling of lightness on stage that enhanced my interpretation of Prayer and several other roles."

Yvonne's gaunt appearance became an issue after Danilova left the tour to prepare for restaging Petipa's full-length *Raymonda* with Balanchine for the company's spring season at City Center.

I had heard comments behind my back about how emaciated I looked. But I was so idealistic, it never occurred to me that without Mme Danilova around some of those comments would be shared with Denham. Before I realized what was happening, he called me into his suite and said he was sending me home to gain ten pounds. I was so mad, the only thing I remember was that he said several people had "expressed their concerns, that the pressure seemed to be taking its toll on the baby." So I went home, and Momma fattened me up in record time. She loved to cook and made sure I ate lots of biscuits and gravy with every meal. Before she went to teach at Fort Defiance, she was trained as a dietician and agreed I needed to gain a little weight, but she didn't think my strange diet had been unhealthy.

The unexpected respite was as good for her as the home cooking she ate without complaint. Roughly two weeks and twelve pounds later, Yvonne returned to the company. With a green light from Denham, she resumed her duties as a soloist without blinking an eye. To her relief, the incident had no impact on her progress. Balanchine cast her in the Hoop Dance in his new ballet, *Night Shadow,* and she was given a leading soloist role in *Raymonda,* dancing opposite Maria Tallchief, Ruthanna Boris, and Marie-Jeanne. "Of course, with Mme Danilova back, I took off some of the extra weight I didn't need, and no one said a word."

Chapter Twenty-Eight

Center Stage

During her third season with the Ballet Russe, Yvonne began to attract media attention. She was featured in popular women's publications such as *Town and Country* and *Woman's Home Companion,* and her photograph often appeared with reviews of the company in newspapers and dance publications. In the December 3, 1945, issue of *Life* magazine, Yvonne and Patricia Wilde were pictured balancing on the railroad tracks in front of the train station in Cresco, Iowa. The photograph created quite a sensation in Oklahoma, and news stories carrying the date and page number and a brief profile of Yvonne appeared in most local and statewide papers. Publicity pictures were not all that Yvonne collected during the 1945–46 tour. She amassed an impressive assortment of good reviews. Among her most treasured was a review written by the Fort Worth critic Marian Fitzgerald. Citing Massine's *Le Beau Danube,* featuring Danilova as the street dancer and Yvonne as the daughter, as the highlight of the evening's performance, Fitzgerald wrote, "Danilova, who danced with Diaghilev [and] reigned supreme over the company as prima ballerina, danced with confidence. Chouteau danced with hope and joy."

For Yvonne, the physical challenge of spending six to twelve hours a day on the train, performing almost every night, doing matinee and evening performances on weekends, and rehearsing anywhere and anytime the schedule permitted was exhausting, but that was life as a ballet dancer.

It was very hectic and sounds inhumane, but it was all part of the magic of ballet. The conditions we lived through gave us something onstage that I don't see in dancers today. We worked hard to get onstage, and when the curtain went up, it was all worth it because we got to dance. We performed in cities that had never seen ballet before, and because so many of us had been inspired to dance by the first ballet performance we saw in our own hometowns, it was exciting to be part of that magic circle. We were there because we loved to dance, and making the best of difficult situations was a small price to pay.

The company did not even spend the night in some of the cities where it performed. Where one slept was determined by the distance between cities and train schedules.

When we did stay overnight, the train would leave between 6:00 and 7:00 A.M. and arrive in the next city in time to check in at the hotel and grab something to eat on the way to the theater. After performance, if management succeeded in convincing a restaurant or the hotel to keep their kitchen open, we'd eat dinner, get to our rooms by 1:30 or 2:00 A.M., and be ready to leave for the station between 6:00 and 7:00 A.M. the next day. If we were going on to the next city after performance, we could usually get food at the station or on the train and settle into the sleeper cars. Two-day trips were rare and wonderful. We could sleep as long as we wanted the first day, and by the time we'd arrive at our destination, we would have had a day and a half off! During the war, when we gave our Pullman cars up to the troops, you learned to sleep anywhere.

Even without wartime delays and related inconveniences, the company suffered its normal complement of strains, sprains, viruses, and unexpected ailments during the course of its seventy-nine-city winter tour. Arriving in New York barely ten days before the February 17, 1946, opening night of its six-week season at City Center put tremendous pressure on the dancers. That rehearsals of the season's most significant premiere, a Balanchine-Danilova restaging of *Raymonda,* had been subjugated to rehearsing on tour in hotel lobbies, ballrooms, and other equally unsuitable spaces raised the level of anxiety. Creating a streamlined version of Petipa's popular nineteenth-century Russian classic, set to Alexander Glazunov's score of the same name, was an undertaking of mammoth proportions that to succeed needed the more traditional working environment available in New York.

All of the pieces began to fall into place once we began working on it in New York. Mr. Balanchine and Mme Danilova were setting the ballet as they remembered dancing it at the Maryinsky Theatre. They took out a lot of the pantomime and reworked some of the variations but concentrated on maintaining the Petipa style throughout. I adored the ballet, especially because it was the first time I had a solo created for me. The two of them took me into a small studio to set my variation. Mr. Balanchine looked at me, twitched his nose, and said to Mme Danilova, "Well, we must do something suitable for a sixteen-year-old." So my variation was very sweet and lovely.

As the American dance audience had long been denied the opportunity to enjoy the spectacle of a full-length Russian classic, Denham discarded his pinch-penny habits and commissioned Alexandre Benois to create sets and costumes reminiscent of the Russian Imperial style. Partially out of concern that *Raymonda* would not be ready in time and that sustaining box office sales for six weeks would be difficult, Denham scheduled the ballet's premiere late in the season. As anticipated, opening night drew a sold-out crowd that included a large contingent of Russians involved in the New York dance scene, dance critics from major publications across the country, and an excellent showing of noted observers of both art and dance history. Audience response was excellent, and congratulations were passed around backstage with unabashed enthusiasm.

Unfortunately, the reviews published the following day were less than sensational. Although individual performers, including Yvonne, were praised for their execution of brilliant variations, the ballet itself drew conflicting opinions. Having resumed his post as dance critic for the *New York Herald-Tribune* after a distinguished tour of duty in the U.S. Army, Walter Terry captured the gist of the ambivalent critical reaction with the succinct comment: "Stunning—But Silly." Taking a deep breath, Yvonne says, "A full-length ballet set in medieval times with a knight in shining armor, a menacing ogre, and a beautiful damsel just wasn't what audiences and critics wanted to see in 1946. So the first two acts were cut back until we ended up with a one-act ballet that became a staple in our repertoire."

Regardless of the dubious fate of *Raymonda,* Yvonne enjoyed her most successful New York season to date, winning praise from the critics and inclusion in Terry's season wrap-up. The latter cited Yvonne along with Marie-Jeanne, Pauline Goddard, Gertrude Tyven, and Nora White as the most interesting of the company's younger soloists. Yvonne also attracted an audience following. Blushing, she says, "It was not unusual for soloists to have people who came to see them perform certain roles. Mme Danilova always made a point of how important fans were, so I always took the time to see anyone who was allowed backstage to see me." Yvonne also found herself among the favored few who were extended frequent invitations to lunches, dinners, and after-performance soirées hosted by the company's loyal, wealthy supporters. "I remember Joseph Cameron Cross would send elegant invitations to dinner and have a limousine waiting at the stage door for us after performance. It was great fun."

Although Yvonne's father was no longer directly involved in her career, he had not stopped promoting it, as he had since her days on the powwow circuit. "That's how I ended up in *Ripley's Believe It Or Not* syndicated cartoon! Of course, Denham never approved of recognition you received that he didn't arrange, but that didn't stop Daddy." In addition to noting Yvonne's distinction as the youngest American to ever join the Ballet Russe de Monte Carlo, the Ripley illustration pointed out that her family name was pronounced "Show Toe."

By the conclusion of the 1946 spring season at City Center, it was clear that Yvonne's career had entered a new phase. She had gained the technical skills to handle the demands of a far more extensive repertoire and had proven herself at the box office. The unparalleled lyricism, purity of classical line, and haunting, ethereal qualities that had inspired Denham to hire her at age fourteen had been the harbinger of rare artistry and infinite potential. "Everything came together at the right time," Yvonne says. "I finished growing, my technique fell into place, I turned seventeen and graduated from high school, the contractual restrictions were lifted, and I had a firm sense of direction about my career." Yvonne's "coming of age" also coincided with Balanchine's exit as resident choreographer and the beginning of the company's total reliance on independent choreographers. Yvonne fared well under the new regime and immediately found herself cast in the leading role in Nijinska's *Snow Maiden*. Although no ballet would ever unseat *Les Sylphides* as her favorite, Yvonne admits, "There was never a role I loved as much as the Snow Maiden. It was such a joy to perform. That summer we went to Jacob's Pillow for the first time, and I met Ted Shawn!"

A living legend in the American dance world, Shawn is revered for his role in breaking barriers for male dancers, bringing recognition to religious, ethnic, and modern dance styles, and fostering the development of innovative achievements in music. Yvonne says of him, "He seemed to have a great sense of inner peace and strength. I found him inspiring and a very kind, unassuming person." Shawn also was impressed by Yvonne and showed interest in her lyricism and presence onstage. It was the beginning of a lifelong friendship that remains one of her most treasured memories.

The highlight of the Jacob's Pillow engagement was the premiere of Ruth Page's *The Bells*. Originally created for Page's company in Chicago, the ballet was based on the Edgar Allan Poe poem of the same name, with a commissioned score by Darius Milhaud and sets by Isamu Noguchi. The sets were extremely complicated and collapsed around the dancers, creating a visually shocking and somewhat disturbing effect. "Mme Danilova was cast in the role of the Bride, Ruthanna was second cast, and I was the understudy," Yvonne says. Between the ballet's premiere in Jacob's Pillow and its New York debut during the company's September 1946 season at City Center, Danilova decided the ballet was bad luck and asked to be relieved of the role.

227

Ruthanna took over before we left on tour. But when we got to Toronto, Canada, Ruthanna got sick. It was a very difficult ballet to learn, the music was terribly hard to count, and I had found it impossible to throw myself into it the same way I did with my other understudy assignments. So I had twenty-four hours to learn the ballet. Thank heavens for Ruthanna. She had the entire ballet written down, and I learned it from her notes in the hotel. It wasn't a pleasant experience, but it taught me a lesson.

Despite the circumstances, Yvonne's debut in the role won both popular and critical acclaim. The Toronto critic Rose MacDonald did not mince words in her review the following day, calling her performance a red letter occasion. In addition to praising Yvonne's sensitive portrayal, MacDonald wrote, "The performance revealed, in fuller light than has been hitherto possible, the quality of her dancing gift."

Yvonne credits her early childhood for helping her prepare for the rigors of touring. "The powwow circuit and exhibition performing wasn't an easy road for a youngster. I wasn't performing technically difficult dances, but I had to learn to keep my wits about me in different settings. And there were times I didn't get enough sleep and had to push myself to go out and do a good job." She also attributes her good health and lack of injuries to her mother. "Momma was very nutrition-conscious. I always remember her steaming vegetables and telling me that fatty meats and fried foods weren't good for me. I'm convinced I developed proper eating habits that fostered a natural resiliency that kept me in one piece on tour."

Nothing, however, prepared her for being involved in a serious train wreck.

We were going across Indiana and the train hit something on the track and derailed. It was horrible. Three railway workers were killed, but the only injuries anyone in the company suffered were from baggage thrown from the racks above us. Harding Dorn and I were taken to a nearby hospital for observation, but they released us in time to catch up to the company the next day.

Aside from the train accident, Yvonne remembers the tour offering ample opportunity to satisfy her appetite and eagerness to dance.

I was still doing my share of ensemble roles, and enjoyed stepping in for someone in the corps as much as performing a special role. I loved to dance, and to me, being a dancer meant doing whatever needed to be done. I never felt that I was too good to dance in the corps or that by dancing in the corps I was hurting my image. I was very secure with my position in the company and didn't worry about protecting it.

Her feelings about getting involved in company politics were similar.

There was too much work to be done to waste time or lose sleep over anything except your responsibilities onstage. What anyone else did or didn't do was between them and management. The only "free" time I remember was on the train, and that's when I caught up on my sleep.

Yvonne's diligence in maintaining her technique and constant attendance at company classes taught by Danilova and Franklin did not go unnoticed within the company. Nor did her consistently favorable reviews. In Milwaukee, Edward P. Halline was essentially unimpressed by the company as a whole during its October 1946 engagement there but found Yvonne to his liking. Reviewing what he considered a lackluster performance of Massine's *Le Beau Danube*, he wrote, "One bright moment was the girlish, graceful dancing of Mlle Chouteau." Halline also took umbrage at Balanchine's *Mozartiana* with one exception. "[The ballet] had it moments, particularly in the lovely 'Preghiera,' exquisitely danced by Yvonne Chouteau."

With a triumphant smile, Yvonne notes, "It was the first tour that every critic who mentioned me didn't refer to my age!" Yvonne's image as the baby of the company did not change, but any doubts that she brought a mature presence to the stage were laid to rest. Gradually Yvonne began to realize that barring some unforeseen development, her future with the Ballet Russe de Monte Carlo had no limitations other than those she chose to impose.

I knew what I did well. I was not a bravura-style technician who could whip off thirty-two fouettés without blinking an eye or a classical ballerina in the purest sense. I preferred roles I could put my heart and soul into that often were technically challenging but demanded more than executing steps. Every dancer has an individual forte, and mine was being able to create an illusion and express a mood onstage. I gravitated toward those roles, and what is interesting is that Daddy always said he wanted me to be a lyrical or romantic ballerina. And that was the path my career followed.

Chapter Twenty-Nine

Guest Engagements

Although Yvonne's career took her far from the windswept prairies and golden wheat fields of Oklahoma, her growing fame remained a source of pride in the halls of the State Capitol. In the spring of 1947, Yvonne was named the youngest recipient of the state's highest honor, induction into the Oklahoma Hall of Fame. During the layoff following the March 30, 1947, conclusion of the company's City Center season, Yvonne returned to Oklahoma to celebrate with her parents. "It was a great honor for me and extremely significant for my parents," Yvonne says. "All of us were disappointed that I wouldn't be able to attend the ceremonies in November, but in all fairness to Denham, the company really wasn't large enough to spare anyone unless it was an emergency. Personally I thought it was wonderful because Momma received the honor for me!"

During her trip home, Yvonne was also baptized in the Roman Catholic church.

After years of going to Mass, it had started to bother me that I couldn't receive Communion. My friend Judy Aaron worked out the arrangements and I was baptized in the Church of the Sacred Heart in Oklahoma City. She was my sponsor, and I still have the missal she gave me to commemorate the beginning of my life as a Catholic. So it may have been one of the shortest layoffs the company ever had, but it was one of the most important in my life.

Extended layoffs were no longer part of life for the Ballet Russe de Monte Carlo. Denham had succeeded in expanding tour bookings to keep the company on the road between City Center seasons essentially without stop. "Daddy's favorite saying was 'Don't stop to look back, just keep going.' And it might as well have been the motto for the Ballet Russe. Once the season started, you just put your head down and kept going." Although Denham devised a triple bill consisting of *Swan Lake* (Act II), *The Nutcracker* (Act II), and *Scheherazade* that reduced the cost of one-night engagements and drew enthusiastic audience approval, it had little appeal to the dancers.

We called it the "ham and eggs program" and hated it. *Scheherazade* always closed the program, which made it difficult because practically the entire cast wore body makeup, and few theaters had showers back then. We used a water soluble powder called "Texas Dirt," that ran when you sweat and rubbed off on your clothes. It was bad enough when you could take a shower at the hotel, but going on to the next city by train ruined your clothes. Women were not allowed to wear slacks in the Ballet Russe, and the men had to dress nicely as well, so it was very hard to maintain a personal wardrobe.

The whirlwind schedule, however, proved exciting and productive for Yvonne. During the 1947–48 season, she made her debut in the pas de deux in *Les Sylphides* and appeared in both the role of the Page and the Ballerina in company soloist Ruthanna Boris's *Cirque de Deux*.

It was Ruthanna's first commissional work for the company and it premiered during our August engagement at the Hollywood Bowl. It was a parody of the classical pas de deux, featuring two couples in a circus scene, set to Gounod's Walpurgis Night music from *Faust*. Ruthanna was the Ballerina, Patricia Wilde was the Page, and I was second cast for both of them. It was a different kind of ballet for me, and challenged my ability to exhibit a sense of humor onstage.

The only other new works that season were staged by Ruth Page and featured Yvonne as the Angel of Innocence in *Billy Sunday* and the Flirtatious One in *Love Song*. Both premiered on the road, but only *Billy Sunday* was presented during the 1948 spring season at City Center, which, ironically, drew sharp criticism for the lack of new works. "Denham was wrapped up in planning the company's gala tenth anniversary season. There were all kinds of rumors about leaving City Center for the Metropolitan Opera House and what Denham's plans were for the big gala."

As it turned out, the 1948 anniversary season was to be presented at the Met, and the company did boast a full complement of guest artists returning to re-create the glorious past of the Ballet Russe de Monte Carlo. "Massine came to restage *Seventh Symphony* and *Rouge et Noir*. And guest artists included Alicia Markova, Mia Slavenska, Agnes de Mille, Anton Dolin, and José Torres. Dolin set *Pas de Quatre* for Danilova, Markova, Slavenska, and Krassovka, de Mille performed *Rodeo,* and Torres staged *Spanish Dances*." Ruthanna choreographed *Quelques Fleurs,* which was tied in with the unveiling of the Houbigant fragrance of the same name and was underwritten by the perfume company. "It was a wonderfully silly ballet! Gertrude Tyven, Patricia Wilde, and I were cast as the Fragrant Ladies and had great fun doing it. Everyone was excited about dancing at the Met, and it was a gala season in all senses of the word. It was very special and I was thrilled because Massine was with us again."

The anniversary season drew standing room only crowds and prompted critics to declare that the glory of the Ballet Russe de Monte Carlo had returned. Before the Met season ended, word arrived from Chicago that the company's engagement was sold out, a scenario repeated in city after city throughout the duration of the tour.

At nineteen, Yvonne's career was on solid ground and she was discovering maturity. "I fell in love. Or, at least, I thought I had fallen in love. Actually, I think I was trying to prove how mature I was, when in fact I was proving just the opposite." Against everyone's advice, Yvonne married Pierre Monteux, the son of Ballet Russe conductor Claude Monteux. "I was young and convinced I knew better. Of course, I didn't, and we ended up having the marriage annulled in a very short period of time." In spite of the chaos in her private life, Yvonne's command of a repertoire, ideally suited to her ethereal qualities, won tremendous popularity with audiences and critics and earned her top soloist billing following the company's final season at City Center in the spring of 1949.

After her photograph appeared on the cover of the August 1949 issue of *Dance Magazine,* Denham announced she would portray Lady Poverty in the often-promised and long-awaited revival of Massine's *St. Francis* during the company's fall season at the Met. There seemed to be little doubt that the Ballet Russe was preparing to claim its own "baby ballerina." Shrugging her shoulders, Yvonne says,

Denham went back on his word, again. And I essentially gave up hope of ever performing *St. Francis.* That was the point in my career that I began to realize how great a limitation the company's lack of a resident choreographer was for me, and for the rest of the soloists. Without a resident choreographer, it is essentially impossible to develop an artistic identity. Dancers need roles that develop their individual strengths with a sense of continuity and clear artistic focus. Massine was the closest I came to working with a choreographic mentor, and had he been allowed to do the ballets for me he wished, it would have been completely different for me.

Although destined to shape her career without the benefit of a guiding choreographic force, Yvonne was never without an ample supply of new roles. In addition to earning a soloist's role in Danilova's *Paquita,* Yvonne was designated second cast to Danilova in the ballet's leading role. She also was cast opposite Nina Novak as a Junior Girl in a new production of David Lichine's *Graduation Ball* and understudied Novak in the leading role of Antonia Cobos's *The Mute Wife.* The season proved successful at the box office, but with the exception of Lichine's ballet, the critics faulted the company's new offerings as little more than choreographic trifles. At the same time, a number of critics took umbrage at the expanding repertoire of the company's fastest-rising soloist, Novak.

According to Yvonne, the Polish-born dancer had joined the company as a soloist in 1948 at the recommendation of Tatiana Chamié, a noted teacher and choreographer as well as a good friend and frequent adviser to Denham. "Nina was a talented dancer with a flair for certain kinds of roles. She was exceptional as a caractère dancer, but lacked a solid classical foundation. Later that year, Denham brought *Prince Igor* back to the repertoire, and Nina did the best Polovtsian Girl I ever saw." Politely sidestepping comment on the controversial private side of the issue, Yvonne acknowledges that Denham was determined to make Novak a classical ballerina and steered her career in that direction. Contrary to the traditional pattern of ascension in the Ballet Russe, negative reviews citing lack of technical finesse did not impede Novak's acquisition of leading roles. Ultimately the situation proved detrimental to the company, but it was deemed little more than a passing fancy after Denham announced that Paris Opéra ballerina Yvette Chauviré would be joining the company as a guest artist for the 1950 spring season at the Met.

In keeping with standard guest artist policies, Chauviré's contract stipulated that several works from her repertoire would enter the Ballet Russe lineup. In addition to making her debut in the Ballet Russe de Monte Carlo *Swan Lake* and *Giselle,* Chauviré was scheduled to perform former Paris Opéra ballet master Victor Gsovsky's *Grand Pas Classique* and adaptations of Serge Lifar's one-act *Romeo et Juliette* and *Mort du Cygne,* staged by her husband, Constantin Nepo. As expected, Chauviré won tremendous popular acclaim as well as the enthusiastic approval of the New York critics. While some critics took exception to the material she performed, ranking it little more than an excuse to highlight her elusive lyricism, Denham was applauded by others for bringing the American dance world a treasure from abroad.

For the first time in her life, Yvonne was exposed to a ballerina whose ethereal quality onstage and individual strengths were similar to her own. "Chauviré was completely different from any ballerina I had ever seen before. She presented herself beautifully and her face was exquisite, especially as Juliette. She made a lasting impression on me and, really, the entire company."

Unfortunately, Chauviré's triumphant debut season at the Met was her only opportunity to perform in New York with Denham's company. Beginning with the 1950–51 season, New York was dropped from the schedule. Whether unable or unwilling, Denham canceled New York appearances rather than come to terms with the American Guild of Music Artists over a new ruling guaranteeing unemployment benefits for dancers performing in the city's musical theaters during layoffs.

Eliminating our New York seasons was the beginning of the company's downfall. As crucial as touring was financially, New York audiences and critics were the measuring stick for artistic progress. In addition to eliminating the company's only facsimile of home seasons, the decision created serious internal problems. A lot of leading dancers quit, and choreographers who wanted their works seen in New York lost interest.

Despite the development, Chauviré continued to make guest appearances with the Ballet Russe through 1952. The French ballerina did, however, limit her appearances to engagements in major cities and resumed a full performing schedule in Europe.

Having found a kindred spirit in Yvonne, Chauviré expressed great interest in her from the moment she joined the company. But it had not occurred to Yvonne that that would lead to the most important role of her career. "I was completely stunned when she insisted that I be given the opportunity to perform Juliette. She wanted me to do the role and made sure that I did. Being coached by Chauviré was an incredible experience. She was very thorough and made it very clear that she trusted me with the role. There was so much to learn from her, it was a very special opportunity for me." At Chauviré's request, Yvonne was cast opposite Oleg Tupine. "Oleg was wonderful. We danced together in several ballets, but he was always my favorite Romeo."

In addition to working with Chauviré on *Romeo et Juliette,* Yvonne was poised to make her debut in the "Bluebird" pas de deux opposite Leon Danielian, as Cerrito in *Pas de Quatre,* and as the Soubrette in Gsovsky's final work for the Ballet Russe, *Nocturne.*

Shortly after the October premiere of *Nocturne* in Chicago, Chauviré returned to Europe, leaving Yvonne to perform Juliette in her absence. "I had to pay to have my own costume made to perform the role. Denham did a lot of things like that, and we just came to accept them." After making her unofficial debut in the role in a small town in New Jersey, Yvonne's first performance of Juliette in a major city took place on December 1, 1950, in Los Angeles. "Chauviré's absence made it possible for me to perform the role, but when the time came, my only regret was that she wasn't there." Leafing through the pages of a leatherbound scrapbook meticulously put together by a close friend of the family, Yvonne says, "Here is the telegram she sent me from London." Neatly covered with a plastic flap, the Western Union Telegram bears its message forty years later in clear bold type, "GOOD LAKE [sic] FOR ROMEO 1 DECEMBER MY TENDRESSE. YVETTE CHAUVIRÉ."

Closing the book, Yvonne says,

I so much wanted her to see my first performance, but that wasn't possible. Mme Danilova was very excited for me. And since she had coached me in the role after Chauviré left, she was very much a part of my success. Juliette was the first role that I learned to put my heart into and express myself. What was most interesting, for me, was that it wasn't until I actually performed the role that I understood how crucial it was for my development. It felt like no other role I had performed. There was a sense of communication with the audience that was deeply fulfilling and had a significant effect on my attitude about performing. Aside from the major impact it had on my career, it took me a step closer to fully realizing my potential as a performer.

In addition to thunderous audience response, Yvonne was greeted by enthusiastic congratulations backstage. Danilova and Franklin were elated, and the usually noncommital Denham made a point of expressing his approval. The following day, the Los Angeles critics echoed the sentiments of the evening before, hailing Yvonne as a ballerina of exceptional beauty and grace. After all the years spent growing up in the company, Yvonne had unequivocally fulfilled the expectations of her mentors. Before the company left Los Angeles, Yvonne Chouteau was promoted to the rank of ballerina.

Amid a rush of impromptu celebrations honoring her change of status, Yvonne felt an incredible sense of accomplishment and pride. For her parents, her promotion was the realization of a lifelong dream. "Of course, as usual they didn't express any great emotion, but I could sense that they were pleased." Rattling off a string of extraneous benefits ranging from a slight increase in pay to better Pullman accommodations, Yvonne catches herself in midsentence.

What really mattered to me had nothing to do with all of that. I didn't dance to get ahead or make money or become famous. I danced because I couldn't live without it. Dance mattered more to me than anything in the world. It was my life. And as much as I considered it an honor to bear the title ballerina, I was excited because it took me a step closer to performing more fulfilling roles.

Chapter Thirty

Farewell

Following her midseason promotion, Yvonne added two more leading roles to her repertoire, the Snow Queen in *The Nutcracker* and the
Glove Seller in *Gaîté Parisienne*. Looking forward to her first full season as a ballerina, she ignored the usual *St. Francis* promise but felt
confident that everything else Denham spoke of for the 1951–52 season would materialize. According to Denham, there was to be a new
full-length *Swan Lake* in addition to several other new works, and
Massine and Mia Slavenska were slated to join the guest roster. Given
his past success in mustering eleventh hour financial resources to pull
off wildly ambitious plans, it is likely that Denham fully expected to
be able to deliver the season he promised to the American public.

Unfortunately, he failed. With the exception of Massine's *Capriccio Espagnol,* the entire repertoire was drawn from the two previous seasons. And by the conclusion of the tour's opening engagement in Chicago, the star roster had been decimated by the loss of Massine, Slavenska, Franklin, and Danielian.

With Chauviré's appearances few and far between after Chicago, the company set off across the country with no new ballets and a star roster that audiences and critics quickly discovered had nothing to do with reality. Box office sales plummeted, and review after review queried, in not so many words, how long the gems of seasons past could be considered worth the price of a ticket.

The public's dwindling infatuation with the company had little effect on Yvonne's steady rise to fame. Scanning the contents of a large envelope tucked in the back of a souvenir book, Yvonne explains that her father collected reviews. Pulling an oversized glossy collage of review clips from the manila envelope in her hands, she says, "This was one of his favorites." Although pieced together with little regard for the name of the newspaper or critic, each bears a neatly handwritten date—1951. One still attached to a *St. Louis Globe-Democrat* masthead reads, "Topping the bill was the youthfully eager and fresh dancing of Yvonne Chouteau and Alan Howard in the 'Bluebird' pas de deux." Another reads, "Miss Chouteau matches a limpid technical style with a meltingly tender expressiveness. To see her work is to be bewitched." Her portrayal of Juliette was described as "exquisitely youthful, touching and passionate," and her appearance in Boris's *Cirque de Deux* prompted one critic to write, "Many will remember Mlle. Boris herself dancing this merry circus scene some seasons ago, but she would be hard put to top Yvonne Chouteau." The most evocative summary of Yvonne, however, was captured with the words "She has the unusual quality of being able to give the impression of effortless floating in space, of unreality and detachment from the world."

Personal success aside, Yvonne admits the 1951–52 season headed downhill from Chicago. "I knew Leon Danielian had been invited to guest in Europe, and it had been rumored that Slavenska and Franklin were going to form their own concert company. But I don't think anyone expected Massine to retire from the stage in Chicago! At least I had the chance to perform with him in *Gaîté Parisienne* and *Le Beau Danube,* and to say good-bye." Rapidly becoming disillusioned with the direction the company was heading and seeing the Denham-Novak situation continue to worsen as the tour progressed, Yvonne was not surprised when Danilova announced her resignation as a regular member of the company in December 1951. Danilova's exit fueled speculation in the dance world that the collapse of the company was imminent and left the dancers little reason to believe otherwise.

"After Mme Danilova left, everyone knew it was simply a matter of time. But we still had a long tour ahead of us. Denham had booked an August engagement in Mexico City, and from there we were scheduled to perform in South America. So we danced for the audiences and ignored everything else." When the company returned from South America, the dancers were laid off for an undetermined period of time.

No one was surprised. Actually, I think we were all relieved. We were told a small concert company would be sent out to keep the company name alive and that full operation would resume after a major reorganization had been completed. Most of us decided to give Denham a year to get it back together before we started looking elsewhere.

It was the best year in my entire career! It was wonderful to be able to study and concentrate on technique. I made guest appearances with Alan Howard, who was an exquisite classical dancer and one of my favorite partners in the company. And some of us worked in shows or revues put together by other company members, so financially it wasn't devastating. Of course, my parents' first reaction was that I should come home, but they understood how important it was for me to be in New York.

In addition to taking classes at SAB and the Vilzak-Shollar studio, Yvonne worked with Antony Tudor and, for the first time, with Margaret Craske. The latter she credits as having had a major impact on her pointe work. "I never had good feet. But Miss Craske suggested I try working in Freeds, a British-made pointe shoe. The shoes made an incredible difference and my feet changed completely. Of course, it wasn't just the shoes. Miss Craske taught me how to use my feet in ways that no one had ever taught me."

To Yvonne's surprise, Ted Shawn invited her to appear as a guest artist at Jacob's Pillow during the summer of 1953. As it turned out, Tudor had accepted an offer from Shawn as well, under the condition that he could create a pas de deux for Yvonne and Gilbert Reed. In a letter to her parents, Yvonne described the turn of events as the "greatest privilege of all my career and something not to be passed up." Tucked away in the heart of the Berkshires, Tudor created *Little Improvisations* to music from Robert Schumann's Kinderscenen. And the bonds of friendship wove a lifelong alliance between Yvonne and the enigmatic British choreographer. Reviewing the Pillow season for the *New York Herald-Tribune,* Walter Terry cited Tudor's work as the emergence of "a new Tudor" and wrote, "Chouteau has never had a more graceful part and it would be a hard and cold individual who did not lose his heart to her in her dancing." Of greater personal importance to Yvonne was a handwritten note from Shawn reading, "Again, I cannot *tell* you how deeply touched I am by your dancing, and how truly beautiful a *person* is revealed *thru* [sic] your dancing."

Shortly after the first of the year Yvonne received a formal letter from the company office announcing that the Ballet Russe de Monte Carlo had completed negotiations to open a school and would present a 1954–55 season and cross-country tour. The tour was booked under Columbia Artists. Maria Tallchief had signed as guest ballerina, and Massine had agreed to do a new ballet. Among the company's top stars, Gertrude Tyven and Leon Danielian returned, Franklin resumed his dual post as premier danseur and ballet master, and, at Massine's suggestion, Denham hired Argentinean ballerina Irina Borowska to share top billing with Yvonne, Tyven, and Novak. Yvonne was thrilled to be back in rehearsal, and delighted that everyone recognized the difference in her technique. "The first thing everyone noticed was my feet! And because the foot is what shortens or elongates the line of the leg, I had acquired a completely different look in everything I did." In addition to commanding the repertoire she had acquired prior to the company's hiatus, Yvonne was cast as Peep Bo in Antonia Cobos's adaptation of the Gilbert and Sullivan operetta *Mikado* and as the Pilgrim in Massine's *Harold in Italy,* set to the Hector Berlioz score of the same name. Following a chaotic rehearsal period, which required teaching the company's entire repertoire to an essentially new corps de ballet, the company embarked on a thirty-week cross-country tour by bus.

"We were the first major ballet company to travel by bus. And

Yvonne Chouteau and Miguel Terekhov in front of the San Francisco Opera House, 1956. (Personal collection.)

we got to find out how hard it was on dancers' bodies. But it saved management money." Once on the road, the physical strain of traveling by bus was not the only disappointment. Denham wasted little time making it clear he had no intention of letting Novak take a back seat to anyone. To the detriment of Tallchief, Tyven, Borowska, and Yvonne, he insisted on casting Novak in the leading classical role at practically every stop. Faced with what she considered a no-win situation, Yvonne took a long, cold look at her future. "When I realized that my career was not going to advance. I had several alternatives. To stop dancing, go to another company, or begin to make life a little more lively."

Opting for the latter, Yvonne says, "That's when I fell in love with Miguel Terekhov!" Terekhov, the son of a Russian dancer and a native Uruguayan of Indian heritage, also had begun his career at the age of fourteen and rose to acclaim as a soloist in de Basil's Original Ballet Russe. "If I had been passionately devoted to my career, there would have been no time for romance. Gertie [Tyven] and Eugene Slavin had talked me into double-dating a few times in New York, but I was still determined that my career came first. Of course, the minute I showed a change of heart, I found myself in the midst of a whirlwind courtship that led to marriage within a year!"

While the Denham-Novak situation had a chilling impact on morale, Yvonne's attention was divided between performing four ballets a night and enjoying her new-found social life. Had Yvonne needed any encouragement that she was following the right path, the Chicago critic Ann Barzel unwittingly reminded her. After several viewings of *Harold in Italy,* Barzel wrote, "Without a doubt, Massine has found a quality in [Yvonne Chouteau] which has been hinted, but never exploited to its full extent. It is in the realm of true dance."

While Yvonne won popular and critical acclaim and the company as a whole succeeded in garnering a fair share of positive reviews, there was growing dissention over the constant promotion of Novak. After Tallchief made it clear she had no intention of returning to the company after fulfilling her contract, Denham convinced Mia Slavenska to return as guest artist for the company's July engagement at Lewisohn Stadium. While New York critics soft-pedaled their objections to various signs of familiar problems, Denham worked behind the scenes to pull off yet another major coup—signing Alicia Alonso and former Ballet Russe premier danseur Igor Youskevitch for the 1955–56 season. Denham's success in luring Alonso and Youskevitch away from Lucia Chase's Ballet Theatre set off an avalanche of interest from the dance press, but veteran Ballet Russe members deferred comment.

The company's future had, once again, been placed in the hands of outsiders. Growing increasingly aware that she had found a personal relationship that would endure the test of time far beyond the limits of her performing career, Yvonne viewed the arrival of Alonso and Youskevitch as a potential boon.

To have such great artists to learn from was an honor, and most of us responded as such. By that time, Alonso was almost completely blind. We all did things to help her find the wings during performances, and make sure she was where she needed to be for entrances. She picked me to stand in for her during *Giselle* rehearsals and taught me the role. I didn't have the opportunity to perform the role with Denham's company, but I will never forget her telling me, "You must do something new, every time you perform a role."

During the 1955–56 season, Yvonne was cast with Tyven and Howard in Balanchine's *Pas de Trois.* "It was a wonderful ballet, and having the challenge of doing a Balanchine ballet new to me after so many years was exciting. Especially since I knew the history of the ballet." Originally commissioned by the Marquis de Cuevas in 1948 as *Pas de Trois Classique,* featuring Rosella Hightower, Marjorie Tallchief, and André Eglevsky, Balanchine revised the work and renamed it *Pas de Trois* in 1951 for New York City Ballet. "I did the role created for Marjorie, and had great success in it."

In the midst of the company's Chicago engagement, Yvonne and Terekhov were married in a civil ceremony. "My parents had met Miguel when we went through Oklahoma, and liked him very much. So we had their approval. Denham, however, threw a fit. He never wanted any of his 'girls' to get married!"

That season, Yvonne was finally allowed to fulfill her role as Goodwill Ambassadress of Oklahoma. "Denham suddenly decided it was a good thing for the company to have me make an official visit to the mayor of every city on tour to extend a symbol of friendship from the state of Oklahoma. I think the fact that I had been appointed Miss Oklahoma Semi-Centennial and invited to participate in a number of events during the yearlong celebration had something to do with his decision."

Unfortunately, Denham also initiated a policy during the 1955–56 season that called for the curtain to be lowered by the clock at every performance, regardless of whether the final ballet had been completed or not. "All of us were outraged. Youskevitch even issued a statement to the press denouncing the policy. We never knew when the curtain would come down in *Gaîté Parisienne* because it was always the last ballet. More times than I like to remember, we stood there staring at the curtain with part of the ballet left to dance!"

Returning to New York for rehearsals, Yvonne and Miguel wasted no time getting married in a Roman Catholic church. "In those days, your vows had to be read from the pulpit at Mass three Sundays in a row. Since we were so rarely anywhere three weeks in a row, we didn't hesitate."

Despite growing evidence that the artistic future of the company was in great jeopardy, Denham announced the Ballet Russe de

Monte Carlo would return to the Met during the 1956–57 season with Danilova and Franklin augmenting the current guest roster.

Shortly after the Met season was announced, Yvonne and Miguel discovered that they were expecting their first child.

At the time, it didn't occur to us that I would be more than six months pregnant by the opening of the Met season. And since I had no problems, and showed very little, I went ahead and danced. It wasn't exactly the way I envisioned making my farewell performance with the company, but that is the way it turned out. It was a very happy season for me. With Madame Danilova and Franklin back, it was like old times, and I enjoyed quite a bit of success.

On July 31, 1957, Christina Maria Terekhov was born at New York's Lenox Hill Hospital. "I took maternity leave, stayed in New York with Christina, and got back into shape. Miguel went with the company to Puerto Rico and when he returned we decided to resign. We still wanted to dance, but we didn't want to be separated. So we decided to go to the Montevideo State Opera as guest artists and stay with Miguel's parents."

As difficult as Yvonne found it to say good-bye to the Ballet Russe de Monte Carlo and the people who had been part of her life since she arrived in New York in 1941, she admits, "I no longer had the 'do or die' attitude, and it was important to stop before losing focus."

Part III

Shaping the Future of Dance

Chapter Thirty-One

Dallas, Texas

Marjorie returned to New York with her husband after a triumphant farewell performance at the conclusion of the Harkness Ballet's engagement at the 1966 Marais Festival in Paris. "Youra renewed his contract with the company, and I moved into my sister's town house with the boys. Both of them were very well behaved and never had any problems in school or anywhere else. But they were boys, and they were teenagers, and they needed me there."

Having worked very hard to establish and maintain a strong family unit despite the demands of a professional career, Marjorie did not suddenly find herself facing the task of parenting at the eleventh hour. In retrospect, she admits having looked forward to life without touring. "I knew I would miss performing, but as much as I enjoyed aspects of going on tour, I had done my share. I did make a few guest appearances, performing in Canada twice and appearing with a symphony here and there, but that was about it. So the boys and I settled into being on our own. I never really felt completely at ease living in the city without Youra, but we did fine."

As it turned out, Marjorie and the twins did not have to live in New York City without Skibine for very long. Within six months of his wife's departure from the company, Skibine relinquished his post as artistic director of the Harkness Ballet. Marjorie was pleased with her husband's decision. He had succeeded in establishing a strong artistic focus for the troupe and created some excellent works. Skibine exited gracefully, leaving his ballets in the company's repertoire and remaining on good terms with Mrs. Harkness.

Youra liked Mrs. Harkness, and she often called him for advice, which he was more than happy to extend. He really had enjoyed the challenge of building the company. There always was a lot of internal turmoil, but to him that was part of the creative environment. Years later after we had moved to Dallas, Texas, Mrs. Harkness brought her second company to perform in the city. She called Youra aside and said "See, these dancers are well behaved." And his reply was simply, "Yes, but artists are not well behaved."

The initial transition from performer to teacher was difficult for Marjorie.

Shortly after I retired to take care of the twins, they announced they wanted to study ballet. They had been studying piano for years, and actually were quite good. Then, all of a sudden, it was "We want to take ballet classes." Youra and I agreed to let them. But he insisted that they would have to take classes for a full year. Of course, I decided I would teach them myself. Well, I could have killed them both! They were impossible! Finally we decided they needed to go to the School of American Ballet, so Youra made arrangements for them to enroll with the directors of the school, Natasha Gleboff and Eugenie Ouroussow.

It was difficult because Alex and George were already fourteen so you couldn't put them in a child's beginners class. The only place for them was in an adult beginners class. Of course, that didn't last long. They were very unhappy. They would come home and complain that they couldn't possibly learn anything because everyone in their class was a cripple. It was terrible. Natasha wasn't at all surprised, and arrangements were made for the two of them to have private classes with Muriel Stuart. I never went to see them in class, but my husband did. Youra thought Alex showed quite a bit of promise, but neither of them kept up with it. They did their year and that was the end of it.

The experience of teaching her teenage twins ballet had no lasting effect on Marjorie's interest in teaching. It was, instead, a short-lived episode in her otherwise pleasant adjustment to "civilian life." News of Skibine's resignation from the Harkness Ballet prompted a number of offers from companies interested in his directorial talents. Although he was receptive to engagements as a guest choreographer, he showed no interest in directing another troupe. "That's when we moved to Dallas, and I was thrilled. I thought it would be great to go there, retire, and do nothing. Of course, it didn't work out that way because Youra always had to be doing something. But we moved to Dallas and found a wonderful house."

Living in Dallas made trips to Fairfax an easy five-hour drive. And once settled, Marjorie and her husband began teaching. Soon Skibine became involved in establishing a consortium of teachers in the area.

There was very little in Dallas as far as dance when we arrived. There wasn't much of an audience for ballet, with the exception of a small group of supporters. But there were some very good dancers and a lot of good boys. In the beginning, I taught because I thought it was my duty. I just accepted that it was my responsibility to pass on what I was taught by the great teachers I was fortunate enough to have studied with and what I had learned from my own career. Gradually, I started to realize that I really enjoyed it and liked the challenge.

Given the talent at hand, Marjorie was not surprised by her husband's decision to stage a production of *Firebird* to see if community support could be raised to the level necessary to establish a civic company in Dallas. "The only thing I did not like about the idea was that it meant I had to perform again! And it was very difficult because I

251

hadn't been onstage for so long. But it was a wonderful production, the students did extremely well, and it became the catalyst for starting the Dallas Civic Ballet."

The company grew rapidly. The community offered enthusiastic support, and a cadre of volunteers turned ideas into reality without hesitation. A formal board of directors with a guild to augment fund-raising activities was formed, and a small administrative staff was hired to allow Marjorie and Skibine to concentrate their efforts on the school and company. Within a year of entering the realm of civic ballet companies, the troupe won acceptance as a member of the National Association of Regional Ballet (NARB). Participation in NARB festivals followed and the company began gaining recognition outside Texas. "Mrs. Harkness also helped us. She had been very interested in what we were doing all along, and she decided to give us sets and costumes from the company that were no longer being used."

The twins did not share their parents' delight with life in Dallas. "I'm not really sure why, but they didn't like Texas at all. When it came time for them to go to college, they both decided on schools outside Texas. George went to the University of Chicago and Alex went to Tufts University. It was the first time they had been apart since they were born, but that was what they wanted." Once in college, both boys decided to pursue careers in law. Again, they chose different law schools, George completing his law degree at the University of Minnesota and Alex completing his at Northwestern University.

"Today," Marjorie says, "Alex is a law professor in Utah and George is director of gaming for the Bureau of Indian Affairs. They are still very close, but I don't think they actually spend much time together. Alex and his wife, Jackie, have two children, Sasha and Natalie. George and his wife, Gail, have two boys, Adrian and Trevor." Talking about the twins, Marjorie expresses pride in the fact that they have found success in their chosen careers and, more important, seem to be enjoying life. To her surprise, neither of the boys have shown any interest in returning to Europe where they spent so much of their childhood. "They keep in touch with friends there and always are glad when one of them comes to visit, but they have no desire to go back themselves."

Once the twins went off to college, Marjorie and Skibine were free to focus their undivided attention on building the company in

Dallas. By the mid-1970s, the troupe was successfully touring in the South and Midwest and beginning to attract dancers from outside the region. Consistent and swift progress led to considerations of expanding the troupe beyond the realm of its "civic" ballet company roots. "That's when Youra took the lead in efforts to develop a professional wing within the NARB. There was quite a bit of interest among the member companies to expand the scope of the organization to include companies taking the next step, but nothing ever really came of it. Finally, we went ahead with our own plans and became a professional company known as the Dallas Ballet."

As the company grew, production budgets grew and Skibine launched rehearsals for a full-length *Coppélia* with sets and costumes designed by his cousin. "It was a great success," Marjorie says, pointing to elegantly framed illustrations of the first act backdrop and costume designs. The troupe continued to build a solid reputation and in late 1980, negotiations were launched for a summer residency in Santa Fe, New Mexico. During the course of completing the contract, it became apparent that Skibine was ill. He was diagnosed as having Guillain-Barre syndrome, a disease that attacks the central nervous system. On January 14, 1981, he succumbed. Marjorie does not discuss her husband's death but credits her sons with handling details in Dallas while Maria and Buzzy helped with arrangements for her move to Chicago. Although Marjorie immediately made known her intention to leave Dallas, she stayed on to help with the transition to a successor and saw the troupe through the Santa Fe residency as planned.

Having spent a fair amount of time in Chicago, Marjorie adjusted to her new surroundings quickly. "But I never got used to the cold. I had to buy a fur coat for the first time in my life!" The weather was not the only thing she found cold in Chicago. "I don't really know why, but Chicago is not a good town for ballet. Coming from Dallas, where we had so many people supporting what we were doing, it seemed to me people were trying to defeat what my sister was trying to do in Chicago." Taking charge of the faculty at the school, which had been in existence just shy of two years, Marjorie focused her energies on improving the roster of teachers. "We had some very good dancers and the studios were wonderful. The school came along very nicely and we built a very solid foundation." Marjorie also was instrumental in developing a successful summer residence program to attract students from out of state.

Initially the school's reputation as a superior training ground for preprofessional dancers proved sturdy enough to weather the side effects of the widely publicized demise of the Chicago City Ballet. "We lost some students for a short time, but that was as much because of the confusion created by the way the company was taken away from Maria than anything else. And it had no effect on the students we attracted from outside Chicago. Our 1987 summer residence program attracted students from twenty-eight states and Canada." Unfortunately, shortly after former New York City Ballet principal dancer Daniel Duell was hired to replace Maria Tallchief as director of the Chicago City Ballet in 1987, the school once again became a political football.

Chapter Thirty-Two

Florida via Chicago

In 1989, amid the battle for control of the School of Chicago Ballet, Marjorie received an invitation to take over the reins of the dance faculty at the Harid Conservatory in Boca Raton, Florida. As had been the case throughout her distinguished twenty-two-year performing career, the offer was extended rather than solicited. In Marjorie's eyes, the fact that opportunity continues to preclude the need for a plan in her life is of little consequence. "That is how it has always been." A charter member of the roster of internationally renowned guest teachers at the fledgling conservatory, Marjorie was approached to take the position by longtime friend and Harid founding director, Jeannot Cerrone.

Marjorie's decision to leave the position she had held at her sister's Chicago school since her husband passed away in 1981 drew enthusiastic support from Maria.

She was all for it. Maria thought going to Boca Raton was a wonderful opportunity and kept saying "Go, the potential is unlimited. And because Jeannot is there, everything will be done right." And, of course, Alex and George agreed wholeheartedly. They thought it would be great if I lived in Florida so they would have to go to Florida to see me. At that point, only Alex had children and they came to visit quite a bit. Sasha and Natalie loved going to the Chicago Zoo and we would have picnics in the park across the street from my apartment. The boys also enjoyed seeing Maria, Buzzy, Elise, and Saruth, who they still call Sou. They both worked for Buzzy on construction jobs during the summers when they were younger, and it was a good experience for them. Even today, when they get together with Elise it is amusing because the three of them fight the way they did while they were growing up. I guess it will always be that way.

For Marjorie, the privately endowed, comprehensive arts education program established in 1988 in Boca Raton offered more than a change of scenery. Modeled after the state-supported conservatories of Europe and the Soviet Union, the Harid Conservatory admits only those students who demonstrate academic proficiency and sufficient talent in auditions held annually across the country to qualify for scholarship assistance. It is a bright spot on the horizon of preprofessional dance training in America, offering high school and university-level academic courses. The conservatory owes its existence to the largesse of an anonymous donor: in return for a $30 million contribution, the donor requested simply that a conservatory bearing the name Harid be created to provide study and living space for gifted students irrespective of their ability to pay tuition.

"The situation at the conservatory is ideal. The approach is very Renaissance, and more like the opera schools in Europe than what we have here in America. The students are handpicked in nationwide auditions and committed to becoming dancers or at least working in the field of dance." Harid students live on campus and attend academic courses at the College of Boca Raton and a nearby private high school. The academic curriculum at Harid is hardly reminiscent of

Marjorie's high school experience, which permitted early graduation for successfully completing a horticulture course at home. In addition to standard academic courses that include financial management and computer basics, students are required to study music and dance history, music theory, drama, and Labanotation. "The students work very hard. And for those who have studied only classical ballet, taking classes in modern, jazz, character, and Spanish technique is a new experience. It isn't easy being a professional dancer either."

Watching Marjorie teach and coach young dancers is testimony to her even-tempered personality and unlimited patience. The antithesis of her stern mentor, Bronislava Nijinska, in the classroom, Marjorie cajoles elements of classical style from her students with gentle prodding and untiring repetition.

Raising two boys taught me a lot of things and having patience was one of them. Ballet is constantly evolving, and today's young dancers are different than we were. I remember the first time I worked with Mr. Balanchine, he didn't want the extension in arabesque to rise above the middle of the spine. A year or so later, his dancers had their legs up around their ears in arabesque. My own attitude toward teaching has changed over the years as well. I used to put more emphasis on physical characteristics, but now I feel that the student who truly wants to dance, will dance. And that there will be a place for that dancer—somewhere. It is no longer so much whether you are tall, short, thin, or muscular but the illusion you give. How you use your body is more important than meeting some current aesthetic preference.

She is adamant, however, that as good as change is, there are rules.

I don't agree with people who contend that dancers today are technically more proficient than dancers were years ago. There is so much less emphasis on style, role interpretation, and exact positions today that few of the recent revivals of major works I have seen bear any resemblance to the originals. Ballet is more than steps, and it really doesn't matter how many pirouettes you can do. If you ignore the style and do away with the clean positions demanded by the choreography, I don't think you've accomplished anything.

After taking the reins at Harid, Marjorie continued to be involved with the school in Chicago, returning as a guest teacher and to help prepare the students for concerts. "I went back when I was needed and Maria joined our guest faculty at Harid for the 1989–90 school year. It worked out very well, and I kept track of my students in Chicago." Discussing the advantages of Harid, Marjorie explained that the students were exposed to former stars as well as contemporary choreographers, artistic directors, and heads of major schools around the world. The list of guest teachers engaged since the conservatory opened in 1988 reads somewhat like the guest rosters popularized during the era of the Ballets Russes, with an impressive mix of legendary European, Russian, and American artists. Until her resignation from Harid in 1993 to explore life without daily classes and schedules, Marjorie fully enjoyed being immersed in an atmosphere reminiscent of Nijinska's Hollywood studios where she came of age and the European environment where she took her place in the history of dance.

In November 1991, Marjorie returned to Oklahoma to be inducted into the Oklahoma Hall of Fame and attend the unveiling of a mural honoring the state's Indian ballerinas created by the Oklahoma Indian artist Gary Larsen in the Great Rotunda of the Oklahoma State Capitol. "It was a great honor for me and very exciting. Alex and George were there, and so was my uncle George Tall Chief, who brought other relatives from Fairfax."

Today, Marjorie is as happy-go-lucky as ever and enjoying retirement. "I really find it quite nice and don't miss teaching or coaching at all. I did my share and now I do whatever I feel like doing. And, of course, Alex and George and their families visit frequently and when Maria and Buzzy are here we spend time together as usual. It is really quite nice not having anything to do."

Chapter Thirty-Three

Cannes, France

In 1988 I watch Rosella Hightower Robier teach class at her Centre de Danse International Rosella Hightower in Cannes. The pristine white studio in its lush setting looks as I have remembered it. And the glances of good-natured chagrin her young students exchange are reminiscent of those shared by Harkness Ballet dancers when Rosella demonstrated difficult combinations of turns and jumps with breathless precision. She steps nimbly up on a chair to see the dancers in the back row as the pianist begins to play. Within seconds, she claps her hands to stop both movement and music. As she jumps down from her perch and taps her ear, she signals the pianist to begin the introduction. "Regardez!" Standing in fifth position, she exaggerates

Rosella Hightower teaching class, Cannes, France, 1986. (Personal collection.)

bringing her back foot from fifth position to begin the combination simultaneously with the first note of the melody. Resuming her perch, she signals the pianist and dancers to begin again. "Violà! Tres bien," she remarks as the first group scatters, and the second steps into position.

Later, Rosella blushes slightly when asked how she has managed to sustain the undeniable spark of virtuosity. "I don't realize it. People tell me I do things in class that surprise me. Once I get warmed up, it happens without thinking. I guess it's second nature, at least to the degree it takes to demonstrate a combination." Talking about her school, Rosella radiates a vibrancy that bounces off the walls of the tiny room she shared with the former school administrator, the late Jean-Luc Barsotti.

The energy must come from the top. If I am dragging myself around, then everyone else will. I have to set the example for the other teachers. So it is very important for me to keep on top of what I am doing. That way, everyone does, and we create a sort of energy pool that can be drawn from when needed. The students work so hard, they need to see our energy or they won't be able to sustain the pace. It is very difficult for them here. We have students from twenty-two countries and we only speak French at the school. On top of that, this is the first time most of them have had their academic achievement measured as much as their progress in the studio.

In addition to offering the standard French college preparatory diploma, the school is enrolled in the International Baccalaureate Degree Program. The latter, established in Geneva, Switzerland, in 1967, is based on uniform academic requirements set to establish a benchmark of academic excellence around the world. It is currently offered in more than sixty nations and is considered the most demanding academic curriculum extended at the high school level. Course studies emphasize analytical skills over memorization, and students must score four out of a possible seven points on the program's final examinations to qualify for a diploma. Independent study assignments include preparing a fifteen-page research paper and completing a creative, aesthetic, or social project requiring a minimum of one hundred hours. In keeping with the international scope of the program, final examinations and research papers are graded independently from the issuing school. Although Rosella was aware that the International Baccalaureate program had been introduced in America in 1970, she was pleased to hear that it has been offered since 1984 at Booker T. Washington High School in Tulsa, Oklahoma. "I certainly hope the program is successful enough in Tulsa to find its way to more than one school in the state. It offers tremendous opportunity and challenge for students, no matter what career plans they have."

Acknowledging that her Choctaw ancestry may account for her interest in education, Rosella adds, "The caliber of the academic program we offer our students is as important to me as what they learn in the studio. They need to be challenged on a mental as well as physical level to develop the discipline to succeed in life. It puts more pressure on them while they are here. But if they pass the entrance requirements, we know they are capable of succeeding, and the end results are simply a matter of application."

Challenge, opportunity, discipline, and application remain the cornerstones of Rosella's approach to life. Watching her teach, finding her working in her office long after everyone has left, and listening to the observations of those around her remove any doubt that, much like her virtuoso quality, her insatiable appetite for hard work remains intact. It is evident that the school is a manifestation of Rosella's commitment to passing on the legacy of ballet, as she knows it. In 1995 the school faculty list included founding members Rosella and Jean Robier and former Grand Ballet du Marquis de Cuevas dancers Arlette Castanier and José Ferran.

In 1988 there were one hundred sixty students, sixty of whom were enrolled in the resident program. Space to accommodate dance, music and academic classes and rehearsal space for Le Jeune Ballet International, a semiprofessional company then under the direction of the American teacher Edward Cook, was scarce. Although space has been a problem since 1988, a solution has been found. At the beginning of the 1995–96 school year, the school boasts a new facility, new to the school, but hardly new to Cannes. Rosella explains, "We took a historic hotel and converted it into exactly what we needed. There is still lots to be done, but somehow we will be ready when school opens."

In addition to having little difficulty placing dancers in professional dance companies around the world, the school has become the primary training ground for prospective teachers.

In Europe, much like the United States, we have many people opening schools who do not have the proper training. It is impossible to take those people away, but we succeeded in establishing a national standard for dance teachers in France. I made a great effort to see this become a reality. Now to teach dance in France you must have a State Teaching Diploma. It is a crucial element of our school. We developed a program designed to train teachers and prepare them to pass the State Teaching Technical Exam to obtain the diploma.

The teaching program is open to graduate students and focuses on extended course studies in kinesiology, dance and music history, theory of choreography, and musical composition as well as hands-on teaching experience under the supervision of the school's faculty.

Rosella explains, "All of our prospective students must 'audition' during the summer or by attending a mini-spring session to enroll in the full-year program. Sometimes we make exceptions, but generally we insist the students come first for the short session or the summer. That way, they see what it is like and our faculty has the necessary time to properly evaluate their abilities."

Student evaluations are a constant part of life. A computer monitoring system developed by Barsotti reads bar-coded student identification cards to track attendance, grades, meals, and participation in outside activities. Because of the academic challenge facing the students, testing is done every three months to determine if tutoring or other assistance is needed. Test results are included in progress reports sent to parents with comments from faculty members involved with each individual student. Parents also receive updates from Hélène Dore, headmistress of the academic program.

Students who do not speak or read French when they enroll enter a four-month accelerated course that has proven extremely successful. "We are the ideal immersion camp. When your only means of communication is French, you learn very quickly. Usually, before students have been here six months, they have completely mastered the language." Acknowledging that learning a second language offers the students an advantage in meeting the language requirement for an International Baccalaureate diploma, Rosella says, "So you see, as difficult as their academic schedule is, they have little difficulty meeting the language, art, and creative project requirements."

The school also employs dieticians who dictate menus, prepare the food, and instruct the students in proper diet.

It's very interesting to watch the students react to different foods and different combinations of foods from what they are used to eating. Quite naturally, coming from all over the world, they bring their own ideas of what is a balanced diet. But once they see the benefits of what we serve them in the mirrors in the studios, they start to understand why we make so much noise about it. Since dancers today can afford to eat properly, they must learn good dietary habits.

With the noonday Mediterranean sun filtered through translucent windowpanes illuminating her smile, Rosella says softly, "And here I am. Where I told people in Kansas City I would be more than half a century ago."

Chapter Thirty-Four

At the Artistic Helm

Watching a soft rain drench the neatly trimmed lawn edged with brightly colored flowers in the courtyard of their villa in the hills above Cannes, Rosella and Jean Robier share a mirthful look. Speaking in a thick French accent, Robier says, "Rosella is always go, go, go," as he makes a delicate flicking movement of his hands, "There is no slowdown or what you call retirement. It is the same, always." Rosella explains,

I am like my mother, who would come visit us for exactly two weeks every year because that was how long she could be away from her work. When she didn't have to work anymore, she opened a residence in Kansas City

265

where airline pilots and crew members stayed. She loved working there and wouldn't consider putting someone else in charge because that would have left her with nothing to do. Some of us have no interest in doing whatever it is people do when they retire.

Since her late 1965 appearances with the Grand Ballet Classique de France in China, she has encountered more opportunities than even her vision for the future held.

For me, China was the end of my performing career. I continued to appear in galas to raise funds for the school for some time, but it was never the same after China. Claude Giraud booked a Far East tour for the company, shortly after de Gaulle reopened diplomatic ties with China. It was terribly exciting for everyone. In the company, we had students from the school, a few professionals, and myself, Nina Vyroubova, Liane Daydé, and Juan Giuliano. We were very well received and had great success.

In addition to generating international interest in the school, the Far East tour brought Rosella the distinction of being named to the French Legion of Honor. Established in 1802 by Napoleon to recognize outstanding achievement in military or civil life, the national society of merit remains the highest tribute extended by the French government. Robier explains, "There is no greater recognition in France. There are three levels of decoration, but only by receiving the first may you receive the second, and third." Rosella adds quickly, "I have now received all three. The first was given in honor of our success in China and the second after I completed my term at the Paris Opéra. Now, I have just received a letter notifying me I am to receive the third for my work here at the school. It is always a surprise to be honored. I like to think it is because dance is important in France that my work is considered a great service to the nation."

Between 1969 and 1986 one opportunity led to another and commuting became a way of life. "It started when I was asked to take over direction of the opera ballet in Marseille. After working with the company for three years, I helped bring Roland Petit to take over my post and I moved on to the company in Nancy." Three years later, she left that company in the capable hands of Janine Monin and returned to Cannes. A combination of Rosella's success in Marseille and Nancy,

266

the wisdom of her choice of successors, and her tremendous popularity in the French dance world led to her appointment as director of the Paris Opéra Ballet in 1980. Accepting the post required hiring a full-time teacher and an administrator to take over the lion's share of Rosella's daily work. "I felt that after almost twenty years, if the school wasn't structured well enough to stand alone, then I had really made some very great errors along the way. Of course, having built the school from scratch, I wanted to think I was indispensable. But I wasn't." Commuting back and forth actually proved beneficial for Rosella. "It was very helpful for me. I could do my paperwork on the train without any interruptions. When I arrived here, I would teach a few classes at the school, make sure everything was in order, and spend the train ride back thinking about decisions that needed to be made. It was hectic, but very rewarding."

Rosella takes pride in having devised a structure for the Paris Opéra company that gave everyone more flexibility, and ultimately more opportunity to perform.

What I did was divide the company into three groups or what I call "programations." The largest concentrated on the classics and traditional repertory suitable for the stage and audience of the Paris Opéra House. The second, more compact division focused on more contemporary works in both the ballet and modern idioms that were suitable for touring and appearances at the Champs-Élysées Theatre. The third consisted of a dozen volunteers, concentrated on experimental works under Jacques Garnier in the Groupe de Recherche Chorégraphique de l'Opéra de Paris. The GRCOP, as it is called, performed at the Opéra-Comique and toured regional cultural centers. I used the term "programations" because at the Opéra programming is done a year in advance. I allowed the dancers to have some say in which programation they were to be assigned. Principals or étoiles were free to move from one to the other, and I was very clear that assignments were to be made every year. That way, a dancer would not be forever destined to perform only one kind of repertoire or locked into a touring or nontouring situation. You cannot expect to do everything you wish at the Opéra. But it is possible to have an impact.

Among her other accomplishments in Paris, she cites elevating a total of eight dancers to the status of étoile, achieving an equitable balance in the repertoire between the traditional classics and contemporary creations and bringing audiences across France a long-overdue glimpse of the nation's primary national ballet company. According to Madame Josseline Le Bourhis, Paris Opéra Ballet archivist, Rosella's contributions to the Opéra were far more significant. Speaking with the help of an interpreter, Le Bourhis says,

She was very well liked by the dancers. And that was essential because Rosella was appointed at a difficult time at the Opéra. The entire staff was in a state of change, Bernard Lefort had just been appointed to complete the term of Rolf Liebermann as administrator general, and Rosella replaced Violette Verdy, who had resigned before her term had expired. So there was much confusion and upheaval for the one hundred fifty dancers. Rosella was very clever. She developed a new structure for the company and put in tremendously long hours to make it all work. She made many changes, but she showed great reverence for the traditions of the Opéra."

Les Saisons de la Danse editor, Andre Philippe Heresin, concurred.

Rosella worked very hard for the dancers, and in return, they worked very hard for her. She reorganized the structure, sent a group from the Opéra to tour cities across France, and brought back the "Grand Défilé," or procession of the entire company at performance end, which had not been done since Lifar in 1945. She also put into practice the old rule that guest artists do not appear with the company on tour. She was amazing for all the hours she put in. It was as if she never slept. I remember seeing her leave the Opéra on her way to Cannes loaded with satchels of paperwork, and two days later she would be back here teaching class as if she had never left the city. Her stamina was unlimited, and I think it was perhaps that element which the dancers sensed and responded to with her. They knew she was going back and forth to her school, and still never showed fatigue or any loss of energy.

Repeating the pattern of her directing career, Rosella held the post for a single three-year term and enthusiastically welcomed Rudolf Nureyev as her successor. "I thought he was well suited to the environment at the Opéra and could be effective without being drawn into the infamous politics of the institution. When Nureyev put his foot down, people jumped, and in some ways that is what it takes at the Opéra." Before leaving Paris, Rosella received an invitation to assume the post of director of the ballet at La Scala.

I accepted, because I felt it would be a good opportunity to apply what I had learned in Paris.

You have to remember that in Europe all of the government-supported opera houses have ballet companies. Each has its share of limitations as to how many hours the dancers are allowed to work, how many dancers are employed, and for how many years dancers may continue performing. At La Scala the company is very much a family affair, which makes it even more difficult to bring younger dancers up quickly. But I was able to make some progress in that direction and in bringing some contemporary choreographers in at the same time.

Another major problem Rosella faced in Italy was the constant threat of workers going out on strike in the middle of the night.

I remember going to the theater in Milan one morning to teach class and discovering that it was closed. The reason was simple—the custodians were on strike. By the time I got back to my hotel, I found out all the housekeepers were on strike and guests were responsible for cleaning their rooms, changing their linen, and so on and so forth. Now it's funny, but at the time it was very frustrating. I can't remember how many times I repeated my great-grandmother's words, "Life goes good, life goes bad, and you must live through both phases."

In mid-1986, two and a half years after taking over the company in Milan, Rosella turned the reins over to Patricia Neary.

I felt she was the right person for the situation there, and she did a very good job. I am proud of what I was able to accomplish with each company. And for being able to help place the right people in each situation when I left.

Chapter Thirty-Five

The Adventure Continues

Rosella's success as a director proved beneficial for her school. Enrollment had reached an all-time high by the conclusion of her term at La Scala. On her return to Cannes in late 1986, she immediately resumed a daily schedule of classes and other duties at the school to ease the pressure on other faculty members.

The school had grown tremendously, partially because of my work and partially because we were beginning to get "second-generation" students. Many of our graduates who enjoyed successful careers had left the stage to teach or run companies and began sending students to study in Cannes. Maina Gielgud, for instance. She was an exceptionally gifted dancer and

271

had a fabulous career as a ballerina in Maurice Béjart's company, London Festival, which is known today as the English National Ballet, and as a guest artist in major companies around the world. Maina came to take classes here on a regular basis, and when she took over as director of the Australian Ballet in 1983, she began sending students to us. She also has been back as a guest teacher several times. It is very rewarding to see students of former students come to us, and to see that they have been well trained.

The list of companies boasting alumni—among others, the Royal Danish Ballet, Pina Bausch's Wuppertal Dance Theatre, Les Grands Ballets Canadiens, the Martha Graham Company, the Paris Opéra, Béjart's Ballet Lausanne, the Stuttgart Ballet, the Maguy Marin company, London Festival Ballet, and Chopinot—is testimony to the eclectic training offered at the school. Chopinot is the company Rosella's daughter, Monet, worked with during the late 1980s.

They do fantastic creations that incorporate elements of theater, costume design, and decor in very unusual ways. She has learned how to fly on wires and studied boxing for a recent piece. Hearing her talk, I didn't see how any of that could possibly have much to do with dance. But after seeing the company in performance, I was quite impressed. It's definitely at the outer edge of the spectrum, but their productions are fascinating.

Talking about their daughter, Rosella and Robier express tremendous pride.

It was very interesting because Monet decided to become a dancer as abruptly as I did. For her, it was a performance of Béjart's company that struck a nerve. Her reaction to Béjart was the same as mine had been to the Blum–de Basil Ballets Russes. From that moment on, she was determined to be a dancer.

Monet's interest in Béjart's work was taken no more lightly by her parents than Rosella's interest in ballet had been viewed by her Aunt Maxine. In 1970, Béjart choreographed a divertissement featuring mother and daughter.

It was a wonderful experience. He had been here at the school many times, and Jean had done his portrait. So Béjart decided to do a piece for Monet and me. Of course, that was all Monet needed to commit herself to the goal of getting into his company. What I was not expecting was for her to go off to audition for Béjart's company with several of her classmates from the school the following year. But she did, and he hired her! She stayed with the company almost six years and since then has focused on experimental dance working with Dominique Bagouet and Régine Chopinot, and ultimately started a small company in Montpellier. Now, in 1995, I'm happy she has come back to teach at the school. It is important for her to move into this area of her career. And she is a very good teacher.

Now that the school has added a new facility, Rosella is creating a formula for the future.

I am determined that everyone who has invested time and energy to making the school what it has become, will be protected when the day arrives that I cannot go on. Because the École Supérieure de Danse is a state school subsidized by the Ministry of Culture, the city of Cannes, and other non-profit-seeking organizations, the naming of a successor will be decided by a panel. So we are working on a plan that can be utilized that will assure that the school, the faculty, and the two performing groups we have established can then be assured of continuing as they are, regardless of my participation. There is a perfect chemistry now among the faculty, and everyone makes a unique contribution to the school. I have always encouraged my teachers to do things their way. If they have a problem, I am there to help. All of us make mistakes, it is natural. To look over their shoulders would inhibit them. I put tremendous effort into knowing each student and seeing what each has to offer or what his or her strong points are. But I leave my staff to do their work, their way.

And then, every year, we have six months time to prepare for the annual spectacle here in Cannes. It takes the entire faculty and student body working in all of the available studios we have to pull it together. It's always a madhouse by the end, but it is an excellent learning experience and valuable challenge.

Attending a performance of the 1988 musical production based on Howard Richardson and William Berney's brooding, supernatural tale *Dark of the Moon* brought the entire focus of the school into perspective. In addition to exhibiting excellent command of classical,

273

modern, and ethnic dance techniques, the young cast excelled in both solo and group vocals, brought dramatic intensity to the portrayal of complex characters, and projected a stunning energy across the footlights. The quality of the performance was comparable to that offered by most American regionally based companies and surpassed the fare offered by authorized touring companies of popular Broadway musicals.

Noticing that the rain has stopped, Rosella lets her German shepherd, Baptiste, out into the yard, then returns to talk about projects on the calendar for 1988 through 1990.

I have been invited to stage Bronislava Nijinska's *Rondo Capriccioso* for Arthur Mitchell's Dance Theatre of Harlem. It will be exciting because the company is doing a program in honor of Nijinska. Then, I have been asked to return to the stage playing my own age in the "Harold and Maude Story," being choreographed by Joe Saveno. Ann Barzel also has invited me to Chicago to be interviewed at the Newberry Library for the *Stone Camryn Series* featuring prominent dance figures.

Rosella also took the time in 1991 to return to Oklahoma for the dedication of the mural in the Great Rotunda of the State Capitol honoring Oklahoma's ballerinas. "I arrived in Oklahoma City the evening before the dedication and flew back the same night. But it was very important to me to be there."

Letting Baptiste back in, Robier comments, "It is what you say (in America) is perpetual. But that is how it should be." Rosella protests, "Since I finished in La Scala, life has been much easier. We spend time at home, go skiing on weekends, and this year we went away on our first vacation." Since 1988, the couple has vacationed on the islands off Bretagne.

I think it was good for the faculty and administration to have the school closed for two weeks. It is different for the students because they have a short break after our spring performances and summers off. For the rest of us, spring break is spent looking at students who want to enroll for the coming year, and then we have our summer program. Because it worked so well last year, I think it is good to give everyone two weeks off before we begin the fall semester. It is wonderful to have no classes, no students, no worry for almost two weeks. We swim in the Arctic water and ride bicycles all over the island. It is great fun.

Responding to a query about "Arctic water and bicycling," she says with a laugh, "Well you don't just go on vacation, you have to earn that too!"

Chapter Thirty-Six

Chicago, Illinois

The fierce intensity that Maria Tallchief brought to the stage for more than two decades has not waned in the years since her retirement. Much like the five-star general to whom she likened herself in carrying out her responsibilities as a ballerina, Maria Tallchief Paschen continues to bear the markings of a commanding officer, though long retired from active duty. The austere grandeur of her carriage reflects both her aristocratic Osage ancestry and her unprecedented reign as America's first and foremost prima ballerina. Aggressively enthusiastic and forthright, she views the world through untinted lenses and shares her opinions in absolute terms. She exudes a distinct sense of urgency that often catches people off guard and creates an illusion of impatience. Underneath the seemingly impervious exterior, however, Maria is still very much the little girl named Betty Marie. She makes constant reference to the "good fortune" that has allowed her to enjoy the rewards of both career and family. "I am very lucky. So many dancers miss out on having a family. I didn't. And I can't imagine what it would be like without Buzzy and Elise." She loves to cook, relishes searching the supermarket aisles for good buys, boasts of having made a friend of the butcher, laments the nagging foot problems that have left her able to wear only the most expensive or cheapest of shoes, and admits that speaking engagements terrify her.

When asked what, if anything, she would like to have seen happen during her career that did not, she responds,

It would be much easier to say what I could have done without than to name something I missed. The only thing I can think of that would have enhanced my career would have been having the kind of television exposure that today's dancers enjoy. The quality and quantity of dance on television today is eons ahead of where it was thirty years ago. I remember when we did the "Bell Telephone Hour" in 1959, they had to change the choreography a little because there were only two stationary cameras. It was very primitive, and none of those early shows were filmed onstage. We danced on concrete floors in television studios, and I really don't know how we did it. But it had to start somewhere to become what it is today. Now, we use videotape in the studio to set ballets and watch full-length productions taped live from the Metropolitan Opera House in our living rooms.

With regard to significant developments in the technique of dance, Maria takes exception to the popular belief that today's dancers are more technically proficient than their predecessors.

I think there are more good dancers today than there were thirty years ago, but I've seen too many revivals of ballets that don't have all the steps in them to agree that technical advances have been made. If the hops on pointe that make a variation difficult are taken out, then the variation isn't what it was. So there is no basis for comparison between a dancer who doesn't do the hops on pointe with one who did.

I'm not sure when or why, but it appears that dancers are being allowed to do whatever they feel like. I want to know what happened to finishing pirouettes in fourth position. It was always a nightmare to do two pirouettes and stop in fourth, and now, no one seems to bother. Technique is not just execution, it is control. Doing two pirouettes isn't hard, but stopping is. When I see dancers crashing out of turns, I don't see the technical merit of the turns.

Making a point of saying that she is impressed by a number of very fine dancers, she voices serious concern over the quality of direction and coaching available today.

I see dancers performing major roles with almost no relation to the music, nuances of style, or dramatic interpretation that are integral to breadth of the role. Recently, we saw a performance of *Coppélia* and Freddie Franklin was sitting behind us. During intermission, I asked him why no one was dancing on the music. He looked at me, shook his head and said sadly, "It just is not the way it used to be." Well, it isn't and it shows. I don't see the same gut-wrenching effort being made onstage or the determination to learn in the studio or rehearsal hall that we grew up with.

A former student of mine, who had difficulty getting a job after our company was dissolved, called me one evening to say that she was so sorry that she had resisted what I was teaching. She proceeded to tell me, "Well, I didn't always think everything had to be as absolute as it seemed." I told her I couldn't believe what she was saying because she had been there, in class. All she had to do was to see the results on somebody else and say "I want to look like that" and accept that to look like that she had to do what I was saying.

That's what I did. When I saw Mary Ellen Moylan dance for the first time, I knew that if I was ever to achieve that look I had to go to Balanchine's school. So I did. And when I got there, I did exactly what I was told to do. Obviously, there are still some dancers who are applying themselves that way, but judging from what I've seen recently, there are very few. I remember when I joined the Ballet Russe, all of us learned every role we possibly could on our own, hoping to have the chance to step in at the last minute and prove we were worthy of being more than corps de ballet dancers. That's how it used to work and that's what made great dancers.

As a teacher, Maria brings to the studio her uncompromising dedication to preserving the standards of ballet and combining the classical purity of the Balanchine technique with a teaching style reminiscent of the disciplined approach of Bronislava Nijinska. "I teach what I was taught," she says. Much like Nijinska, she makes it clear to her students and their parents that succeeding as a dancer requires both talent and hard work. Watching her teach in 1988, it was apparent that Maria had one purpose in mind—work. Her shoulder-length auburn hair was tucked neatly under a simple kerchief and barely a trace of makeup accentuated her angular features. She wore pink tights, a black leotard, a black wraparound jersey skirt, and soft leather ballet slippers. After chatting briefly with the pianist and bidding her students good morning, she began class with a series of slow, easy pliés. Backing away from the barre, she demonstrated a tendu combination, beginning and ending in an impeccable fifth position. Pacing up and down the rows of students for the remainder of the barre exercises, she stopped to guide an errant heel in tendu, demonstrate the proper alignment of the hip to the little toe in dégagés, and gently coax the soft arching of a foot in cou-de-pied. Corrections and praise were delivered with a minimum of words, and she constantly urged the students to use the mirror to ferret out their own errors. Adjusting a supple young girl's position in arabesque during center work, Maria chided, "There, now look at the difference yourself and remember to do it that way from now on. Use your head. Dancers have to be intelligent with their minds as well as their bodies."

If there was resistance to what Maria was saying, it was far beneath the surface of the sweat-soaked bodies straining to attain soft, graceful head and arm movements while their legs and feet executed ferociously athletic steps in time with the music. "Listen and let the music help you," she remarked, calling a student forward to demonstrate a combination for the class. "That is what I mean. Now, let's all do it again, that way." Much as it began, class ended quietly with Maria leading the traditional *grande révérence,* or choreographed bow. Following enthusiastic applause, a semichaotic dash erupted as students for the next class gingerly headed for their favorite spots at the barre while Maria's students gathered up dance bags, woolen leggings, and plastic pants piled in heaps under windows stretching the entire length of the studio. On the way to her office, Maria stopped to help a lanky young boy wrap an Ace bandage around a tender knee and queried another about the afternoon rehearsal schedule for an upcoming concert performance.

Ducking into a small dressing room separating her office from a long, narrow conference room, Maria said, "Balanchine was the one who told me I needed to have a dressing room of my own. He came to look at our studios before they were finished to make sure they were done right. He was very pleased, and he was right, I need my own little room here." After changing into a beige wool pants suit, she explained it was Buzzy's idea to convert the two top floors of the building, owned by Paschen Contractors, Inc., into a studio for her company and school. "It's a wonderful space," she said, removing the kerchief and brushing her hair out with a few quick strokes. "The floors were put in properly, and we have just laid down new linoleum that is supposed to be the best surface for dancers." On a quick tour of the two-story facility, Maria pointed out a fully equipped kitchen and dressing rooms complete with stall showers, metal lockers, and solid wooden benches on the way to a smaller studio at the end of the hallway. On the way down a steep staircase to the floor below, she explained dryly that the dressing rooms and lower studio, roughly two-thirds the combined length of those above, had formerly served as home to the Chicago City Ballet. Entering a large foyer area flooded with sunlight from narrow, south-facing windows adjacent to the studio entrance, she said, "Actually, this reminds me very much of the Madison Avenue studios where Balanchine started the school and the company. They were wonderfully airy and bright and had a great sense of space."

Maria's penchant for bright, open spaces was further evidenced in the Paschens' elegant Lake Shore Drive apartment offering unobstructed views of Lake Michigan and the towering skyline of downtown Chicago. Admitting she had never stopped to think about it, Maria rapidly scans the panorama, noting enthusiastically that it is reminiscent of the expansive view from the Tall Chief home in Fairfax. As she gently sets a bowl of fresh-cut flowers on a low table that separates two delicately carved straight-backed chairs facing a cushioned window seat, she remarks, "Well, maybe there is a connection after all. Come, I want to show you one of my prize possessions." As she enters a sunny room fitted with double-height barres and glass shelves brimming with flowering plants facing neatly hung plaques,

281

citations, and awards, she points to a single daguerreotype photograph encased in its original cabochon oval carved frame. "That is Chief Bigheart. Unfortunately, so many of the family heirlooms have been lost or misplaced over the years, but not this one. It means a lot to me to have it. He was a great man with incredible vision. And because he spoke and read English, he was able to secure the future of the Osage. I remember hearing my grandmother talk about going to Washington for the signing of the treaty and what a great moment it was."

Stepping back to view the wall and its contents, she makes a point of explaining that the array of handsomely framed awards, commendations, diplomas, and honorary degrees bore as many Paschen as Tallchief inscriptions. "I'm not the only one in the family who has won recognition!" Indeed, Buzzy's and Elise's honors hold their own opposite Maria's Oklahoma Hall of Fame, Indian of the Year, Capezio Award, Woman of the Year plaques, and a slew of honorary degrees. "Elise took ballet for a while and was quite promising, but her interests were more toward her studies. I remember my mother telling me that I could not raise Elise the way I had been raised. And she was right. At least, it's been much easier for me to determine Elise's progress than it was for my mother! And we too are very proud parents."

After graduating from Harvard with honors in 1982, Elise earned a master's degree in twentieth-century literature at Oxford University and continued there to pursue a Ph.D. She taught tutorials on William Butler Yeats while completing her dissertation, "Yeats's Revisions of his Female Personae Poems." During her academic career, Elise was named Harvard College Scholar (1981–82), and won the Richard Selig Prize for Poetry in 1984. She served as cofounder and editor of *Oxford Poetry* (1983–88). Since earning her doctorate from Oxford in 1988, Elise has held the post of executive director of the Poetry Society of America and has been widely published both in America and overseas.

Chapter Thirty-Seven

Turmoil in Chicago

Maria's pride in her daughter's accomplishments is equaled only by concerns over her safety, diet, and propensity to put work before play.

I'm ready to be a grandmother and Elise hasn't even considered getting married yet! I have tremendous respect for her work, and she knows that, but I still kid her about the fact that everyone I know, including my sister, already has grandchildren.

Talking about her husband, Maria says,

We have a wonderful life. And on top of everything else, we are very good friends. He is so sweet and cares so much. At times, it was very difficult for him. I remember the first time he was backstage. I came off into the wings and he tried to put a towel over my shoulders the way you would a prize-fighter. I remember pushing him away because I couldn't breathe, and all I wanted was air. Later, of course, I explained it to him and told him I appreciated the effort but that it wasn't what I needed. He understood. But then, that's Buzzy. He carries a tremendous amount of responsibility, but he never lets it show. He's always cheerful and we have a lot of fun.

Looking at her watch, Maria says, "Even after Elise went off on her own, I still try to arrange my schedule so I am here when Buzzy comes home from the office. He hates it when I'm not here." As if on cue, the sound of the elevator coming to a stop at their floor-through apartment, Maria rises to her feet. "We're in here," she calls out, heading for the hallway. After exchanging queries about the other's day, the two appear at the library door. Wearing an impeccably well-cut suit and unpretentious grin, Buzzy suggests relocating to the front room to watch the late afternoon sunlight skip across the lake. He announces it's his turn to cook dinner and disappears into the sunny galley kitchen boasting soft yellows and gleaming white tiles inset with delicate hand-painted tiles.

Hardly the image of the quintessential, hardboiled Chicago tycoon who started out working as a water boy for the family-owned and operated Paschen Contractors, Inc., in 1938, Henry Paschen, Jr., "Buzzy," is the antithesis of what one might expect a life spent in the contracting and construction field in Chicago to produce. On his way to the living room, he stops to pinch a scraggly leaf off one of two giant ficus trees flanking the dining area. After taking a seat, he wastes no time exhibiting a charming wit, a delightfully inquisitive mind, a penchant for getting people to talk about themselves, and the fact that he has no more use for rose-colored glasses than does his wife. He also makes it clear that he considers himself as "fortunate" to be married to his wife as she does to him. Abruptly turning the conversation toward what he is convinced will soon be declared a culinary masterpiece, he disappears once again into the kitchen. Without further ado, dinner is served, and the results of Buzzy's efforts win high marks.

Gradually, the conversation turns to how the couple ended up in the midst of a highly controversial ballet war. Maria sets her fork on the plate and sighs.

I should have known better than to try to do something in Chicago. When I first retired, I had no intention of doing anything except take care of my family. It was wonderful not having to feel responsible for setting the tone for an entire ballet company, and to be home with Elise and Buzzy. I was appalled at the quality of dance teachers in Chicago and the lack of arts education in the schools, but getting involved would have taken time away from my family. Of course, I did exercises every day, and Buzzy turned one of the rooms in our other apartment into a small studio for me. Well, that led to a friend asking if she could join me and then a few of her friends came along, and all of a sudden I was teaching a regular exercise class. Then, I let them talk me into working with the singers at the Chicago Lyric Opera, and before I knew it, I was pulling together a small group of young dancers to work with the opera.

So, in 1974, I went against my better judgment and started an "instant ballet company." At that point, Elise was in high school and the Lyric schedule was flexible enough that it wasn't an intrusion into family time. I didn't have any intention of expanding my role or taking on any more responsibility than selecting and preparing the dancers to appear in Lyric productions. Balanchine collaborated on a production of *Orpheus* and approved of what I was doing. So I was content with how it was working out.

With a slight edge to his voice, Buzzy adds,

That is, until the Lyric decided to cut costs by eliminating the dancers from the budget. Then all hell broke loose. During dinner one night, Maria got a frantic call from the Lyric demanding that she get to the theater as quickly as possible because the dancers were throwing pointe shoes out the dressing room windows onto Wacker Drive. The police had already been called, so we left dinner on the table and raced over to the theater to try to diffuse the situation.

Taking the dancers' side, Maria says,

They had every right to be angry. They had worked very hard to do a good job and had. So when they were told that they represented nothing more than a line item on the budget, it hurt. Plus, the Lyric only gave them a week's notice. I sympathized with them totally, but I certainly didn't expect them to do anything so radical.

Doing her best to stifle laughter, Maria adds, "Pointe shoes are quite hard, and being thrown from forty-two stories up, they could have seriously hurt or even killed someone. So Buzzy and I calmed everyone down and came back home to talk." The incident had no impact on the dancers' job status with the Lyric, but it fueled Maria's determination to find a solution for the unfortunate ordeal.

Chapter Thirty-Eight

Priorities Rule

With Balanchine's blessings, and with both Balanchine and New York City Ballet ballerina Suzanne Farrell serving as artistic advisers, Maria launched the Chicago City Ballet in late 1979. Buzzy says, "I knew Maria felt responsible for providing the dancers fired by the Lyric with an opportunity to continue their careers. And when she couldn't place all of them in other companies, I didn't see any other solution except to get involved in helping her establish a school and company." Maria adds,

Before I started the company, a close friend said, "Maria, you are never going to be able to raise any money. Everyone is going to expect your husband to pay for everything." But I was convinced a city the size of Chicago needed a ballet company. And that the people who so willingly turn out to see American Ballet Theatre and Joffrey would, if for no other reason than to support local talent, get behind our efforts. But I underestimated the apathy for local talent and ballet.

"Here in Chicago," Buzzy says,

you can get a reputation as a dance aficionado on the social circuit by attending a performance of any of the major touring companies that come through here every year. But it takes a sincere commitment to dance to support a local company twelve months out of the year. It isn't all parties and performances. It's a business. And the original board was essentially made up of well-meaning society people who weren't prepared for the reality that to make a ballet company work, it takes work. So attendance at board meetings was minimal, fund raising was treated like an unwanted stepchild, and when funds were needed, everyone turned to me. But I was committed to supporting Maria's efforts and making it all work.

After watching the company work out of rented studios for several months, Buzzy offered to convert two floors of a building owned by Paschen Contractors, Inc., into dance studios and donate the space to the school and company. "Maria was responsible for everything. So we discussed the possibility of bringing in support staff. Maria had a veteran fund-raiser in mind, and Suzanne Farrell suggested that her husband, Paul Mejia, would be an excellent choice for assistant director and resident choreographer." Maria liked the idea of bringing Mejia in very much. "He was a product of the School of American Ballet, had been in New York City Ballet, and, before he married Suzanne, was being groomed as a choreographer by Balanchine himself."

With preparations under way to bring Mejia on board, the company seemed to be making progress. Fund-raising efforts were taking shape to mount a full-length *Cinderella* choreographed by Mejia and starring his wife, on loan from New York City Ballet. Ironically, the woman who created the role of the Sugar Plum Fairy in Balanchine's historic 1954 production of the holiday classic could not present the ballet or reap the financial benefit *The Nutcracker* has proven to be for American dance companies. Nationwide, *The Nutcracker* accounts for approximately one-third of the annual total ticket revenues raised by ballet companies in America. It also has become a powerful audience builder because of the large number of children included in the cast.

Maria explains, "Balanchine offered me his production, but the biggest and most successful charity fund-raiser in Chicago was, and is, Ruth Page's *The Nutcracker*. I certainly was not about to interfere. Which is why Paul did *Cinderella*. It was a big ballet, featured a number of children in incidental roles, and, like *The Nutcracker*, could be done every year to amortize the production costs over several seasons. But it didn't solve all of our problems."

Buzzy admitted he began to chafe under the burden of being the company's resident emergency funding source. "It was irritating to say the least. Here I was, bailing the company out every time there was a crisis, and Maria was being openly criticized for not doing her share of the fund raising. It didn't take a rocket scientist to figure out that she was bringing in the lion's share of the operating funds through me." Despite the company's inability to reduce its long-term debts, a supportive attitude within the financial community allowed operations to continue as usual. That is, until the Federal Deposit Insurance Corporation took over Continental Bank in 1984. Continental was the Chicago City Ballet's major creditor, and when the FDIC demanded payment, foreclosure seemed to be imminent. A feasible payment plan for the Continental debt was negotiated in 1986, but the crisis took its toll. The company's general manager and several board members resigned and the local financial community tightened up. At that point, the board restructured the corporation to allow the company and its affiliated school to function as separate entities.

With the threat of bankruptcy behind them, the board began questioning artistic decisions and raising objections to the predominantly Balanchine-style repertoire. "I really don't understand what makes people who have spent their entire lives in the business world think they know how to run a ballet company," Maria says.

I founded the company on the same artistic guidelines as New York City Ballet. Between Paul and me, that artistic integrity was maintained. And as far as we were concerned there is no higher artistic standard to aim for than that of George Balanchine. But not according to some of our board members. They decided to have a market research survey done. Of course, it showed that the three hundred people they selected to participate wanted to see more light, jazzy, or whatever kind of ballets that stir the public's curiosity. If they had put the same energy, time, and money into coming up with an aggressive marketing plan, I am convinced our problems would have been solved. The solution wasn't changing our repertoire, it was letting people know we existed.

The board then demanded that Mejia prepare a five-year plan responsive to the findings of the survey. Mejia declined, according to Maria, much as Balanchine would have. "He said very little, and let his artistic product stand on its own. They didn't understand that, so of course it was taken the wrong way." With a disgruntled look, Buzzy adds, "That's when the discussions started about letting Paul go. We voiced our objections and made our feelings clear. But we had to go out of town." Interrupting, Maria says, "Before we left town, I sat here in this apartment with two members of the board and told them why I was against letting Paul go. Then while we were gone, they fired him—and made statements to the press saying that Buzzy and I supported the decision because there were problems between Paul and me! I was outraged. Paul took it in stride and despite our so-called rift we have continued to work together since he took over as artistic director of the Fort Worth Ballet. I was very upset."

The death knell had sounded, Buzzy contends. "But Maria and I were too busy trying to make the company work to see the foundation crumbling around us. There was a lot of pressure to find a replacement for Paul, and Maria was trying to use her contacts to find someone who could do the job and generate some publicity by taking the position." Having been trained almost exclusively by Russians, Maria thought bringing in a Russian or other prominent international dance figure was a viable solution. "All that I think ever came out of that was a brief airport meeting with Alexander Godunov that I wasn't even invited to attend."

The fatal blow for the Paschens was struck during the board's August 1987 meeting. At that meeting, former New York City Ballet principal dancer, Daniel Duell, was hired by unanimous vote to serve as artistic director of the Chicago City Ballet, and Maria was officially named founder and adviser. "I was still operating under the concept that Duell was coming in to replace Paul," Buzzy says. "The next thing

I remember is the board telling Maria, 'It must be a great relief for you to not have to worry about the company any more,' and I realized they had taken her out of the picture. By the time it sank in, it was a done deal or I would have raised the roof." Picking up where her husband left off, Maria says, "They kept putting words in my mouth, saying I had recommended Danny for the job, when I hadn't. And telling me how hard I had worked, and that the rest would be good for me. All I can remember is feeling like the rug had just been pulled out from under me and I had just woken up with a concussion. When Buzzy and I left the meeting, I think we were both in shock."

Breaking the tension with a quick laugh, Buzzy says,

In some ways, it was so ludicrous it was funny. After everything they did, they expected me to keep letting them use the studios rent-free! I remember wanting to ask them if they would like me to kick Maria out on the street and let her fend for herself. But I don't do things like that. Everything I had done was in support of my wife's attempt to make a ballet company. When they kicked her out, I had no reason to continue my support. Then I was painted as the bad guy. I didn't kick the dancers out of the studio and I never asked anyone to leave. All I did was demand that they pay rent. And even though I never expected to be paid, I sent them a bill for the cost of converting the warehouse space into dance studios. Under the circumstances, I don't think those requests were out of line. I don't regret anything I did, and I think the company Maria created from nothing made a tremendous contribution to the cultural development of the city.

Maria concurs, "I'm proud of what was accomplished and just sad about how it ended. I kept my school going to get some of my students ready for companies. The board dissolved the Chicago City Ballet and went into business as Ballet Chicago."

In 1992, Maria and Buzzy returned to Oklahoma to attend Marjorie's induction into the Oklahoma Hall of Fame. The following day, the two sisters were honored during the unveiling of a mural, "Flight of Spirit," in tribute to the achievements of Oklahoma's American Indian ballerinas. The work was created by the American Indian artist Gary Larsen and sponsored through the combined efforts of the State of Oklahoma, the State Arts Council of Oklahoma, and the State Capitol Preservation Commission. Within a year, Maria closed her school. And approximately two years later Buzzy followed suit and officially retired from Paschen Contractors, Inc.

"It was very special, watching Marjorie be given the recognition in Oklahoma she was due," Maria commented in September 1995. "She was in Europe long enough that people in Oklahoma heard very little about her career." Of whether the trip to Oklahoma prompted thoughts of retiring, Maria will only say, "It was time. It really is very nice. We get to choose our schedules and enjoy sitting on the porch with a beautiful view." Since selling their Lake Shore Drive apartment, Maria and Buzzy go back and forth between their residence in Martha's Vineyard, their Highland Park home outside Chicago, and their recently purchased home in Delray Beach, Florida. "We are having a great time. Elise comes to visit when she can, and we play poker with our neighbors. I still teach and coach and lend my support to New York City Ballet and the recently established Balanchine Foundation. But only the things I want to do. We're having too much fun!"

Chapter Thirty-Nine

Oklahoma via Montevideo, Uruguay

With a jaunty coral pink and turquoise knit cap pulled down over her ears against a brisk north wind, Yvonne Chouteau Terekhov nimbly leads her yellow Labrador retriever through his daily training exercises. Nigel's thick-muscled chest and broad head accentuate Yvonne's delicate frame as the two prepare for an upcoming dog show. After gingerly praising Nigel for his prompt, eager response to her commands, Yvonne remarks, "It's funny. After all the years of performing without even a hint of stage fright, I'm a nervous wreck in the dog ring!" Once Nigel is secured in the back seat, she starts the engine and turns on the heat.

Yvonne rubs her hands together for a second before heading

Yvonne Chouteau and Miguel Terekhov with daughters Christina and Antonia and Papa Terekhov. Montevideo, Uruguay, 1958. (Personal collection.)

home from the park and begins to describe the odyssey that led to Oklahoma in 1960.

A few months after we got settled with Miguel's parents in Uruguay, we discovered I was expecting a second child. So I danced very little with the Montevideo State Opera. After Papa Terekhov became ill, Miguel took over his tobacco business and we helped his mother with her ballet store.

We stayed very much in touch with the dance world. When the de Cuevas came through, Rosella came to dinner and we had a wonderful time. I will never forget seeing her perform *Piège de Lumière* and how homesick I felt when she left.

Among her favorite memories of Uruguay, she mentions letters from friends, having the pleasure of meeting Margot Fonteyn for the first time, and being given the opportunity to help Antony Tudor reconstruct *Little Improvisations*. About the latter she says, "Tudor sent me a letter asking for help remembering it for a student concert at Juilliard. So I wrote out the entire ballet on a legal pad and sent it to him."

Mounting political tensions prompted thoughts of returning to the States following the birth of their second child, Antonia Elizabeth

Terekhov, in 1959. "My parents were very concerned, and for good reason. Being a free spirit from Oklahoma, I was not about to let anything keep me from taking the babies to the park across the street from the university every day! But it got worse and finally Miguel said, 'We must leave this country.' His parents were very sad to see us leave, but they understood."

Staying in New York just long enough to see friends and discover that everyone wanted them to start teaching immediately, Yvonne, Miguel, and the children left on a brief visit to Oklahoma. "My parents had come to visit us in New York after Christie was born, but they only knew Toni through pictures. So they were very glad to see us, and only mildly surprised to find that Christie could speak Spanish but very little English!"

C.E. had a surprise for his daughter and son-in-law as well. In preparation for their visit, he had arranged a meeting for them with George Lynn Cross, then president of the University of Oklahoma.

Daddy had told Dr. Cross that we were going to be visiting for a while, and thought he might like to have us make a guest appearance or teach a few classes at the university. Cross was interested in finding out what kind of response ballet would bring on campus. The only thing going on as far as dance at OU were modern classes that Helen Jane Gregory was teaching for the Department of Physical Education. So we agreed to teach a few classes a week during the second semester, to see if there was enough interest to start a dance program. Dr. Nat Eek, who was director of the School of Drama, found a room to turn into a studio for us, and F. Donald Clark, the dean of the School of Fine Arts, helped us recruit students.

The idea of developing a college dance program similar to what the University of Utah and Indiana and Texas Christian universities had done was very exciting for Miguel. And the more we talked, the more excited he got. He was impressed with the beauty of Oklahoma, and keenly aware that the regional ballet movement was just getting started. Doris Hering was organizing the National Association of Regional Ballet and ballet seemed to be on the verge of becoming extremely popular. There were so many possibilities, we had to give it a try.

As we arrive at the Terekhov home, Yvonne lets Nigel into the fenced backyard, then leads the way inside. "Of course, my parents

295

were elated and did everything they could to help. We also did some guesting in the area and taught a few classes in the city at the Bishop McGuiness High School after school hours."

In the beginning Yvonne did not find teaching rewarding.

Then, I found my niche. My great love was teaching youngsters. I let them start at five and worked with them until they were twelve, to start shaping their bodies and giving them a good correct base. I wanted them to embrace ballet through the stories I told them about the great artists. There is so little heritage today because no one teaches history anymore, unless you go to college. Five is really too early to start, but you teach them to jump over the mountain and keep the love there so at eight, they are ready to learn technique. With older students, my forte is coaching, much like Mme Danilova. It's funny, how there are always certain words that never leave you. Some of the first words Mr. Balanchine said to us in class were, "If you ever teach, you must always demonstrate everything, down to the fingertips. Children do not understand words. You have to show!"

Between teaching in the city, a little guesting, and making the thirty-mile trek to and from the OU campus in Norman several days a week, the couple began preparing for an April concert in the university's Holmberg Hall.

We were adamant from the start that we would focus on developing a program geared toward performing skills. It was extremely important to us because we expected to be working with more students who wanted to be teachers than performers. And we knew some of them would not be interested in performing. So to make sure they got the performing experience needed to teach others to perform, we were determined that it be a course requirement. We were very fortunate to have six young ladies who had previous training. So between Miguel and me, and the six of them, we put on a very good concert. No one expected us to be able to pull anything together so quickly. And certainly not a performance that showed several of our own students to good advantage.

After the concert one thing led to another, and suddenly Yvonne and Miguel were appointed artists-in-residence and given the responsibility of starting a full-fledged dance program within the OU

Yvonne Chouteau rehearsing University of Oklahoma Dance Department students, Norman, Oklahoma, 1962. (Personal collection.)

School of Drama. Miguel took the helm of the fledgling program and enthusiastically plunged into the tasks at hand. Yvonne says, "We continued to perform at OU for years but essentially stopped making guest appearances in 1961. Making the transition from teaching a few classes to building a college dance program and a student performing group at the same time you are raising two children was not easy." Miguel also inherited the task of integrating the modern dance classes into the Department of Dance to offer dance majors the choice between ballet and modern and working with Dr. Eek to begin laying the foundation for curricula leading to a bachelor's or master's in fine arts in either discipline. Yvonne explains, "It was a pioneer effort. For us and the university. I think everyone involved sensed that what we did in Oklahoma had the potential of influencing the development of future dance programs at colleges across the nation."

Yvonne and Miguel soon began to think about opening a private studio in Oklahoma City. Their reputations as stars of the Ballet Russe de Monte Carlo and Yvonne's celebrity status in Oklahoma provided more than just a solid foundation for such an endeavor.

The final encouragement came from noted dance critic, historian, and then managing editor of *Dance News,* P. W. "Bill" Manchester. "Bill came right out and said 'you must open a studio.' And she was right. As much as we were doing at OU, we weren't working a full-time schedule on campus and we had had a very good turnout for the classes we had taught in the city. So we bought a small studio and opened the Chouteau-Terekhov Academy of Ballet in 1961."

Once again, opportunity found its way to their doorstep. John E. Kirkpatrick, a devoted supporter of the cultural and educational future of Oklahoma whose philanthropic portfolio represents a stunning example of private sector investment in the community at large, invited Yvonne and Miguel to relocate their studios in a facility he was building for the Oklahoma Science and Arts Foundation at the State Fairgrounds. Describing Kirkpatrick as a dear friend whose loyal support of the arts and dance goes far beyond contributing funds, Yvonne says, "He built the studios exactly as we asked, and added a touch of his own. He wouldn't let them hang ceilings. He said he didn't want me to hit my head when Miguel and I did overhead lifts! I have no idea where dance in Oklahoma City would be today without John."

Chapter Forty

Changing Roles

In 1963 the Chouteau-Terekhov Academy of Ballet moved into its new home and Kirkpatrick galvanized a cadre of local dance and arts supporters to launch a civic ballet company. Yvonne and Miguel wasted no time acquiring a volunteer team to keep production costs as low as possible. Yvonne and Miguel donated their services as founding artistic directors, students from the OU School of Drama served as the production design staff, students from the OU dance program were selected to create an ensemble, and an in-kind donation from the Oklahoma Science and Arts Foundation provided all administrative and managerial services.

In December 1963 the Oklahoma City Civic Ballet made its

debut with a production of *The Nutcracker* featuring Maria Tallchief and Royes Fernandez. "They were so wonderful," Yvonne says. "They donated their services and then paid their own way!" The company's debut in the city's Municipal Auditorium, known today as the Civic Center Music Hall, sold six thousand tickets and the box office was forced to turn away several hundred people. "We never expected that kind of community support. I realize it was *The Nutcracker,* but ticket sales remained strong for other programs, including those without the lure of visiting stars. We knew how important it was for our dancers and audiences to be exposed to great artists from the professional world of dance."

While the civic company was making strides, OU broke ground for the construction of the $1.5 million Fine Arts Center and Rupel J. Jones Theatre, which today serve as home for both the OU School of Art and the School of Drama and the Department of Dance, respectively. "The complex was completed in 1965 and Miguel began staging a full-length production of *Giselle*. Up to that point, we had restaged several ballets from the Ballet Russe repertoire, Mr. Balanchine gave us permission to mount several of his ballets, and Miguel had started choreographing. *Giselle* was a landmark for me, Miguel, and the department. To have the opportunity to perform the role I had trained my entire career to dance was one of the most fulfilling experiences of my career. "The production was immensely successful and drew a glowing review in an article in *Dance Magazine* written by Jack Anderson, the *New York Times* dance critic, historian, and author.

Without any warning Nigel leaps off the couch and makes a beeline for the front door. "He heard the key, which means 'T' is home. We're in here," she calls out at the sound of her husband's deep baritone query, "Chiksy?" Filling the doorway to the family room with his six-foot-four frame, Terekhov gives his wife a warm hug and makes a fuss over Nigel. As he looks at the scrapbooks strewn on the table, he says, "So. I see you've been busy." Reaching across the table to retrieve a newspaper clipping with a color photograph of the couple with their daughters in the studio, he exclaims, "Ah! Mama, remember this?" Speaking in thickly accented words, Terekhov says, "Christie and Toni were talented. But they chose not to dance, and that was fine with us."

Yvonne adds, "The girls grew up in Oklahoma surrounded by all the things Oklahoma has to offer. They went to parochial schools, including my alma mater Villa Teresa, and because of my parents they were exposed to the history of Oklahoma and the Chouteau family. I taught them Indian dances, and they have a great love for dance today." Patting Nigel's head, Terekhov says, "And they had animals and parents who didn't go off on tour. Now, they are all grown up and happy. One lives in St. Louis, the other in Florida. Christie and her husband, Kevin, have two boys, and Toni is going to nursing school in Orlando. We visit back and forth a lot. And we're all looking forward to attending Toni's graduation in 1996!"

By 1971, the OU program had progressed beyond all projections. Terekhov had emerged as a formidable choreographer, attendance at student concerts had led to an expanded performance schedule, and students were applying for admission from across the nation. As a result Terekhov had to go on a full-time schedule and resign his post with the Oklahoma City Civic Ballet. "I was very firm about not being a person to direct a company," Yvonne says. "It is not my nature. So I told them I would keep the company in shape, teach company class, and continue the lecture-demonstration program in the schools until they could get a director. I did that for a year, and then New York City Ballet veterans Conrad and Joy Ludlow came to direct." "Well, you see," Terekhov says, "the search for a new director was complicated because no one else was willing or able to work for nothing. So a lot of things had to be changed."

The company was renamed the Oklahoma City Municipal Civic Ballet, which has since become Ballet Oklahoma. After more than its share of upsets along the way, the company has blossomed under the direction of former New York City Ballet soloist Brian Pitts, who took over the artistic helm in 1985. Yvonne says, "I have coached Brian's wife, Laura, who also danced with New York City Ballet. I worked with her on several of the roles I performed before she retired in 1993 to help take some of the load off Brian. I like what they are doing with the company."

In 1972, the fortieth anniversary of Yvonne's debut as a performer drew a citation from the State Legislature and festivities were held in her honor, concluding with a performance featuring her in excerpts from her most treasured roles in the Rupel Jones Theatre at the University of Oklahoma in March 1973. "Miguel choreographed wonderful roles for me and I still felt fine onstage, but the strain of performing was taking its toll. So I performed only rarely after that." The following year Yvonne received the Distinguished Service Citation from OU and an honorary Doctorate of Humanities from Phillips University. In 1975 she was named to the Commission of Presidential Scholars by President Gerald Ford, and in 1976 she received an Oklahoma Governor's Art Award.

Later that year Yvonne returned to the stage to perform what she considers one of the most important roles of her career, at the Kennedy Center of Performing Arts in Washington, D.C., in observance of Oklahoma Bicentennial Day.

Performing the *Snow Maiden* in the Ballet Russe, I first realized the power projecting emotion can have on an audience. Dancing Juliette was the final realization of that indefinable quality and fulfillment. But the ultimate and most deeply fulfilling roles I performed were *Giselle* and *The Trail of Tears,* a variation Miguel choreographed for me which I performed at Kennedy Center. That solo was the fullest definition of what I wanted to do and be as a dancer.

With a photo of her parents in her hand and a smile rising from her eyes, Yvonne says, "Daddy never told me I did something well or he liked what I did until two years before he died. He looked at me and said, 'Well, you've done everything I've ever wanted you to do, Yvonne. I'm very proud of you.' That was all he ever said, but it took me off the hook and I will never forget it."

In 1981 Yvonne took early retirement from the University of Oklahoma to dedicate more time to her academy. That year, the couple bought a home overlooking Lake Gibson not far from the Chouteau family farm in northeastern Oklahoma. After Miguel retired from his post at the University in 1988, Yvonne closed her academy.

When I first closed the academy, I went back and forth between being elated because I did not have to teach six days a week and feeling as though I had forgotten something. Every once in a while I still coach Ballet Oklahoma dancers and lend my name and presence to a multitude of fund-raising events benefiting Ballet Oklahoma, the Oklahoma Arts Institute, the University of Oklahoma, and others.

Of all the award ceremonies, fund-raisers, and other appearances I have made, giving the introduction for Marjorie Tallchief Skibine when she was inducted into the Oklahoma Hall of Fame and watching Miguel receive the Governor's Arts Award in 1995 were the most rewarding.

Not unlike her mentor, Alexandra Danilova, Yvonne sets an example of artistic and personal integrity with exceptional grace and pride.

Chronologies

MARIA TALLCHIEF

1925	Born, second child of Ruth and Alex Tall Chief.
1942	Professional debut, Ballet Russe de Monte Carlo.
1943	Adopts name Maria Tallchief, Ballet Russe de Monte Carlo.
1944	Promoted to soloist, Ballet Russe de Monte Carlo.
1945	Ballet Russe de Monte Carlo.
1946	Marries George Balanchine, New York, New York; guest ballerina, Paris Opéra Ballet.
1947	Joins Balanchine's Ballet Society.
1948	Ballet Society becomes New York City Ballet; guest ballerina, Ballet Theatre; rejoins NYCB.
1949–51	NYCB.
1952	NYCB; appears in MGM feature film *Million Dollar Mermaid*; marries Elmourza Natiroff.
1953	Rejoins NYCB.
1954	NYCB.

1955	Guest ballerina, Ballet Russe de Monte Carlo; rejoins NYCB, Bordeaux, France.
1956	Marries Henry Paschen, Jr., Chicago, Illinois.
1956–58	NCYB.
1959	Birth of Elise Paschen, Chicago, Illinois; rejoins NYCB, winter season.
1960	Guest ballerina, American Ballet Theatre; Dance Magazine Award.
1961	Guest ballerina, Chicago Opera Ballet and the Chicago Lyric Opera.
1962	Guest ballerina, Royal Danish Ballet.
1963	Indian of the Year Award, Anadarko, Oklahoma; rejoins NYCB.
1965	Resigns NYCB; Capezio Award; guest engagements.

ROSELLA HIGHTOWER

1920	Born, only child of Eula May and Charles Edgar Hightower.
1938	Professional debut, Ballet Russe de Monte Carlo, Monaco; marries Mischa Resnikov; promoted to soloist.
1939–40	Ballet Russe de Monte Carlo.
1941	June, International Dance Festival, Jacob's Pillow; joins Ballet Theatre, soloist.
1942–44	Ballet Theatre.
1945	Promoted to ballerina, Ballet Theatre.
1946	Joins Original Ballet Russe, ballerina.
1947	Original Ballet Russe; joins Marquis de Cuevas's company, leading ballerina, Vichy, France.
1948–50	Grand Ballet de Monte Carlo; name changes to Grand Ballet du Marquis de Cuevas
1951	Marries Jean Robier, Paris; Grand Ballet du Marquis de Cuevas through 1953.
1954	Resigns Grand Ballet du Marquis de Cuevas; joins Leonide Massine for filming of *Neapolitan Carousel;* returns to Kansas City, Kansas.
1955	Birth of Dominique Robier, Kansas City, Kansas; rejoins Ballet Theatre, ballerina.

1956– mid-57	Ballet Theater.
1957	Rejoins Grand Ballet du Marquis de Cuevas, ballerina and artistic consultant.
1958–61	Grand Ballet du Marquis de Cuevas.
1962	Grand Ballet du Marquis de Cuevas dissolved; Centre de Danse International, Cannes, France opens; forms concert group with Arova, Bruhn, and Nureyev, European engagements through 1963.
1964–65	Grand Ballet Classique de France featuring students from the school and other guest artists; named to first level of the French Legion of Honor.

MARJORIE TALLCHIEF

1927	Born, third child of Ruth and Alex Tall Chief.
1944	Professional debut, soloist, Ballet Theatre.
1945	Ballet Theatre through mid-1946.
1946–47	Joins Original Ballet Russe as leading soloist.
1947	Joins Marquis de Cuevas's Nouveau Ballet de Monte Carlo, second ballerina, Vichy, France; marries George Skibine, Vichy.
1948–51	Grand Ballet du Marquis de Cuevas.
1952	Birth of twins, George and Alex, Paris; rejoins Grand Ballet du Marquis de Cuevas, performing through 1955.
1956	Gala Performance, Stoll Theatre, London; invited to join Paris Opéra Ballet as premiere danseuse Étoile; guest ballerina, Chicago Opera Ballet.
1957	Joins Paris Opéra Ballet, Étoile; guest ballerina, Chicago Opera Ballet.
1958–61	Paris Opéra Ballet, Étoile.
1961	Guest ballerina, Teatro Colón, Buenos Aires, Argentina; resigns Paris Opéra Ballet.
1962–63	Guest engagements throughout Europe.
1964	Joins Harkness Ballet, prima ballerina, New York, New York.
1965– mid-1966	Harkness Ballet.
1966	Resigns Harkness Ballet.

YVONNE CHOUTEAU

1929	Born, only child of Lucy and Corbett Edward Chouteau.
1943	Professional debut, Ballet Russe de Monte Carlo.
1944	Ballet Russe de Monte Carlo.
1945	Promoted to soloist, Ballet Russe de Monte Carlo.
1946	Ballet Russe de Monte Carlo.
1947	Inducted into the Oklahoma Hall of Fame; Ballet Russe de Monte Carlo.
1948	Marries Pierre Monteux; Ballet Russe de Monte Carlo.
1949	Promoted to leading soloist, Ballet Russe de Monte Carlo.
1950	Promoted to ballerina, Ballet Russe de Monte Carlo.
1951	Ballet Russe de Monte Carlo.
1952–54	Ballet Russe de Monte Carlo suspends normal operations; dancers laid off.
1952	Guest engagements.
1953	Guest artist, Jacob's Pillow, premiere of Antony Tudor's *Little Improvisations*.
1954–55	Ballet Russe de Monte Carlo resumes normal operations.
1956	Marries Miguel Terekhov, Chicago, Illinois; Ballet Russe de Monte Carlo.
1957	Birth of Christina Maria Terekhov, New York, New York; resigns Ballet Russe de Monte Carlo; guest ballerina, Montevideo State Opera, Uruguay.
1959	Birth of Antonia Elizabeth Terekhov, Montevideo, Uruguay.

Select Bibliography

The books and articles listed here are the sources I used to corroborate the veracity and specific details of the events described in this book. The reader should bear in mind that a written record of the history of ballet in the United States did not exist prior to the grand-scale arrival in this country of ballet "à la Russe" between 1933 and 1936. The careers of the American Indian ballerinas coincided with the establishment of an American dance press, and for this reason only a small body of published books and articles documents their careers. In addition to these books and articles, I relied on the souvenir books, touring schedules, performance programs, and related memorabilia I have collected since my childhood.

Select Bibliography

BOOKS

Anderson, Jack. *The One and Only: The Ballet Russe de Monte Carlo.* New York: Dance Horizons, 1981.

Chujoy, Anatole, and P. W. Manchester. *The Dance Encylopedia.* New York: Simon & Schuster, 1967.

Danilova, Alexandra, and Holly Brubach. *Choura: The Memoirs of Alexandra Danilova.* New York: Alfred Knopf, Borzoi Books, 1986.

Eakins Press Foundation. *Choreography by George Balanchine: A Catalogue of Works.* New York: Viking Press, 1982. Limited edition.

Fly, Shelby M. *The Saga of The Chouteaus of Oklahoma.* Oklahoma: Levite of Apache, 1988. Limited Edition.

Lido, Serge. *Masques.* Paris: Revue Internationale d'Art Dramatique, 1947–1949. Photography Collection.

Mitchell, Jack. *Dance Scene: U.S.A.* Cleveland, Ohio: World Publishing Co., 1967.

Payne, Charles. *American Ballet Theatre.* New York: Alfred Knopf, 1978.

Reynolds, Nancy. *Repertory in Review: 40 Years of the New York City Ballet.* New York: Dial Press, 1977.

Taper, Bernard. *Balanchine.* New York: Harper & Row, 1960. Reprint. New York: Times Books, 1984.

Twysden, Elizabeth. *Alexandra Danilova.* New York: Kamin Dance Publishers, 1947.

White, Anne Terry. *The American Indian.* The American Heritage Book of Indians Series. New York: Random House, 1963.

Wright, Muriel H. *A Guide to the Indian Tribes of Oklahoma.* The Civilization of the American Indian Series, vol. 33. Norman: University of Oklahoma Press, 1986.

Zotigh, Dennis. *Moving History: Evolution of the Powwow.* Oklahoma City: The Center of the American Indian, 1991.

PERIODICALS

Boroff, David. "Interview with Marjorie Tallchief and George Skibine." *Dance Magazine,* December 1956, 14–17.

Como, William. "A Reverie: In Search of the Red Shoes." *Dance Magazine,* September 1983, 58–65.

Crowle, Pigeon. "Maria Tallchief: Her Early Years." *Dance Magazine.* February 1956, 46–51.

Dupuis, Simone. "Avant-Première: Casse-Noisette." *Les Saisons de la Danse,* December 1982, 40–41.

—-. "L'Opéra de Paris: Projets pour une nouvelle equipe." *Les Saisons de la Danse,* October 1980, 44–45.

Gruen, John. "Tallchief and Mejia's Chicago City Ballet." *Dance Magazine,* December 1984, H25–H27.

Hardy, Camille. "Chicago's City Ballet: Such Stuff As Dreams Are Made On." *Dance Magazine,* December 1984, 70–76.

Henderson, Felicia. "Informal Report: Oklahoma's Indian Ballerinas and Their Families." *Dance Magazine,* December 1957. 17–23, 67.

Heresin, André-Philippe. "Spectacles du Mois." Ongoing series in *Les Saisons de la Danse.* "A l'Opéra: Hommage au Ballet," December 1980, 8–11; "A l'Opéra: Don Quichotte," April 1981, 10–12; "Au Palais des Congres: La Belle au bois dormant." March 1982, 8–10; "A l'Opera: Le Songe d'une nuit d'été." June 1982, 12–14.

Horosko, Marian. "One Hundred Years at the Metropolitan Opera Ballet." *Dance Magazine,* May 1984, 44–49.

Joel, Lydia. "Closeup: The de Cuevas Ballet." *Dance Magazine,* July 1960, 34–37.

Katz, Leslie George, Nancy Lassalle, and Harvey Simmonds. *George Balanchine: A Reference Guide.* New York: Ballet Society, 1987.

Lerouvillois, Monique. "Provence Côte d'Azur: Les moyens de créer." *Les Saisons de la Danse,* March 1988, 34.

Lidova, Irène. "Lidova raconte." Ongoing series in *Les Saisons de la Danse.* "Le Marquis de Cuevas, personnage haut en couleur, prend la fête du Ballet de Monte Carlo en 1947," December, 1986, 44–45; "Dans les années 1952–1953, je suis happée par les saisons, de plus fréquentes, du Ballet du Marquis de Cuevas," June 1987, 44–45.

Merrill, Bruce. "Rosella Hightower: New Director of the Paris Opera." *Dance Magazine,* July 1981, 54–55.

INTERVIEWS

Barsotti, Jean Luc. Tape recording, Cannes, France, April 1988.

Castanier, Arlette. Cannes, France, April 1988.

Cata, Alphonso. Tape recording, Roubaix, France, April 1988.

Cerrone, Jeannot Baptiste. Tulsa, Okla., November 1982; Houston, Tex., May 1982; telephone conversations, 1983–90.

Cook, Edward. Tape recording, Cannes, France, April 1988.

Emerson, Jane. New York, N.Y., December 1987.

Ferran, José. Tape recording, Cannes, France, April 1988.

Franklin, Frederic. Tape recording, New York, N.Y., December 1987. Interviews in Tulsa, Okla., 1977–present.

Heresin, André-Philippe. Tape recording, Paris, France, March 1988.

Le Bourhis, Josseline. Tape recording, Paris, France, March 1988.

Lidova, Irène. Telephone conversations, April 1988 and November 1995.

Mejia, Paul. Telephone conversations, February, 1989.

Paschen, Elise. New York, N.Y., December 1987. Telephone conversations, December 1990–present.

Paschen, Henry ("Buzzy"). New York City, N.Y., December 1987; tape recording, Chicago, Ill., February 1988; telephone conversations, 1988–91; Oklahoma City, Okla., November 1992; telephone conversations, December 1990–present.

Paschen, Maria Tallchief. Tape recording, Chicago, Ill., February 1988; Oklahoma City, Okla., November 1992; telephone conversations, 1988–present.

Pothier, Claude. Tape recording, Cannes, France, April 1988.

Robier, Domonique. Cannes, France, April 1988.

Robier, Jean. Tape recording, Cannes, France, April 1988.

Robier, Rosella Hightower. Tape recording, Cannes, France, April 1988; Oklahoma City, Okla., November 1992; telephone conversations, 1988–present.

Skibine, Alexander Tallchief. Telephone conversation, March 1989; Oklahoma City, Okla., November 1992.

Skibine, George Tallchief. Telephone conversation, March 1989; Oklahoma City, Okla., November 1992.

Skibine, Marjorie Tallchief. Tape recording, Chicago, Ill., February 1988; Oklahoma City, Okla., November 1992; telephone conversations, 1988–present.

Tall Chief, George. Tape recording, Fairfax, Okla., May 1989; telephone conversation, October 1990; Oklahoma City, Okla., November 1992.

Tall Chief, Vaden. Tape recording, Fairfax, Okla., May 1989.

Terekhov, Miguel. Tape recording, Oklahoma City, Okla., March 1990; Oklahoma City, Okla., November 1992; telephone conversations and interviews, Tulsa, Oklahoma City, and Norman, Okla., 1978–present.

Terekhov, Yvonne Chouteau. Tape recording, Oklahoma City, Okla., March 1990; Oklahoma City, Okla., November 1992; telephone conversations and interviews, Tulsa, Oklahoma City, and Norman, Okla., 1978–present.

Index

315

Index

Index

Index